The Discovery of the Fact

Edited by Clifford Ando and William P. Sullivan

UNIVERSITY OF MICHIGAN PRESS
ANN ARBOR

Published in the United States of America by the
University of Michigan Press
Printed and bound by CPI Group (UK) Ltd, Croydon, CR0 4YY

First published July 2020

A CIP catalog record for this book is available from the British Library.

Library of Congress Cataloging-in-Publication Data

Names: Discovery of the fact (Conference) (2016 : University of Chicago) | Ando, Clifford, 1969– editor. | Sullivan, William Peyton, editor.
Title: The discovery of the fact / edited by Clifford Ando and William P. Sullivan.
Description: Ann Arbor : University of Michigan Press, 2020. | Series: Law and society in the ancient world | Includes bibliographical references and index.
Identifiers: LCCN 2020008301 (print) | LCCN 2020008302 (ebook) | ISBN 9780472131884 (hardcover) | ISBN 9780472126644 (ebook)
Subjects: LCSH: Law, Greek—Congresses. | Roman law—Congresses. | Evidence (Greek law)—Congresses. | Evidence (Roman law)—Congresses. | Law and fact—Congresses.
Classification: LCC KJA172 .D57 2020 (print) | LCC KJA172 (ebook) | DDC 347.38/06—dc23
LC record available at https://lccn.loc.gov/2020008301
LC ebook record available at https://lccn.loc.gov/2020008302

Cover photo: Neumagen, Rent payments. Courtesy Rheinisches Landesmuseum, Trier.

Contents

Digital materials related to this title can be found on
the Fulcrum platform via the following citable URL:
https://doi.org/10.3998/mpub.10113490

Introduction

The Discovery of the Fact

Clifford Ando

People are generally familiar with courts as arbiters of truth. Popular culture is rife with representations of courts and legal institutions as adjudicators of questions of fact. Indeed, such representations go back to the high Roman Empire. The *Metamorphoses* of Apuleius and even his life turned on madcap scenes wherein the veracity of the seemingly unknowable was settled—or at least temporarily stabilized.[1] Likewise, in ideologically freighted literatures, the righteousness of empire was often enacted through the performance of justice, in staged trials wherein the validity claims of the imperial power were vindicated through its adherence to proper procedure and standards of substantive justice. In those literatures, the ability of forensic procedure to actualize standards of justice was often understood to rest on the percipience of inquisitorial authorities, who hewed to justice because they saw the truth—often, in popular narrative, despite the false representations provided by those who wielded social power.[2]

This aspect of Roman imperial self-regard finds a modern corollary in traditions of scholarship—in legal history, legal theory, and comparative law—that study the so-called fact/law distinction. In their literatures, the drawing (insiders might say, the *recognition*) of a distinction between so-called questions of fact and questions of law was a necessary and historically localized step in the emergence of law as science. In historical scholarship, it has long been argued that this step was first taken by jurists at Rome. In that body of work, the crafting of a distinction between questions of fact and questions of law takes place within a broader set of intellectual and political moves that ushered in the erection of a firewall between, on one hand, the articulation and application of law and, on the other, all manner of ethical, political, and theological considerations.[3] One notable feature of that historical literature is the extent to which it accords with the ideological self-understanding of many modern (Western) legal systems. The Roman (and not Semitic) triumph in distinguishing questions of law—to be subjected to rationalized analysis by disinterested experts—from questions of fact (which may be submitted to lay judges and juries, with citizenly expertise in the evaluation of material social conditions) was therefore also a Western triumph.[4]

The modern version of this narrative, which is to say, the one influential in twentieth-century legal theory, received its initial, significant articulations in nineteenth-century German scholarship. But the roots of this and similar tales of origin in respect to modern law go back at least to the Enlightenment. In that age, reflection on the long history of progress by which the West surmounted judicial combat and trial by contest was a trope of Whiggish histories of both justice and knowledge, and sophisticated efforts were made to chart the conjoined trajectories of forensics, proof, and science in the late medieval and early modern periods—trajectories that led, as it were, from them to us.[5]

Virtually every aspect of this metanarrative of Western legal history has been subjected to scrutiny and revision in recent decades. The historical conditions in which a notion of autonomous law emerged in Rome, as well as the limitations on its realization, have been subjected to profound historical analysis by Bruce Frier.[6] Similarly, the actual content and operation of the fact/law distinction at Rome has been elucidated as never before by Nicolas Cornu Thénard,[7] while the long history of the notion of the fact between medieval jurisprudence and modern legal philosophy has been profoundly reassessed by Pierre Thévenin.[8] The literature of those three men contributed to inspire this project, and it is a pleasure and an object of this volume to make some aspects of the work and arguments of Cornu Thénard and Thévenin available to Anglophone readers.

Two further contexts of this project are established by modern movements in legal theory and by the history of knowledge. Where legal theory is concerned, the rise of legal realism, with its rejection of the metaphysical and deontological priorities that informed early self-conceptions of law, created space for a range of new explorations of the relationship between legal rules and the worlds they regulate.[9] In the most basic terms, the assertion that laws and legal systems constitute social institutions that arise from historically contingent patterns of material social relations—or, more specifically, from particular understandings of those patterns—opened the door for bravura new movements in legal analysis. This expansion has included problems that we might understand as analogous to those with which the Roman jurists explicitly wrestled: for example, problems of generality in legal language; the normative status of fact patterns that one recognizes as constituting a problem at law; and the crafting of conventionally acceptable legislative forms and modes of legal reasoning that might render instances and limit cases justiciable *ex post*, with all appropriate respect for issues of legal legitimacy.[10]

Where the history of knowledge is concerned, this project draws inspiration from Michel Foucault and the multiple forms of work that he inspired. At issue in particular is the network of connections he drew in lectures in 1977 and 1978 between the interests of the state and the developing sciences of government.[11] That material has contributed to motivate work in a dizzying array of fields and contexts, on the powers of the state, its aspirations to knowledge, and the forms of subjectivity to which these have given rise. Scholars of ancient history have not systematically engaged the periodization(s) that undergird that work. Without seeking to question that body of work as a history of government, the present project asks whether a complex array of interests and social needs contributed to endow intertwined institutions of public power—such as archives, census officials, makers and keepers of cadastral records, and institutions of dispute resolution—with lasting authority over fundamental knowledge interests, not simply in respect to relations between persons and the state, but intersubjectively as well.

This volume assembles papers from a seminar in which speakers were invited to respond to the robust historical landscape here described, with particular attention to the emergence of notions of facticity in the operations of legal theory and legal institutions, as well as to the social and material contexts of their production. Although the historiography of the fact/law distinction lies behind this endeavor, the project of the contributors was not to respond narrowly to that literature's claims on behalf of Rome and, correspondingly, its dismissal of Greek law. Instead, our point of departure encompassed the wider field of debates on the fact/law distinction in modern legal theory, in addition to the historiography of the modern fact. The contributors to this project were trained in the United States, the United Kingdom, and Europe, in a wide variety of disciplines, including classics, history, law, political theory, and philosophy. The issues central to the chapters include the relationship between rules of evidence and contemporaneous forensic science; the existence and importance of a distinction between social and legal facts; the influence on courts and society of the operation of statal institutions of knowledge production; and the confrontation of legal systems with problems of slaves as persons and tools, insofar as they might be accorded both agency and intent. Throughout our inquiries, we have sought to respect the specificity of the historical regimes under study, by allowing for a certain theoretical eclecticism in the volume, as we believe that historical arguments must arise out of consideration of particulars. The volume as whole, however, seeks to make two substantial claims, for ancient legal history as a domain for the study of the history of knowledge and, recursively, for the relevance of questions of historical epistemology to ancient legal history. A brief review of the book's chapters will make this intention clear.

In chapter 1, "Were the Ancient Greeks Epistemic Democrats?," Daniela Cammack opens the volume by throwing down a gauntlet. Her chapter proceeds by means of a double challenge, one philological, one interpretive. First, Cammack asserts that although translations of Athenian oratory make frequent reference to "facts," the Greek texts in question employ a vocabulary that is largely devoid of such epistemic commitments. Second, she considers whether Athenian juries and assemblies understood their interpretive (and political and moral) questions as having objectively correct rather than merely situational answers. To frame these issues, Cammack turns to contemporary concerns for vindicating the utility of democratic politics by reference to the advantages of aggregating knowledge or judgment. Her chapter elegantly uses these concerns to frame her reading of the ancient material, while the conclusions that she draws have recursive implications for how contemporary arguments in favor of democracy on epistemic grounds might often be posing the wrong questions. Political decisions often concern the future, which is inherently unknowable—and the Greeks knew that. This orientation to the future is why political decisions are (creative) acts of judgment; indeed, it is part of what makes them political in the first place, which is why contests erupt over who gets to make them.

In chapter 2, "The Legal Construction of the Fact, between Rhetoric and Roman Law," Nicolas Cornu Thénard likewise commences by establishing a homology between ancient and modern theory—in his case, that between facts and the law. But where modern courts seek to adapt their rulings to the truths provided by facts, Roman jurists, according to Cornu Thénard, asserted the distinction between truth and facts in order to sustain a vastly more robust view of the autonomy of law. To demonstrate this, he carefully considers a number of argumentative moves standard among the Roman jurists (and taught in the course of rhetorical training), including acts of definition, so-called qualification, and analogical reasoning. In each case, he urges that Roman lawyers departed from a concern for what we might term simple facts and focused instead on the abstraction of fact patterns of salience to legal argument. In this way, what turns out to count as facts in Roman law are those things the law defines as such. One might say that at Rome, the law extracted facts from the world to suit itself.

Chapters 3 and 4 take up aspects of the law of slavery in Crete and Rome. Their respective ambitions are conditioned by the evidentiary bases of their inquiry. In "Legal Knowledge in Gortyn: Debt Bondage Laws and the Liability of Slaves in Gortynian Law," David M. Lewis studies clauses of an inscribed code of law from classical Crete. The inscription itself is one of the longest of all Greek inscribed documents, but Crete itself provides neither contextual information about the material and social conditions of slavery nor the sort of literary sources that might reveal the self-interpretive positions of owners or slaves. Lewis therefore proceeds by examining recent efforts to strip away interpretive approaches to the Gortynian code based on assumptions about its historical context; he also insists on the insufficiency of law codes as maps to the social realities that they claim to regulate. In his view, Gortyn's law code provides information on how to understand only itself. It is likely that the social reality of slavery on Gortyn was substantially more messy than the law and hence deliberately underdefined by it.

In "Free in Fact? Legal Status and State in the Suits for Freedom," Nicole Giannella studies Roman jurisprudential literature regarding lawsuits for freedom, in which a person challenged the legal status in which that person or another was held. The basic premise of all such cases was that a person's "true" legal status and the condition or state in which that person existed might diverge. That there might regularly be uncertainty in this regard belies, Giannella argues, much modern writing on the ideology of the slave/free distinction in Roman culture. Focusing on problematic categories—the runaway slave, who might pass as free; slaves who are judged free in one trial but as slaves in another; and self-sale as an instrument in crimes of fraud—Giannella suggests that jurists confronted a world of greater uncertainty in respect to status than we might expect and that they reacted by constructing a firewall around the limits that legal inquiry might achieve. In this way, as in the argument of Cornu Thénard, the Roman jurists are revealed as deeply concerned with the legitimacy and autonomy of the law.

The next pair of chapters treats, from very different perspectives, the rules of evidence and fact-finding ambitions of Athenian courts. In "Gossip, Slander, Hearsay, Truth: Oral Evidence in Athenian Courts," Esther Eidinow takes as her point of departure standard treatments of gossip as expressing and enforcing social norms. However, she reveals the use of gossip within Athenian courts to have been conditioned by legal and epistemic commitments—not only by anxieties about the reliability of hearsay, but also by concerns for issues like character, motivation, and cause, which the frameworks of understanding provided by the standard situations and narrative patterns of so-called gossip are perfectly suited to reveal. In "Truth and Athenian Court Verdicts," Adriaan Lanni demonstrates how Athenian courts declined to develop procedures to distinguish efforts at fact-finding from the issuing of normative judgments on those facts. Employing, as she puts it, a "discretionary rather than formal or numerical approach to proof," Athenian courts declined to bind themselves in respect of judgment on facts. Instead, the possibility that a jury might issue a verdict contrary to the facts was consistently entertained, in keeping with normative criteria whose salience it was free to determine. Lanni's reading of the Athenian system mirrors that which obtained in many Roman courts, where arguments over evidence concerned not issues of admissibility—unlike in American courts, nearly everything was admissible—but, precisely for that reason, questions of the weight and interpretation to be accorded to evidence.

The penultimate chapter in this book, "The Certainty of Documents: Records of Proceedings as Guarantors of Memory in Political and Legal Argument," studies the representation of adversarial argument in judgments published by Roman legal authorities. The earliest extant decrees of the Roman Senate already contain representations of the arguments advanced by the parties who came before it. In other words, the Roman Senate—and other institutions of Roman public law—systematically cited the factual basis on which they acted. "The Certainty of Documents" argues that this was common practice well before we have evidence for the stenographic recording of proceedings. On one level, the practice amounted to a broad-based advertisement for the rationality of the Roman government's procedures. As a further matter, the procedures and immanent rules of evidence of Roman tribunals came to exercise a profound influence on the memory cultures of institutionalized communities throughout the Mediterranean.

The capstone to this volume is provided by Pierre Thévenin. His chapter, "Fact as Law: An Archaeology of Legal Realism," pursues an agenda similar to that of the chapter by Nicolas Cornu Thénard, but by a very different route. Thévenin concerns himself with two aspects of legal history and its contexts: (1) the relationship between legal philosophy and procedure in the reception of Roman law in the high Middle Ages and its influence on the notion of the fact and issues of epistemology and method in emergent science in the seventeenth century; and (2) the rejection of metaphysics and its attendant fetishization of legal "concepts" by American legal realists. In both cases, Thévenin highlights similar efforts to reorient the machinery of reasoning around (inquiries into) the facts themselves. But in a sweeping and remarkable turn, Thévenin turns back to Roman law itself and to the late medieval reception of the Justinianic codification, to question whether Roman modes of legal reasoning, and medieval ways of explicating Roman texts, had been as concerned with autonomy and as divorced from practicalities as is often argued. He concludes by urging that the late medieval glossators' interest in words did not issue in an understanding of law as a transcendent system of rules operating on a different hypostatic plane. That was not their self-conception. Instead, he urges (through appeal to but also revision of Max Radin), they understood facts to arise from law, and law from facts. Whatever the self-understanding and ideological commitments of late medieval lawyers and American legal realists, Thévenin suggests, their practice and argument recognized a far more complicated imbrication of law in books and law in action than scholarship has heretofore acknowledged.

Notes

1. Maud Gleason, "Truth Contests and Talking Corpses," in *Constructions of the Classical Body*, ed. James I. Porter (Ann Arbor: University of Michigan Press, 1999), 287–313.

2. Thomas Sizgorich, "Reasoned Violence and Shifty Frontiers: Shared Victory in the Late Roman East," in *Violence in Late Antiquity. Perceptions and Practices*, ed. H. A. Drake (Aldershot: Ashgate, 2006), 167–76; Ari Bryen, "Martyrdom and the Politics of Procedure," *Classical Antiquity* 33 (2014): 243–80; Clifford Ando, "Substantive Justice in Provincial and Roman Legal Argument," in *The Impact of Justice on the Roman Empire*, ed. Olivier Hekster and Koen Verboven (Leiden: Brill, 2019), 138–56; "Performing Justice in Republican Empire," in *Legal Engagement: The Reception of Roman Law and Tribunals by Jews and Other Inhabitants of the Empire*, ed. Katell Berthelot, Natalie B.

Dohrmann, and Capucine Nemo-Pekelman (Rome: École française de Rome, forthcoming).

3. Yan Thomas, *Mommsen et "l'Isolierung" du droit: Rome, l'Allemagne et l'État* (Paris: De Boccard, 1984). This history is discussed in Pierre Thévenin's contribution to the present volume.

4. A notable work of this kind is John P. Dawson's *A History of Lay Judges* (Cambridge, MA: Harvard University Press, 1960). Further literature in the history of legal epistemology in both civil- and common-law legal systems is cited in Pierre Thévenin's contribution to the present volume.

5. See, e.g., William Robertson, *The History of the Reign of the Emperor Charles V, with a View of the Progress of Society in Europe, from the Subversion of the Roman Empire, to the Beginning of the Sixteenth Century, in Four Volumes* (London: Strahan, Cadell, 1769; repr., 1792), 46–78. For modern histories, see Lorraine Daston, "Baconsche Tatsachen," *Rechtsgeschichte* 1 (2002): 36–55, and the contribution in the present volume by Pierre Thévenin, both with extensive bibliography. Questions kindred to those posed in this volume are asked in James Chandler, Arnold I. Davidson, and Harry Harootunian, eds., *Questions of Evidence: Proof, Practice, and Persuasion across the Disciplines* (Chicago: University of Chicago Press, 1991).

6. Bruce W. Frier, *The Rise of the Roman Jurists: Studies in Cicero's "Pro Caecina"* (Princeton: Princeton University Press, 1985); see also Dario Mantovani, *Les juristes écrivains de la Rome antique: Les oeuvres des juristes comme littérature* (Paris: Collège de France, 2018), 17–78.

7. Nicolas Cornu Thénard, "La notion de fait dans la jurisprudence classique: Étude sur les principes de la distinction entre fait et droit" (PhD diss., Université Paris II, 2011).

8. Pierre Thévenin, *Le monde sur mesure: Une archéologie juridique des faits* (Paris: Classiques Garnier, 2017).

9. It may suffice to cite the classic account of Morton Horwitz, *The Transformation of American Law, 1870–1960: The Crisis of Legal Orthodoxy* (New York: Oxford University Press, 1992).

10. See, already at the gloaming of Horwitz's period (see the preceding note), H. L. A. Hart, *The Concept of Law* (Oxford: Oxford University Press, 1961), 124–54; Ronald Dworkin, "The Model of Rules," *University of Chicago Law Review* 35 (1967): 14–46. For bibliography and a distinctively "economic" analysis of modes of legislation along these lines, see Louis Kaplow, "Rules versus Standards: An Economic Analysis," *Duke Law Journal* 42 (1992): 557–629.

11. Michel Foucault, *Power/Knowledge: Selected Interviews and Other Writings, 1972–1977*, ed. Colin Gordon, trans. Colin Gordon, Leo Marshall, John Mepham, and Kate Soper (New York: Pantheon Books, 1980); Foucault, *Security, Territory, Population: Lectures at the Collège de France, 1977–78*, trans. Graham Burchell (New York: Palgrave MacMillan, 2007).

CHAPTER 1

Were the Ancient Greeks Epistemic Democrats?

Daniela Cammack

Though the primary focus of this volume is the discovery of the fact in the context of legal reasoning, this chapter considers the place of facts—defined as things that can, in principle, be known (i.e., that might be the object of the Greek verbs *oida* or *epistamai*, "know," or described as *epistêmê*, "knowledge")—in the wider ancient Greek political context. This analysis takes in assemblies as well as law courts, particularly (owing to the abundance of evidence) those of classical Athens. It is not too controversial to regard the classical Athenian courts (*dikastêria*) as political bodies.[1] Many plainly political decisions were made by judicial panels, not only via the *graphê paranomôn* (the indictment for proposing an illegal decree), but also through other charges, such as treason, lying to the demos, and offering or taking bribes. Pre-office scrutinies and post-tenure audits were likewise decided by judges and were a standard part of the political process in Athens and elsewhere.[2] Indeed, though ancient Greek courts have often been represented by scholars as accessories to the main decision-making body of a polis, they were arguably equally significant,[3] as suggested by, among other things, Aristotle's representation of "What is advantageous?" and "What is just?" as preeminent political questions. The advantageous (*to sympheron*) was typically decided by assemblies, the just (*to dikaion*) by courts.[4] Both bodies were equally political in that they made decisions on behalf of the polis.[5] They generated actions that were treated as those of the community as a whole.

My topic here is the limits of claims to knowledge in these contexts. Interestingly, there was no ancient Greek equivalent to our word *fact*, though it commonly appears in translation. What is so translated is usually a pronoun, such as "this" (*touto*) or "these things" (*tauta*), and sometimes a participle, such as *to gegenêmenon*, "what has happened."[6] Both assemblies and courts were, as noted, decision-making bodies; they heard arguments and then voted to approve or to reject a proposal and to confirm or to dismiss an indictment. In the course of those arguments, a great many appeals were made to the way things are, have been, or will be—appeals that we may plausibly characterize as appeals to fact. I here investigate something slightly different: the perceived relationship of the decision-making process itself to fact, knowledge, or truth.

Specifically, I ask to what extent the questions considered by ancient Greek assemblies and courts—all of them variations on the basic formulations "What is advantageous?" and "What is just?"—were understood not merely as involving appeals to matters of fact but as themselves inquiries into fact. When an assembly considered whether or not a particular policy (e.g., declaring war against Philip of Macedon) was advantageous, to what extent did its members believe that an objectively correct answer to their question existed? When a judicial panel considered whether, for example, Ktesiphon's proposal to award Demosthenes a crown was illegal, how far was the answer to that question conceived of as something that existed independently of the views of the judges? I ask, in other words, if invocations of fact in arguments about advantage and justice were separated, by a perceived boundary, from the decisions subsequently made, or if, instead, the notion of "facticity" slid into the way the ancient Greeks conceived of those decisions themselves.

I hope to show, against some recent arguments, that there was such a boundary. The ancient Greeks did not regard themselves as working their way toward an objectively correct answer when they decided political questions. On the contrary, their political terminology reveals that they conceived of decision-making as a strictly situated activity, inseparable from the perspective of the decision maker. A decision was a judgment made from a particular point of view, not an attempt to square up to an independently correct order of things. That understanding, I suggest, reveals a grasp of the nature of political action superior to the epistemic conceptualization popular in some quarters today.

The Current Intellectual Context

An influential defense of democracy is the epistemic argument, also known as the argument from collective wisdom.[7] According to this argument, democracy is superior to other forms of government because it offers the best chance of arriving at correct answers to political questions.[8] Support for this claim is often drawn from Condorcet's jury theorem (1795), which shows that, assuming any given juror has a better than random probability of being right, a majority of jurors is almost certain to be right about a defendant's guilt or innocence; in addition, the greater the majority, the higher the probability of a correct conviction.[9] Similar logic has been held to apply to such questions as "Should we build a bridge over the channel or not? If so, should it be a four-lane, a two-lane, built now or later?" and "Should France ratify the EU constitution?"[10]

Epistemic democrats hold that there are correct (or at least epistemically better and worse) answers to such questions. They hold that these answers exist independently of any decision-making procedure but can be approximated by decision makers to some degree (if not known with certainty), and they agree that large, cognitively diverse groups are more likely to approximate correct answers than small groups or individuals (including groups of experts), because the former have access to more diverse knowledge about the world. In the words of Hélène Landemore, "More is smarter."[11] For some, such as David Estlund, this justification of democracy is not merely sufficient but necessary: "Democratically produced laws are legitimate and authoritative because they are produced by a procedure with a tendency to make correct decisions."[12]

There is some plausibility to these claims. In several cases, the "wisdom of crowds" has been shown to answer certain kinds of questions better than individuals, however expert. Two frequently cited examples are a 1906 competition for guessing an ox's weight, described by Francis Galton, and a 1968 search for a missing submarine. More recently, James Surowiecki has documented the same phenomenon when asking members of the public to guess the number of jelly beans in a jar and even, on a radio phone-in program, the number of books in his office.[13] In every case, the average guess of the crowd resulted in something very close to the independently verifiable truth.

These experiments have prompted a great deal of interest among political theorists. But it is not quite clear what their political implications may be, since we have no way to verify "true" or "correct" answers to political questions.

Other kinds of supporting evidence must be found if the epistemic argument for democracy (or any other political system) is to seem credible.

Into this breach, perhaps unexpectedly, step the ancient Greeks. Aristotle is regularly cited in this connection;[14] Protagoras (as represented by Plato) has also been deployed.[15] Most significantly, Josiah Ober has recently championed classical Athens as a "case study in participatory epistemic democracy."[16] What Ober calls the "remarkable" success of Athens can, he argues, be explained at least in part by the "epistemic functions of democratic institutions."[17] "Overall and over time," Ober writes, "democratic Athens fared well enough to outdo all its city-state rivals," and "the postulated value of aggregated knowledge solves the riddle of Athenian success."[18]

Ober's claim is open to two interpretations. It may be read as a purely external or objective account of the Athenian political system: that is, regardless of the Athenians' intentions or self-understanding, the effect of their political system was to aggregate a great deal of politically useful knowledge. If that reading is right, Ober offers a "black box" analysis of Athenian democracy, an "as if" or functionalist-evolutionary account that harkens back to his brief but ringing endorsement of behavioral studies of human society in his major early work *Mass and Elite in Democratic Athens*.[19] Like all "as if" explanations, moreover, such an account could not be disproved on its own merits, given its implicit reliance on circular reasoning.[20] It could only be deemed more or less plausible in relation to competing accounts.

Alternatively, Ober's claim may be read in a more internal or subjective vein, as suggesting that the Athenians consciously deployed democratic institutions in order to maximize knowledge aggregation. If so, Ober's argument is staked at least partly on the territory of political thought as well as practice. It suggests that ordinary Athenians conceived of political decision-making along epistemic lines and actively supported democracy on that basis, not merely that they unwittingly enjoyed its epistemic effects.

Much of the time, Ober has left open which interpretation is to be preferred. This is understandable given the relatively little evidence available on the Athenian council, which Ober describes as the city's most epistemically valuable institution.[21] In at least one version of the argument, however, Ober has favored the second interpretation. Democratic Athens, he writes, depended "directly and self-consciously" on "deploying the epistemic resources of its citizenry to hold its place in a highly competitive multi-state environment."[22]

Unlike a functionalist account, the latter version of Ober's claim concerning

Athens may be assessed directly. We have ample evidence showing how the Athenians and other Greeks conceived of their decision-making processes. Did they favor democratic institutions because they enabled the community to benefit from the epistemic resources of the masses? In particular, did they think of democratic decision-making as a process likely to uncover correct (or at least epistemically superior) answers to the political questions before them? Were they, in short, epistemic democrats? I argue that the answer to these questions is no.

In the remainder of this chapter, I first assess the evidence introduced by Ober and others in support of the view that the ancient Greeks valued democracy on epistemic grounds. Next, I explore the distinction between knowledge (*epistêmê*), understood as information that exists independently of human will, and judgment (*krisis* or *gnômê*), understood as a view produced by and inextricably linked to a particular willing agent. I suggest that while the ancient Greeks certainly believed that knowledge played a role in decision-making, they understood the specific task of decision makers to be asserting how things seemed to them (*edoxe tini*, the language used in the prescript of ancient Greek decrees), not discovering how things really were. This suggests that the concept of a procedure-independent standard of correctness or truth in politics—a necessary postulate of the epistemic view—was largely alien to them. Finally, drawing on political problems such as the Melians' conflict with the Athenians during the Peloponnesian War and the rise of Macedon, I argue that the standard ancient Greek conceptualization of decision-making shows a better grasp of its inherently creative character.

The Evidence for the Epistemic Interpretation

Easily the most-cited evidence for the view that the ancient Greeks supported democracy on epistemic grounds is a section of book 3 of Aristotle's *Politics*, in which he argues that it is sometimes acceptable for a multitude to hold power.[23] The argument itself is fairly brief (though Aristotle frequently refers back to it) and has been much debated. At its heart is a claim that because a large number of relatively ordinary men may collectively possess more of a certain politically salient thing than a few men who are each blessed with a large amount, the large group is able to judge better (*krinousin ameinon*) than the small one.

What is this politically salient thing? Despite some variation among interpretations, the predominant view has been that it is some form of knowledge, such as dispersed information, experience, or expertise.[24] Yet, as I have argued elsewhere, Aristotle does not, strictly speaking, employ epistemic language in this passage.[25] Rather (as shown by his immediately preceding chapters), he takes the crucial criterion for participation in politics to be *aretê*, "excellence" or "virtue," an umbrella term that includes both ethical and intellectual qualities, and he maintains that focus throughout the passage in question. Each man of the many, he says, may have a part (*morion*) of virtue (*aretês*) and prudence (*phronêseôs*), and when they come together, these parts are combined: one man supplies one part, another provides another part, and all together supply the whole (*alloi gar allo ti morion, panta de pantes*).[26]

There is clearly an intellectual aspect to this claim. *Phronêsis*, "practical wisdom," is one of six capacities listed by Aristotle under *logos*, "reason," in his catalog of the parts of *aretê* in its broadest sense.[27] (*Epistêmê*, "scientific understanding" or "knowledge," is another.) Equally clearly, the claim has an ethical aspect. Whenever Aristotle distinguishes between *aretê* and an intellectual capacity (as he does here), *aretê* always refers to a bundle of moral qualities, including (most important for politics) courage, justice, and moderation.[28] But most crucial to our understanding is that in Aristotle's account, these criteria—courage, justice, moderation, and even practical wisdom—are practices, not forms of knowledge. That *aretê* (virtue) is *epistêmê* (knowledge) is an argument famously associated with Socrates and Plato but explicitly denied by Aristotle,[29] according to whom *aretê* is a "power" (*dynamis*) of "providing and preserving good things."[30] Above all, it is practical, realized only in activity.[31] As such, it is quite different from knowledge, which may exist in the mind even when not being acted on.

To the extent that Aristotle had a conception of collective wisdom, then, it seems to have involved not the aggregation of knowledge (conceived of as dispersed information, experience, or expertise) but the aggregation of practical capabilities, including ethical capabilities, in collective activity.[32] Accordingly, his defense of the right of certain multitudes to rule is not "epistemic" according to the modern definition of the term. He never suggests that a multitude ought to rule because it can aggregate more politically useful knowledge than smaller groups. Rather, his view seems to be that a multitude will be justified in ruling if and when, by acting together, it will be braver, fairer, more moderate, and more sensible than some subset of very brave, fair, moderate, and sensible men. I take this argument to be closer to an ethical than an epistemic one.

Losing the support of this passage of Aristotle makes a sizable hole in the epistemic democrat's armory. As well as being the only canonical philosophical support cited in most discussions of collective wisdom, it is the only primary evidence used to demonstrate the Athenians' commitment to the aggregation of knowledge in Ober's 2008 book *Democracy and Knowledge*.[33] Earlier in his career, however, Ober adduced several other passages in the service of a more general argument about the Athenians' faith in the "wisdom of the masses," defined as the "collective knowledge, experience, and judgment of the citizen body as a whole."[34] Unfortunately, those passages also fall short of proving that the Athenians supported democracy on epistemic grounds. Either they reveal respect for the judgment of the masses but do not show that this respect was connected to their possession of knowledge, or they attest to the usefulness of knowledge but do not show that its dispersed possession was believed to justify democracy.

Many sources indicate Greek democrats' respect for the judgment of the masses and their commitment to submitting political decisions to them. One of the best known is a sentence by the Syracusan leader Athenagoras (reported by Thucydides), stating that while the best advisers are the wise (*tous synetous*), the many (*hoi polloi*) judge best (*krinai . . . arista*).[35] As Ober rightly notes, a similar idea appears in Cleon's speech on how best to punish the Mytilenaeans following their revolt: "ordinary men" who "mistrust their own cleverness" generally "conduct affairs successfully" (*orthountai*—literally, "go straight") because they are "fair judges" (*kritai . . . apo tou isou*), unlike those "rivals" who argue with each other from the stage.[36]

At first glance, the passages just cited may look like promising support for the epistemic interpretation. Yet, crucially, neither implies that the basis of the masses' better judgment is knowledge. Cleon, in particular, appears to be suggesting something different: that "ordinary men" judge more soundly because they are not themselves party to a public dispute. That suggestion recalls another argument offered by Aristotle in support of the judgment of the many: that they are less "corruptible" (*adiaphthoron*) than a few, just as a larger stream of water is purer.[37] A single person's judgment (*krisin*), Aristotle argues, is bound to be corrupted when that person is overcome by anger or another emotion, but it is hard to make everyone get angry and "go wrong" (*hamartein*) at the same time.[38] Again, what is at issue seems to be primarily ethical or dispositional.[39] Sound judgment involves being fair to both sides, by practicing the virtue of justice (*dikaiosynê*), a quality commonly lauded in Greek political thought.[40]

A passage from Demosthenes cited by Ober may be interpreted similarly. Ober writes, "Even when berating the jurors for their inconsistency, Demosthenes emphasized their good judgment and claimed that everyone [*hapantes*] quite correctly agreed that bribe-taking politicians were the worst men in the state."[41] Bribery was certainly taken very seriously: a variety of measures were available to bring those involved to court, and if they were convicted, the death penalty might be applied.[42] But it is not clear that Demosthenes' comment reveals a commitment to democracy on epistemic grounds. If the judgment of the masses was deemed superior to that of a bribe taker, the reason for that was surely ethical. Moreover, Demosthenes' suggestion that the judgment of the crowd was the correct one does not amount to a defense of democracy.

In other passages, knowledge plays a more direct role. Hypereides argued that a man's entire life is relevant to his legal defense since "no one in the polis can deceive the mass of you."[43] Similarly, Dinarchus, prosecuting Demosthenes for bribery in 323, remarked that his audience would doubtless "see and know [*epistamenoi*] these facts [*tauth'*, "these things"] much better than I do."[44] Ober argues that since Dinarchus goes on to relate the crimes of Demosthenes in great detail, the prosecutor cannot really have thought this. Rather, Ober suggests, Dinarchus is "expressing solidarity with an ideology that stressed group over individual knowledge."[45]

Ober's interpretation is certainly possible. But the claim "You guys know this even better than I do" remains a fairly common rhetorical gambit, and one would hesitate to argue that every society in which it has appeared is one that prized group over individual knowledge. Moreover, although such remarks are quite common in our extant speeches, they were not above suspicion. Another speech in the Demosthenic corpus includes the lines "[This man] is so unscrupulous that if he has no witnesses to prove a fact [*peri hôn*, "about things"], he will say it is well known to you [*hymas eidenai*] . . . a trick used by all those who have no just argument to advance. If he shall try it, do not tolerate it; expose him. What any one of you does not know [*eidê*], let him deem [*dokimazetô*] that his neighbor does not know either."[46] This advice strongly implies that regardless of the grounds on which ordinary men were invited to pass judgment in court, the possession of prior knowledge was not deemed to be essential.

Most extant ancient Greek speeches, like the aforementioned, concern court cases. Our most valuable evidence concerning speeches made in assemblies is a collection of openings (*exordia*) found among the writings of Demosthenes, and Ober rightly makes the most of them. He draws attention to two in particular. One, *Exordium* 45, recalls the speeches of Athenagoras and Cleon found in Thucydides and quoted above. Ober writes, "When arguing that making a good speech and choosing sound policies are not the same, Demosthenes states that the former is the work of the rhetor, the second of a man possessing intelligence (*nous*). Therefore, 'you, the many' are not expected to speak as well as the orators, but 'you, especially the older ones of you, are expected to have intelligence (*noun*) equal to or better than that of the speakers, since it is experiences (*empeiriai*) and having seen much (*poll' heorakenoi*) that makes for intelligence.'"[47] The special attractiveness of this passage to older citizens is "obvious," Ober remarks, but he also suggests that it "affirms the conviction that collective judgment by the many is superior to individual perception and more important than mere speech."[48]

It is clearly true that the collective judgment of the many was deemed "more important than mere speech." It was, after all, the vote of the mass of listeners, not the opinion of a speaker, that was politically decisive in Athens and other ancient Greek democracies. But the claim that collective judgment by the many was deemed superior to individual perception deserves further consideration. For one thing, Demosthenes does not actually mention perception, individual or otherwise. He is engaged in comparing speech-making and decision-making, and his argument is that different capacities are exercised in each: in speech-making, rhetorical prowess; in decision-making, intelligence (*nous*) based on experience. The modern pro-democracy argument from collective wisdom would be that decisions ought to be made by the many because those who comprise the many have more experience under their collective belt than a single speaker. But Demosthenes does not make that claim. Rather, he takes it for granted that the speaker's role is simply to speak, and he stresses that this function is distinct from the audience's role, which is to decide. Demosthenes goes on to argue that "valorous deeds and bold exploits . . . unless backed by ready armament and physical force, though pleasant to hear, are hazardous in action. . . . All things are easy to say, men of Athens, but not all things are easy to do."[49] Demosthenes' concern is evidently that the audience will make a foolish decision based on its love of fine speeches, rather than a sensible one based on *nous*, which the crowd's older members especially ought to possess. The two dispositive factors here would seem to be age and *nous*, not *epistêmê* or even, necessarily, collective judgment.

The other passage Ober quotes from Demosthenes' *Exordia* offers stronger support for the epistemic case. In it, Demosthenes is outlining the situations in which he would not bother to speak. One is when everyone has already decided to do what Demosthenes considers necessary, in which case a speech from him would be superfluous. The other is when everyone has already decided to do the thing he opposes, "for I should have thought it more likely," he explains, "that a single person like myself should misconstrue the best measures [*agnoein ta kratist'*] than all of you."[50] That line is compatible with the view that the Athenians supported democracy because the knowledge possessed by the assembly en masse made them better able to make good decisions, but it does not constrain that inference. Demosthenes accepts that when he is massively outnumbered, it is more likely that the unsound judgment is his rather than that of his audience. But the basis of its unsoundness is unstated. Most important, the epistemic status of the "best measures" is open to interpretation. Do they exist independently of the crowd, apart from its perceptions and judgments? On one occasion elsewhere, Demosthenes distinguishes between "what seems best to you" (*dokounta beltisth'*) and the "truly best" (*onth' hôs alêthôs*), but it is not clear whether he thought that the "truly best" could securely be apprehended by his audience.[51] Altogether, the second *Exordia* passage referenced by Ober raises the question under consideration here but does not answer it.

Completing Ober's catalog of support for the "wisdom of the masses" is a passage from Isocrates' attack on the Sophists, the itinerant intellectuals who made their living by teaching rhetoric. Though those men professed to have "exact knowledge" (*tên epistêmên*), Isocrates argues that people who relied on *doxai* (opinions, judgments, or views) tended to agree with one another more and to be correct (*katorthountas*, "keep straight") more often than the Sophists themselves.[52] Suggesting that this claim is "not necessarily representative of Isocrates' general beliefs," Ober takes it to show that Isocrates was "willing and able to use the *topoi* of popular ideology for polemical purposes"—the topos in question being "the assumption that groups of individuals lacking special skills and education tended to produce wise decisions."[53] As before, there is no defense of democracy here, epistemic or otherwise. More important is the contrast Isocrates draws between *doxa* (opinion) and *epistêmê* (knowledge). Not only does he counterpose the views of laymen to those of intellectuals, but he specifically distinguishes the judgments of ordinary men from knowledge as such. In the words of translator George Norlin: "There is, according to Isocrates, no 'science' which can teach us to do under all circumstances the things which will insure our happiness and success. . . . All that education can do is to develop a sound judgment (as opposed to knowledge)."[54] On this reading, Isocrates seems very far from making an epistemic claim on behalf of the many.

About Athenagoras, Demosthenes, Hypereides, and Dinarchus, Ober concludes, "All leave a place in the decision-making process for the expert politician, but each affirms that the collective wisdom of the masses must be the final arbiter."[55] Those orators certainly championed the advisory role of politicians, though we should perhaps be a bit cautious about the term *expert*, since that is not how they typically represented themselves.[56] And each certainly wanted the judgment (*krisis*) of the masses to be politically decisive. But to the extent Ober uses the word *wisdom* to mean "knowledge" rather than "judgment," we must demur: we do not have the evidence for that.

Finally, we should consider the sketch of Protagoras' political views given by Plato and recently discussed by Hélène Landemore, who rightly notes that the speech put in Protagoras' mouth is a genuine defense of mass participation in politics.[57] Whether Protagoras' argument amounts to an epistemic defense of democracy is another question. According to Protagoras, all men are originally endowed with the qualities of reverence (*aidôs*) and justice (*dikaiosynê*), which are the bonds of men in poleis; hence all men are born to share in political life.[58] Landemore speculates that the political wisdom inculcated by those qualities is an emergent property of the group, since that interpretation would explain Protagoras' insistence that in addition to being inborn, those characteristics can be further developed through education; Landemore argues that it is only by including everyone that the city will tap "divine wisdom" in the form of collective wisdom.[59] Yet Landemore freely admits the difficulty of calling Protagoras' myth "epistemic." As she rightly concedes, political wisdom appears in this dialogue "as an art, a virtue, but only ambiguously as a form of knowledge."[60] There are slender grounds for interpreting Protagoras' conceptions of either *aidôs* or *dikaiosynê* as epistemic (unlike those of Plato himself). Landemore is right, however, that Protagoras should be significant for epistemic democrats—though for a different reason altogether, as we shall now see.

Knowledge versus Judgment

Ancient Greek democrats were certainly convinced of the wisdom of putting questions to the demos. Yet it is not clear whether that was because the demos itself was deemed wise, at least if by that we mean knowledgeable. *Krisis* (judgment), not *epistêmê* (knowledge), is the key concept associated with decision-making in our sources, and the best case for the epistemic view comes from assimilating the two. But there are good reasons to resist that move.

As far as we can tell from Plato's representation, Protagoras was particularly famous for one idea, formulated by Plato in the *Theaetetus* as "Man [*anthrôpos*] is the measure [*metron*] of all things, of the existence of the things that are and the non-existence of the things that are not."[61] A few pages later, this idea reappears with a noteworthy alteration: *metron* is replaced by *kritês* (judge), cognate with *krisis*, the term meaning "decision" or "judgment" that we have already encountered several times.[62] To paraphrase the assertion of Plato's Protagoras, claims about "what is" express nothing more or less than that they appear to be so to a human being. Whether this amounts to full-blown philosophical subjectivism or relativism may be debated.[63] But according to Protagoras' account, human beings cannot get beyond their own perceptions; the views they adopt are intrinsically and ineluctably attached to them as perceivers as well as to the objects perceived. As Plato's Socrates suggests of Protagoras' view, "Nothing is invariably one, itself by itself, but everything is always becoming in relation to something, and 'being' should be altogether abolished."[64]

Protagoras' position is the target of lengthy and explicit criticism in the *Theaetetus*, and I want to draw attention to the concatenation of ideas associated and contrasted with it. The "man-measure" doctrine is consistently identified by Plato with (1) *krisis* (judgment, decision) and *aisthêsis* (perception), as opposed to *epistêmê* (knowledge);[65] (2) *genesis* (generation) and *kinêsis* (motion), as opposed to *ktêsis* (possession);[66] (3) *to dokein* (seeming)—cognate with *doxa* (opinion)—and *to phainetai* (appearing) and *to genesthai* (becoming), as opposed to *to einai* (being);[67] and (4) political activity, as opposed to philosophy.[68] These patterns admit of concise summarization. At the heart of the *Theaetetus* lies a significant distinction between judgment and knowledge. Judgment is conceived of as an articulation of how things seem to an agent—a changeable articulation generated by and inextricably linked to that agent. Knowledge is conceived of as an articulation of how things really are, which may be possessed by but exists independently of an agent and is not susceptible to change.

From Plato, we understand that the norm in Athens was to care—principally, if not exclusively—about judgment. That Socrates alone is depicted as being more interested in knowledge is to be expected: the self-conception attributed to Socrates as being the Athenians' lone "gadfly" demands it.[69] But, strikingly,

Plato seems to have been right. The evidence is overwhelming that although the ancient Greeks granted knowledge a role in the production of judgments, they saw the essential task of decision makers as being to assert how things seemed to them (a view in which they were themselves implicated), rather than how they thought things really were (an understanding independent of their own views or commitments). In other words, when a political agent chose to follow a particular course of action, it was understood that he (or it, in the case of a collective agent) had not discovered but deemed that particular course of action to be advantageous or just.

One way that understanding is visible is in the widespread use of the terms *krisis* (decision, or judgment) and *gnômê* (judgment, opinion), as opposed to *epistêmê* (knowledge), to describe the verdicts of assemblies, courts, and other decision-making bodies.[70] But it is plainest in the use of the verb *dokeô* (seem) in decision-making contexts. Throughout ancient Greece, that was the term used to establish laws, decrees, alliances, and other political decisions. We have scores of examples of inscriptions beginning with *edoxe tô dêmô* (literally, "it seemed [good] to the demos") or variations (involving other agents or institutions).[71] The verb in these cases is often translated "decided by," "resolved by," or even "voted" (since that was often the action that had taken place), but what was asserted, more literally, was that the chosen course of action had seemed advantageous to the decision-maker.[72] Even the notion of advantage was typically implicit, though it did appear occasionally. Two examples are Lycurgus' description of a decree of 338 to the effect that the council would "hold itself ready to do whatever seemed to be in the interest of the demos" (*ho ti an dokê tô dêmô sympheron einai*) and a line of Demosthenes in which he observed that out of a multitude of proposals, "the selection of the one advantageous to you" (*tên tou sympherontos hymin hairesin*) should not be too difficult.[73] Never merely implicit, however, was the agent to whom the given course of action had seemed appropriate, that is, the identity of the decision maker. That information was evidently deemed an essential part of the political record.

Dokeô was used in a parallel way in judicial contexts: Aeschines reports that the "formula prescribed by law" to be spoken by the herald prior to a vote was "The hollow ballot for he who believes [*hotô dokei*; literally, "to whom it seems"] that [X has committed the charge], the solid ballot for him who does not [*hotô mê*]."[74] The only difference was that in court, the wider issue under consideration was not what seemed advantageous to the judges but what seemed just. Hypereides asked his hearers, when they went to the ballot, to "dispense with the arguments of us all" and "vote whatever seems to you to be just [*ho ti an hymin dokê dikaion einai*] and in keeping with your oath."[75] The speaker in *Against Macartatus*, an inheritance case, "deliver[ed] over to you this boy to be the object of your care in whatever way you deem most just [*hopôs an hymin dokê dikaiotaton einai*]."[76] Similar examples include the injunction "If I seem to have been the victim of wrongful and lawless acts [*ean êdikêsthai kai paranenomeisthai dokô*], render me the aid which is my due"; the plea that the judges come to the speaker's aid "if we seem to be being wronged" (*dokômen adikeisthai*); and the recollection that "you punished him, because he was judged to be guilty [*doxanta adikein*; literally, "he seemed to have done wrong"]."[77] The essential issue was how things seemed to the judges, and the majority view was accepted publicly and, it seems, unhesitatingly—except by Plato—as decisive.

The use of *dokeô* in these contexts, especially the use of *dokeô tini* (seem to [the decision maker]) to mean "decide," militates strongly against the claim that most ancient Greeks supported democracy (or any other decision-making system) on epistemic grounds. A key postulate of the epistemic view is that there is a procedure-independent right answer to political questions, which it is the decision maker's job to approximate and against which the final decision can be judged. But no such conception appears in our ancient Greek sources—as long as we include "agent-independent" under the banner of "procedure-independent," as I think we must. Rather, the evidence suggests that most ancient Greeks were quite comfortable with the idea that decisions simply track the view of the decision maker, however that view might have seemed to others. Only Plato's Socrates, it appears, showed an interest in "right answers" to practical questions beyond the ken of how things seemed to be to the decider, and that position arguably constituted one of the most far-reaching philosophical interventions in the history of political thought.[78]

Paradoxically, today's epistemic democrats would appear to side with the notorious antidemocrat Plato on this issue, against the rest of the ancient Greeks. The standard Greek conceptualization of political decision-making seems to have been closer to the doctrine of Protagoras. And that doctrine, I submit, actually reflects a more plausible account of the nature of political action.

The Nature of Political Action

Among the postulates of the epistemic defense of democracy is the idea that there are right or correct (or, at least, epistemically better and worse) answers to political questions, such as "Should we build this bridge?" and "Should France ratify the EU constitution?" To those queries, we may add some ancient Greek equivalents: "Should the Melians refuse an alliance with Athens?" or "Should the Athenians go to war against Philip of Macedon?" or "Was Ktesiphon's proposal to give Demosthenes an honorary crown illegal?" Epistemic democrats suggest that the right answers to these questions exist independently of the decision-making process and may be approximated by decision makers to some degree, if not known with certainty.

Now let us consider the nature of political decisions. Essentially, they specify and set in train a course of action within the effectual power of the decision maker—in this case, the agent who speaks for the polis.[79] In that respect, political decisions are no different from decisions made by individuals in regard to their personal lives. Both set in motion actions within the power of the decision makers to effect. That characteristic is easy to see in the case of policy decisions, that is, questions of advantage. Whether the bridge is built, the constitution ratified, the alliance made, or war declared is, in the final analysis, simply up to the decision-making agent to decide. Other things may intervene before, for example, the bridge is completed or even begun, but having the bridge built must, in principle, be within the capacity of the decision-making agent.

Accordingly, I suggest, decision-making is an inherently creative act. It can create something new in the world: a bridge, a constitution, an alliance, a state of war. Or it can create a world in which (at least for the time being) there is no such bridge, constitution, alliance, or war, although the potential for it had existed. Either way, something novel is generated purely by the will of the decision maker. That creative aspect suggests that deciding political questions is fundamentally different from answering questions of the kind described earlier in connection with the successful use of the "wisdom of crowds": the weight of an ox, the location of a missing submarine, and the number of jelly beans in a jar or of books in a study. To these examples, we may add one from ancient Greece, not yet, as far as I know, cited in any of the relevant literature: "How high is this wall?" The Plataeans, Thucydides tells us, made ladders as high as their enemy's city wall by severally "counting the layers of bricks in an unplastered section. . . . Many counted the layers at the same time, and while some were sure to make a mistake, the majority were likely to hit the true count."[80] In each of these cases, a right answer really did exist independently of the will of those answering. No matter how much those doing the estimating may have wished otherwise, it was not within their power to alter the weight of the ox, the location of the submarine, or the number of jelly beans, books, or bricks in the wall. The responses given to these questions were not decisions: there was no decision to be made.

In the case of political questions, however (at least when they are being answered by responsible agents rather than by philosophers), the response offered is a decision. It is not an "answer" in the true sense but a creative act, ultimately (in any case where the decision maker is choosing between two or more possible options) dependent on the will of its author. Indeed, it may be a mistake to think that the political agent and the philosopher interested in political issues are even responding to the same question. At the moment of decision, what is asked is arguably not "Should we build this bridge?"—the question that may well have guided consideration up to that point. Rather, what is asked, implicitly or explicitly, is "Shall we build this bridge?"—a question that necessarily draws our attention back to the will of the decision maker.

In short, I am here taking Aristotle's side against Plato on the nature of action. Plato posited that the question "What is right?" may be conceived and therefore answered in the same way in the realms of both philosophy and politics—that in both cases, the answer lies on the terrain of "what is" and therefore of *epistêmê*. In contrast, Aristotle argued that asking "What do I know?" is intrinsically different from asking "What shall I do?" The first question calls on *epistêmê* and scientific reasoning, the second on *phronêsis* and deliberation (i.e., choice-making).[81] The "answer" that results from the latter type of inquiry is a decision rather than a fact—a completely different kind of determination.

Since political decisions, with their creative aspect, cannot be divorced from what the decision maker wills and has the power to do, the postulate that there are right answers independent of the decision maker—that is, independent of its will—must, I think, be considered false. It would be akin to suggesting that there exists a right answer to the kind of poem a poet ought to create. My claim may seem to verge on relativism or nihilism (as David Estlund might argue).[82] Surely, some might say, we can imagine better or worse outcomes from the point of view of the agent, and there will exist an agent-independent or objective answer as to what those outcomes are. For example, we can agree that war, famine, or the annihilation of the polis are undesirable outcomes, while its continued flourishing is a desirable one. Can we not use these eventualities as a standard by which to judge the felicity or otherwise of our decisions? To that question, I would say no, and I think most ancient Greeks would have concurred, for two reasons. First, even when preferred outcomes are agreed on, there may be profound uncertainty about how to establish them and—still more intractable, though perhaps less often considered—wide variation in appetite for the risks involved in doing so. Second, even if things do not turn out as hoped, it does not necessarily follow that the initial judgment of the responsible agents was a poor one. Deciding to pursue a particular course of action, with all the risks it entails, is not the same thing as predicting that the course of action will turn out well. Accordingly, even with the benefit of hindsight, the distinction between judgment and knowledge remains intact.[83]

Uncertainty and risk follow from the obvious point that we decide on actions without knowing their results. As Isocrates argued in *On the Peace*, "in dealing with matters about which they deliberate [*bouleuontai*], men ought not to think that they know [*eidenai*] what the result will be, but be minded towards these contingencies as men who exercise their best judgment [*houtô dianoeisthai*]."[84] Inasmuch as every action creates a new state of the world, we cannot fully foresee its consequences or those of other actions that will be taken in response. The results of our actions are thus susceptible not to knowledge but only to hope and fear. The degree to which we are prepared to accept the risks inherent in any action in order to pursue our hopes and escape our fears will vary from person to person. Consequently, there cannot be an objective standard—at any rate, one accessible to our species—by which to assess the decisions taken by given agents in given conditions.

Consider the situation of the Melians in book 5 of Thucydides.[85] Their options were clear:[86] either they could become allies of the Athenians, paying tribute but preserving their territory, or they could refuse to become allies, trusting in fortune, the gods, and the Lacedaemonians to assist them if the Athenians attacked.[87] As Thucydides has the Athenians point out, the chances that fortune, the gods, or the Lacedaemonians would step in to save the Melians were slim, while the Athenians' position was extremely strong: they had thirty of their own ships and eight of their allies' anchored at Melos, with a force of about seventeen hundred hoplites, three hundred bowmen, and twenty mounted archers encamped on the land, and they had already set about ravaging the Melians' territory.[88] Nonetheless, the Melian negotiators refused the alliance, stating that they would not so readily "rob of its freedom a polis that has already been inhabited seven hundred years"; instead, they would "try to win our deliverance."[89] The sequel is well known. The Athenians commenced a siege, the Melians eventually capitulated, and the Athenians killed all the adult males, enslaved the women and children, and eventually repopulated the town with their own colonists.

Does it make sense to think of the Melians' decision to reject the Athenians' demands as epistemically better or worse than the alternative? The language of knowledge certainly played a role in the arguments. Both sides "knew" (*epistamenous, epistametha*) that "the powerful exact what they can, while the weak yield what they must" and that "the fortune of war is sometimes impartial and not in accord with the difference in numbers."[90] Declaring the Melians' reasoning to be *alogôs* (irrational), the Athenians openly accused them of placing greater confidence in their hopes than in their present resources and of "holding out for the worse alternative."[91] Yet I can see no reason to believe that the Melians decided as they did because they were mistaken about the magnitude of the task before them. They acknowledged that they would find it very difficult to defeat the Athenians, who, for their part, admitted that the favorable contingencies imagined by the Melians might happen.[92] As the Melians argued, "For us, to yield is at once to give up hope; but if we make an effort, there is still hope that we may stand erect."[93]

The Melian negotiators were willing to take an enormous risk—to "stake your all on a single throw," as the Athenians put it.[94] But it does not follow that they made an epistemic mistake. Only hindsight brings certainty; before the event, there will always be room for hope. If the will to tolerate the relevant risks exists, the claim that acting on that will involves a factual mistake seems meaningless. One may, I think, sooner say that the Melians were crazy to act as they did than that they were mistaken, even if their preferred outcome was survival as opposed to an honorable destruction.

Other examples show that the ancient Greeks did not consider all decisions that proved unfortunate to have been mistaken. Take, for instance, the Syracusans' response to the news that the Athenians were coming to invade Sicily in 415. Hermocrates asserted that he spoke with knowledge (*eidôs*), but he was disbelieved; Athenagoras' argument that the Athenians would hardly act so foolishly was based on probabilities (*ta eikota*), and the Syracusan demos agreed.[95] The Athenians did invade, but Athenagoras was not accused of making a mistake. His judgment had been a reasonable one: the Syracusans were not to know how reckless the Athenians could be.

Another example is Demosthenes' self-defense in *On the Crown*. At various points between the late 350s and 322, when the Greek rebels against Macedonian rule were comprehensively defeated, the Athenians had to choose between fighting—as they did, for example, in 352–346, 340–338, and 323—and keeping the peace. Both options risked disaster, either through annihilation by superior military forces, as happened to Thebes in 335, or through the loss of political autonomy, as happened to Athens in 322. Demosthenes' position during that period seems to have been complex and not necessarily consistent, but the defense he offered in 330 was straightforward. His policy of resistance to Macedon had failed, but it had seemed right to him, and he stood by it.[96] More than four-fifths of the judges voted in his favor, rejecting Aeschines' argument that proposing a crown for these efforts was illegal.

Evidently, neither Hermocrates' advice nor that of Demosthenes was interpreted as a form of prediction. Judging well—that is, making (or advising) a decision on what seem reasonable grounds—was, apparently, treated as distinct from one's judgment being borne out by events. Indeed, ancient Greeks seldom spoke of good or wise judgments, let alone correct ones. Rather, they complimented the act of judging. The usual form of praise was to say that someone had judged "straightly" (*orthôs*).[97] Whether or not such "straight judging" turned out to embody a successful prediction was a separate issue. Similarly, making a poor judgment was "going wrong with respect to a judgment" (*gnômê hamartanei*) or "seeming to make a mistake" (*dokoit' an hamartein*). I am not suggesting that criticism of others' views was rare; on the contrary, the Athenians were arguably harsher in this respect than we are today, as revealed by their custom of indicting those who proposed illegal measures or disadvantageous laws. But at stake in such cases was usually the claim that the original judgment had been based on deceit or manipulation of the people or the political process, not that it had been epistemically unsound.[98]

To what extent were the questions raised in Athenian courts—decisions of justice—treated like guesses at the number of jelly beans in a jar, and to what extent were they treated like policy questions of the kind raised in assemblies? To Plato, questions of justice exactly resembled the example of the jelly beans: they were questions with a right answer independent of the views of the judges. Consequently, it was possible for judges to give a wrong verdict, as they had—Plato's works consistently implied—in the case of Socrates. Court cases certainly seem to involve *epistêmê* more than did votes in the assembly. As Aristotle observed, court cases concern the past, not the future, and what happened in the past can, in principle, be known. One might argue, then, that at least where the evidence allowed it, court judgments could be determined directly from the facts at hand.

Knowledge of relevant facts certainly played an important part in court speeches. Aeschines, closing his speech against Timarchos, called on his hearers to "make your decision" (*krisin*) in the following manner: "Let nothing be more credible in your eyes than what you yourselves know [*hôn autoi suniste*] and have been persuaded by. . . . Give your vote with regard to the long term, truth, and your own knowledge [*hois autoi suniste*]."[99] Isaeus and Demosthenes both emphasized the importance of giving one's verdict with a "perfect" or "accurate" knowledge of what had happened,[100] while Isocrates argued, in a pamphlet imitating a self-defense in court, that the "best and fairest defense" was "that which enables the judges to know [*eidenai*] . . . about that which they are about to vote" and which specifically left "no room for them to go astray in their thinking [*dianoia*] or to be in doubt which party speaks the truth [*alêthê*]."[101]

Yet even Isocrates drew up short of suggesting that when the facts of a matter were clear, the judgment that ought to follow was equally plain. Once his readers had "learnt the truth" (*mathontas tên alêtheian*), he said, they would be in a better position to "deliberate [*bouleusesthai*] and pronounce judgment [*diagnôsesthai*] on it."[102] Knowing the truth did not determine what the judgment should be; rather, it enabled the decision makers to judge well. In this context, as with decisions regarding advantage, "seeming" necessarily supervened. Isocrates himself (in the very next line) reverted to the terminology we have seen elsewhere: "Cast your ballots as seems to each of you right [*dokê dikaion einai*] and in accordance with law."[103]

The clearest available example of judicial discretion concerns the Harpalos affair of 324. Alexander of Macedon's treasurer, Harpalos, had absconded with a huge amount of money, sought refuge with the Athenians, been imprisoned in Athens, and then escaped from the city, leaving behind considerably fewer funds than he had had upon arrival. Following an investigation, it was determined by the council of the Areopagus that he had paid enormous bribes to various politicians in order to leave Athens, and the named men were put on trial in the normal way. What is striking is the division of labor between the Areopagus and the courts. Just because the Areopagus had determined that a given man had committed the offense, it did not follow that the judges were expected to punish him.

As Dinarchus explained with respect to another case, "The report of the council was not proved false; it was quite true, but the jury decided to acquit Polyeuctus. The council [of the Areopagus] was instructed to discover the truth [*to . . . alêthes*], yet . . . the court decided [*ekrine*] it was a case for pardon."[104]

Earlier, when prosecuting Demosthenes, Dinarchus had pleaded, "You have taken over the case from the people [*dêmô*], who know the facts [*to gegenêmenon eidotos*]. . . . Will you disregard all that has passed and acquit the first man here before you? Will you, with full power at your command, reject what seemed just [*ta dikaia . . . doxanta einai*] both to the demos and to the Areopagus and indeed to everyone?"[105] These were not merely rhetorical questions. Demosthenes was convicted and severely punished, but letting him go was a real option and would not necessarily have been interpreted as impugning the credibility of the Areopagus. The council was to uncover the facts; the judges were to decide what was just. These were two distinct tasks.

If this seems contradictory, we should remember the extent to which judicial decisions were forward-looking, creative acts, just like those of the assembly. Isocrates took this for granted when prosecuting Lochites: if the judges voted to convict, he remarked, they would not only "judge well" (*orthôs gnôsesthe*) but also "cause other citizens to be more decorous and make your own lives more secure."[106] The principal focus of lawsuits was the judgment of past events, but in every case, the judges also brought something new into being: a conviction or an acquittal, a reparation or a lack thereof. Their decision produced not only a new state of affairs—one in which, for example, Ktesiphon's proposal to crown Demosthenes would or would not count as illegal—but also a new normative benchmark. To put the issue bluntly, judicial decisions create facts. Sometimes, the point is that they create facts where there were none before. Which facts are produced is owed solely, in the final analysis, to the will of the decision makers at the moment they cast their votes.

If we allow that there is even a minor creative aspect to judicial decision-making, it seems to me to follow that there can be no objective right answer to questions of justice, in just the same way that there is none to questions of policy. We are, perhaps, caught on the horns of a dilemma: either judges have no agency in this context and, hence, do not really decide anything but merely assert something to be true, perhaps mistakenly; or they do decide something, in which case we must allow for their agency and thus recognize that even accepted facts and the judgments based on them may diverge. If so, we should consider the possibility that the role of facts even in judicial decision-making may be radically circumscribed. Their significance is for the decision maker to decide. If that seems persuasive, the significance of the discovery of the fact with respect to political action in any context may also be judged quite limited.

Conclusion

Near the beginning of *Infotopia*, Cass Sunstein limits the scope of his investigation: "To keep the analysis simple, I focus not on controversial judgments of value but on questions with demonstrably correct answers, now or in the future. What exactly happened in World War Two? Does a certain nation have nuclear weapons? Will a human being be cloned? Will the government of Saudi Arabia be toppled? Will there be a flu pandemic? Will a terrorist attack hit the United States in the next year?"[107] I suggest that this set of questions makes the mistake of treating two different kinds of inquiry as one. Ancient Greek political terminology helps us to see the difference.

The first two questions in Sunstein's list concern the past and present, both now unchangeable. There is, in principle, a "demonstrably correct" answer to those questions. In contrast, there is no "demonstrably correct" answer now to speculation concerning the results of future human actions, though not because it is difficult to predict such things. On the contrary, prediction is often quite easy, and events may even unfold just as predicted. If they do, it is not, however, because the original prediction had a secure epistemic basis. That is impossible, because the necessary actions had not yet been decided. The reason we can have *epistêmê* about the past, Aristotle suggested, is because the past cannot be changed. In comparison, the future is created by agents whose wills are as yet undetermined. How things seem to the relevant decision makers thus necessarily supervenes in the decision-making process, not only because the outcome of their actions cannot be known, but (more significantly) because what will be created depends on their own wills and what seems tolerable to them, which, in turn, depends not on knowledge but on perception. The distinction to which this necessity points is not between facts and values, as Sunstein suggests, but between facts and unforced actions. Though facts may prove helpful in getting to the threshold of a decision, they cannot finally determine which action to choose.

Why, then, did ancient Greek democrats support democracy, if not because they were persuaded that it led to epistemically superior decisions? One might turn to the argument of Aristotle discussed earlier, but it is a defense not of *dêmokratia* but of rule by a particular kind of multitude, one that meets Aristotle's criterion of adequate *aretê*. Better evidence can be found in two Athenian sources: the *Athênaiôn Politeia* (*Constitution of the Athenians*) found among

Xenophon's writings, written probably between the late 440s and late 420s, and another work of the same name, dated to the late 330s and attributed to Aristotle but more likely produced by a student or students of his.

Pseudo-Xenophon, sometimes known as "the Old Oligarch," was no democrat (at least if we take his text at face value).[108] But there is also no reason to think that he offers an inaccurate picture of democratic ideology. Indeed, his stated intention is to make clear why the Athenians acted as they did, even though he himself would not endorse their actions: "I do not myself praise the political system of the Athenians; but since they have decided to have it so [*edoxen houtôs autois*; literally, "it seems [good] to them to have it so"], I will show how well they maintain it and achieve those other things concerning which the other Greeks think they act mistakenly [*ha dokousin hamartanein*]."[109]

First, says Pseudo-Xenophon, "the poor and the demos there rightly [*dikaiôs*] do better than the wellborn and rich, because it is the demos that mans the ships and brings power [*dynamin*] to the polis." Accordingly, "it seems right [*dokei dikaion einai*] for everyone to have a share in the offices, both randomly allotted and elected, and for any of the citizens to be allowed to speak if he wishes." In other words, what is said to justify the power of the demos within the political system is the power imparted by the demos to the polis. The text does not specify to whom, exactly, this situation appears justified: presumably the demos favored this reasoning, but it seems possible that it was shared more widely—if, as in the case of Pseudo-Xenophon, reluctantly.

He goes on, touching directly on the issues of wisdom and the will: "One might say that they ought not to let everyone speak and serve on the council, but only the smartest [*tous dexiôtatous*] and best [*andras aristous*]." But even in that regard, Pseudo-Xenophon argues, the Athenians "deliberate well" (*bouleuontai arista*). "For if [only] gentlemen spoke and deliberated," he explains, "it would be great for the likes of them, but it would not be great for the men of the demos." The latter "know [*gignôskousin*] that the ignorance and viciousness and goodwill [*eunoia*] of the wretched profits them more than the virtue [*aretê*] and wisdom [*sophia*] and ill will [*kakonoia*] of a gentleman [*tou chrêstou*]."[110] What follows spells out the stakes for the demos, with remarkable matter-of-factness: "For the demos does not want good government under which it is itself enslaved [*douleuein*]; it wants to be free [*eleutheros*] and to rule [*archein*]. . . . If it is good order [*eunomia*] you seek, you will first see the smartest men [*tous dexiôtatous*] making laws in their own interest. Then these gentlemen will punish the lowlifes [*tous ponêrous*]; they will make policy and not allow madmen to sit on the council or to speak or come to assemblies. As a result of these excellent measures, the demos would rapidly fall into slavery [*douleian*]."[111]

In Pseudo-Xenophon's account, democracy seems very far from being pursued on epistemic grounds. On the contrary, it represented an act of openly partisan self-defense by the demos, advanced by the goodwill of its lowly supporters, endangered by the ill will of at least some of the privileged class. This argument is further supported by Pseudo-Xenophon's closing remarks, where he gives several examples of *dêmoi* which, having lost the upper hand, had been enslaved or "cut down" by the upper classes in their polis.[112] We may also recall Aristotle's quotation of an oath sworn in several oligarchical poleis: "I will be hostile to the demos and plan whatever evil I can against it." Apposite, too, is Aristotle's list of the three qualities desirable in candidates for high office: loyalty (*philia*) to the established constitution, capacity to perform the office, and *aretê* and justice, with loyalty listed first.[113] In each case, the disposition of the decision maker is represented as paramount.

To this evidence on the Greek understanding of democracy, we can add the perspective of the Aristotelian *Athênaiôn Politeia*, written around a century later, a few years prior to the end of the classical democratic period. According to its author, the Athenian demos became *kyrios* (supreme or authoritative) over affairs when, following the short rule of the Thirty Tyrants in 404/3, "Having accomplished its return by its own efforts, it seemed just [*dokountos . . . dikaiôs*] for the demos to take over the political system."[114] Once again, "seeming" is of decisive importance, not merely within the established political process but also with respect to the establishment of the political process itself. The author does not specify to whom, exactly, the reestablishment of democracy seemed just, but we can venture a guess. At a minimum, it will have seemed agreeable to the demos, which had the upper hand at that point and could therefore put its judgment into action.

The author of the Aristotelian *Athênaiôn Politeia* goes on to explain what that action entailed: the demos "administers everything by decrees and by courts in which the demos is the ruling power." He adds, "They seem [*dokousi*] to act rightly [*orthôs*] in doing this, for a few are more easily corrupted by gain and influence than the many." This justification, like the preceding one, suggests the importance of the will of the decision maker in forging political action—in this case, with respect to protection against corruption. But this line is, importantly, the author's personal evaluation. From everything that has been said, I do not think it would have seemed necessary to the demos to offer any additional justification of its political supremacy.

Notes

I thank Cliff Ando, Larissa Atkison, David Grewal, Matthew Landauer, Josiah Ober, and George Scialabba for their comments on this chapter. Translations are mine unless otherwise stated.

1. See M. H. Hansen, "The Political Powers of the People's Court in Fourth-Century Athens," in *The Greek City from Homer to Alexander*, ed. O. Murray and S. Price (Oxford: Clarendon, 1990), 215–43; R. Bauman, *Political Trials* (London: Routledge, 1990).

2. Aristot. *Pol.* 1281a–b, 1298a–b, 1300b, 1317b, 1322b; Ps.-Aristot. *Ath. Pol.* 48.4, 59.4.

3. See, e.g., J. K. Davies, *Democracy and Classical Greece*, 2nd ed. (Cambridge, MA: Harvard University Press, 1993), 226; G. Glotz, *The Greek City* (London: Routledge, 1921), 182; K. Raaflaub, J. Ober, and R. Wallace, *Origins of Democracy in Ancient Greece* (Berkeley: University of California Press, 2007), 4.

4. Aristot. *Rhet.* 1358b1–59a6.

5. For this language, see, e.g., Dem. 5.3, "you who deliberate on behalf of the polis" (addressing an assembly); 25.14, "those who deliberate on behalf of the polis and the laws" (referring to judges). On the relationship between deliberation and decision in ancient Greece, see D. Cammack, "Deliberation in Ancient Greek Assemblies," *Classical Philology* (forthcoming).

6. See, e.g., Din. 1.33, 105, trans. Burtt (*Minor Attic Orators*, vol. 2 [Cambridge, MA: Harvard University Press, 1954]). Cf. Dem. 41.25, 50.21, 37, 52.7, trans. Murray (Demosthenes, *Orations* [Cambridge, MA: Harvard University Press, 1930–49]).

7. For an account of this defense and some alternatives, see M. P. Saffon and N. Urbinati, "Procedural Democracy, the Bulwark of Equal Liberty," *Political Theory* 41 (2013): 441–81.

8. D. Estlund, *Democratic Authority* (Princeton: Princeton University Press, 2008); H. Landemore, *Democratic Reason* (Princeton: Princeton University Press, 2013); H. Landemore and J. Elster, *Collective Wisdom: Principles and Mechanisms* (Cambridge: Cambridge University Press, 2012); J. Ober, "Democracy's Wisdom," *American Political Science Review* 107 (2013): 104–22; Ober, *Demopolis* (Cambridge: Cambridge University Press, 2017), 139–52; C. Sunstein, *Infotopia: How Many Minds Produce Wisdom* (Oxford: Oxford University Press, 2006).

9. For this and related theorems, see B. Grofman, G. Owen, and S. Feld, "Thirteen Theorems in Search of Truth," *Theory and Decision* 15 (1983): 261–78.

10. Estlund, *Democratic Authority*, 230; Landemore, *Democratic Reason*, xv.

11. Landemore, *Democratic Reason*, 104.

12. Estlund, *Democratic Authority*, 8.

13. All the examples mentioned are discussed in J. Surowiecki, *The Wisdom of Crowds* (New York: Doubleday, 2004). For another approach toward the same conclusion, see L. Hong, S. Page, and W. Baumol, "Groups of Diverse Problem Solvers Can Outperform Groups of High-Ability Problem Solvers," *Proceedings of the National Academy of Sciences* 101 (2004): 16,386–89.

14. Aristot. *Pol.* 1281a40–82a40, 1286a25–b7, discussed below and in Estlund, *Democratic Authority*, 232–33; H. Landemore, "Collective Wisdom: Old and New," in Landemore and Elster, *Collective Wisdom*, 1; Landemore, *Democratic Reason*, 59–64; J. Ober, *Mass and Elite in Democratic Athens* (Princeton: Princeton University Press, 1989), 163–64; Ober, *Democracy and Knowledge* (Princeton: Princeton University Press, 2008), 110–14; Ober, "Democracy's Wisdom," 109–12; Sunstein, *Infotopia*, 49, 119; J. Waldron, *The Dignity of Legislation* (Cambridge: Cambridge University Press, 1999), 92–123.

15. Plat. *Prot.* 322d–e, discussed in Landemore, *Democratic Reason*, 57–59.

16. J. Ober, "Epistemic Democracy in Classical Athens," in Landemore and Elster, *Collective Wisdom*, 118. Cf. Ober, *Democracy and Knowledge*; Ober, "Democracy's Wisdom."

17. Ober, *Democracy and Knowledge*, 17.

18. Ober, "Epistemic Democracy," 143.

19. Ober, *Mass and Elite*, 311–14.

20. See J. Elster, *Explaining Technical Change: A Case Study in the Philosophy of Science* (Cambridge: Cambridge University Press, 1983), 55–68.

21. Prefacing his original fourteen-page reconstruction of the council's contribution to epistemic democracy, Ober writes, "Lacking any detailed first-person narrative from antiquity, a thought experiment must suffice" (*Democracy and Knowledge*, 143). In keeping with this prescription, the first nine pages of his account cite no primary evidence at all. He offers another hypothetical account in "Democracy's Wisdom" (116–17) and *Demopolis* (146–52). For a discussion of the activity of the council based on available sources, see D. Cammack, "Deliberation and Discussion in Classical Athens," *Journal of Political Philosophy* (forthcoming).

22. Ober, "Epistemic Democracy," 118.

23. Aristot. *Pol.* 1281a40–82a40, 1286a25–b7.

24. R. Balot, *Greek Political Thought* (Malden, MA: Blackwell, 2006); E. Barker, *The Politics of Aristotle* (Oxford: Clarendon, 1962), 126–27; J. Bookman, "The Wisdom of the Many," *History of Political Thought* 13 (1992): 1–12; Estlund, *Democratic Authority*, 232–33; A. Lintott, "Aristotle and Democracy," *Classical Quarterly* 42 (1992): 114–28; R. Mulgan, *Aristotle's Political Theory* (Oxford: Clarendon, 1977), 103–5; M. Nichols, *Citizens and Statesmen* (Savage, MD: Rowman and Littlefield, 1992); Ober, *Mass and Elite*, 163–65; Ober, *Democracy and Knowledge*, 110–14; Ober, "Democracy's Wisdom"; A. Saxonhouse, *Fear of Diversity* (Chicago: University of Chicago Press, 1992); Waldron, *Dignity of Legislation*, 92–123; J. L. Wilson, "Deliberation, Democracy, and the Rule of Reason in Aristotle's Politics," *American Political Science Review* 105 (2011): 263.

25. D. Cammack, "Aristotle on the Virtue of the Multitude," *Political Theory* 41 (2013):

175–202. See also K. Cherry, "Aristotle's 'Certain Kind of Multitude,'" *Political Theory* 42 (2014): 1–23; M. Lane, "Aristotle on Claims to Rule: The Case of the Multitude," in *The Cambridge Companion to Aristotle's Politics*, ed. M. Deslauriers and P. Destrée (Cambridge: Cambridge University Press, 2013).

26. This interpretation is defended in Cammack, "Virtue of the Multitude."

27. Aristot. *NE* 1139b15, 1144a5–10. See, further, Cherry, "Certain Kind."

28. Aristot. *NE* 1098a17–18, 1179b30; *Pol.* 1280b5–10; *Rhet.* 1366b.

29. E.g., Plat. *Meno* 89c. Cf. Aristot. *NE* 1116b, 1144b25–40; *EE* 1216b3–25, 1230a5–10, 1246b30–37.

30. Aristot. *Rhet.* 1366a30–35. See also Aristot. *NE* 1098a15–35, 1100b10–15, 1103b1–30, 1105b10–15, 1106a15–25, 1152a5–10; *EE* 1222a5–10, 1223b10–15.

31. Aristot. *NE* 1099a1–7.

32. For further discussion of the way in which *aretê* may be interpreted as aggregative, see Cammack, "Virtue of the Multitude," 185–90.

33. Ober, *Democracy and Knowledge*, 110–14. It is very doubtful that Aristotle is talking about Athens in this passage, though I do not pursue that issue here. See Cammack, "Virtue of the Multitude," 180; E. Garver, *Aristotle's Politics: Living Well and Living Together* (Chicago: University of Chicago Press, 2011), 14.

34. Ober, *Mass and Elite*, 163–65.

35. Thuc. 6.39.1.

36. Thuc. 3.37.3–5.

37. Aristot. *Pol.* 1286a30–33.

38. Aristot. *Pol.* 1286a33–36.

39. Landemore denies this, arguing that Aristotle's claim is "cognitive, not moral" (*Democratic Reason*, 62). To the extent that Aristotle believed that all *aretê* involved acting in accordance with *logos* (reason), he certainly thought there was a cognitive element in virtuous human behavior (*NE* 1144b26–7). Arriving at one's *krisis* (judgment or decision) is also certainly a cognitive activity. But it is not, in Aristotle's view, exclusively cognitive. He argued explicitly that *phronêsis* (the part of *logos* involved in deciding action) and ethical *aretê* are intertwined (*NE* 1144a13–b17). The cognitive and moral (or—following the Greek terminology—ethical) elements in decision-making are not as distinct as Landemore implies.

40. See, further, D. Cammack, "Plato and Athenian Justice," *History of Political Thought* 36 (2015): 611–42.

41. Ober, *Mass and Elite*, 165, citing Dem. 23.145–46.

42. See C. Taylor, "Bribery in Athenian Politics," pt. 1, "Accusations, Allegations, and Slander," and pt. 2, "Ancient Reactions and Perceptions," *Greece and Rome* 48 (2001): 53–66, 154–72.

43. Hyp. 1.14, trans. Burtt, modified, quoted in Ober, *Mass and Elite*, 165.

44. Din. 1.33, trans. Burtt, quoted in Ober, *Mass and Elite*, 165. Cf. Aeschin. 1.44–45, 55, 65, 70, 73, 89, 189; Andoc. 1.1, 20, 37, 46; Din. 2.2, 3.1; Hyp. 4.22; Is. 3.40.

45. Ober, *Mass and Elite*, 165.

46. Dem. 40.53–54, trans. Murray, modified.
47. Dem. *Ex.* 45.2, trans. DeWitt; Ober, *Mass and Elite*, 164.
48. Ober, *Mass and Elite*, 164–65.
49. Dem. *Ex.* 45.2–3, trans. DeWitt.
50. Dem. *Ex.* 44.2.
51. Dem. *Ex.* 26.1.
52. Isoc. 13.8; cf. 12.9.
53. Ober, *Mass and Elite*, 163.
54. G. Norlin, *Isocrates* (Cambridge, MA: Harvard University Press, 1929), 2:162–63.
55. Ober, *Mass and Elite*, 165.
56. Aristot. *Rhet.* 1359b–60b, Plat. *Alc.* I, and Xen. *Mem.* 3.6 suggest that those who offered political advice were expected to be acquainted with basic information about the resources and organization of the polis; cf. L. Kallet-Marx, "Money Talks: Rhetor, Demos, and the Resources of the Athenian Empire," in *Ritual, Finance, Politics*, ed. S. Hornblower and R. G. Osborne (Oxford: Oxford University Press, 1994), 227–52. But I do not know of any assembly speech where an orator goes so far as to represent himself as an expert, and Plat. *Prot.* 319d strongly implies that neither *technê* (323a) nor the impression of it was required.
57. Plat. *Prot.* 322d-e; Landemore, *Democratic Reason*, 57–58. See, further, C. Farrar, *The Origins of Democratic Thinking* (Cambridge: Cambridge University Press, 1988).
58. Plat. *Prot.* 322d–e.
59. Landemore, *Democratic Reason*, 57–58.
60. Landemore, *Democratic Reason*, 59.
61. Plat. *Tht.* 152a.
62. Plat. *Tht.* 160c.
63. See, e.g., Farrar, *Origins*, 49; H. Segvic, *From Protagoras to Aristotle* (Princeton: Princeton University Press, 2009), 7, 25–26.
64. Plat. *Tht.* 157a.
65. Plat. *Tht.* 151e, 152a–c, 153a–d, 160c, 161c–e, 170d, 179a, 186e, 201b–c, 201e, 210a. Cf. *Prot.* 356c–e.
66. Plat. *Tht.* 152e, 153a–e, 155e, 180d, 182d, 183a, 197a–b.
67. Plat. *Tht.* 151e, 152a–c, 153a, 154a, 157a–d, 166d, 167b–c, 170a, 177c–d, 178d–e, 179a, 183a, 186c. Cf. *Gorg.* 459d–e, 464a, 527b; *Prot.* 340b, 344d; *Rep.* 357a–b, 361b, 362a, 365b–c. See also *Rep.* 477a–b, which explicitly associates "being" with *epistêmê.*
68. Plat. *Tht.* 172a–177d, 201a–c; cf. *Gorg.* 455a–b, 466d–467b.
69. Plat. *Apol.* 30e.
70. For *krisis* and cognates, see Aristot. *Pol.* 1286a33–36; Aeschin. 1.93, 186, 196; Dem. 18.57, 226, 20.87; Dem. *Ex.* 33.3; Isoc. 6.5; Hyp. 2.10. For *gnômê* and cognates, see Aeschin. 1.196; Andoc. 1.2, 3; Dem. 18.8. Cf. Aristoph. *Eccl.* 655; Plat. *Prot.* 340b.
71. R. Meiggs and D. M. Lewis, *A Selection of Greek Historical Inscriptions to the End of the Fifth Century BC*, rev. ed. (Oxford: Clarendon, 1988), §§ 5.11, 5.24, 14.1, 23.2,

31.1, 37.2, 40.1, 46.1, 47.1, 52.1, 58.1, 64.11–12, 65.3, 68.3, 69.3, 70.3, 71.1, 73.2, 82.2, 85.3, 86.3, 88.1, 89.4, 90.2, 91.1, 92.1, 94.5; P. J. Rhodes and R. Osborne, *Greek Historical Inscriptions, 404–323 BC* (Oxford: Oxford University Press, 2003), §§ 1.19, 2.41, 2.56, 4.3, 5.9, 8.1–2, 10.5, 14.3, 15.1, 17.2–3, 18.2, 22.5, 23.1, 25.1, and many others. Cf. Andoc. 1.27; Aristoph. *Eccl.* 395; Aristoph. *Thesm.* 372–77; Lyc. 1.37. Cf. also Thuc. 1.53.1, 125; 2.24.1; 4.118.2, 4, 9, 11; 5.18.8; 5.23.6; 6.47.12.

72. E.g., Aristoph. *Eccl.* 197–98, trans. Henderson (Cambridge, MA: Harvard University Press, 2002): "We need to launch a fleet: the poor man votes yes, the wealthy and the farmers vote no" (*tô penêti men dokei, tois plousiois de kai geôrgois ou dokei*). Cf. 454–57, 764, 854.

73. Lyc. 1.37; Dem. 1.1. Cf. Thuc. 1.36, 87.3, 91.5, 5.47.12; Dem. 1.16; Dem. *Ex.* 5, 18; Isoc. 8.10, 12.248.

74. Aeschin. 1.79, trans. Adams (Cambridge: MA: Harvard University Press, 1919).

75. Hyp. 4.40. Cf. Is. 11.50; Isoc. 15.179. An alternative formulation appears at Dem. 48.52, where the judges are asked to "reach the conclusion regarding us which may seem to you best" (*ho ti an hymin dokê beltiston einai*).

76. Dem. 43.81, trans. Murray.

77. Dem. 38.2, 54.2, 56.55, 59.117, trans. Murray. Cf. 48.52, 53.24.

78. See, further, Cammack, "Plato and Athenian Justice."

79. Cf. Aristot. *Rhet.* 1359a35–b2.

80. Thuc. 3.20.3, trans. Smith (Cambridge, MA: Harvard University Press, 1910).

81. Emphasized at Aristot. *NE* 1140b1–8. For further discussion of Aristotle's understanding of deliberation as choice-making, see D. Cammack, "Aristotle's Denial of Deliberation about Ends," *Polis* 30 (2013): 228–50. See also Segvic, *From Protagoras to Aristotle.*

82. Estlund, *Democratic Authority*, 5.

83. A complicating factor is the extent to which any possible course of action, entertained because it seems a plausible means to the desired outcome, may or may not advance any of a host of other valued ends, of varying importance to the decision maker. One may argue that the notion that there are single "right answers" to political questions is not true to life, because there may be many coefficients (as it were) that we are trying to maximize or many values that we are trying to respect (though it can be easy to forget this when certain forms of modern analysis privilege precisely those questions for which it is possible to measure or quantify or guesstimate outcomes, and they often dominate debate: e.g., will we be better off economically after Brexit?). An epistemic democrat might reply that the "right answer" in such a situation is whatever maximizes the value of all relevant "coefficients." Yet what those coefficients are may be disputed, as well as their rank ordering, and even when there is no dispute, the relevant ends may—as has been much discussed—conflict (or appear to conflict) with one another. In such cases, their relative importance to the decision maker must be weighed, and the decision maker's willingness to tolerate the risks involved in contingently prioritizing one valued end over another will come into play.

84. Isoc. 8.8, trans. Norlin, modified (Cambridge, MA: Harvard University Press, 1980).

85. Thuc. 5.84–115.
86. Thuc. 5.84.3.
87. Thuc. 112.2.
88. Thuc. 5.84.1–2.
89. Thuc. 5.112, trans. Smith, modified.
90. Thuc. 5.89, 102, trans. Smith.
91. Thuc. 5.104, 111.
92. Thuc. 5.104, 111.
93. Thuc. 5.102, trans. Smith.
94. Thuc. 5.103, trans. Smith.
95. Thuc. 6.33, 36.
96. Dem. 18.62, 65–72, 191–95, 199, 206–10. Consider, in particular, 199: "Suppose that the future had been revealed to all of us, that every one had known what might happen, and that you, Aeschines, had predicted and protested, and shouted and stormed . . . even then the city could not have departed from that policy if she had any regard for honor, or for our ancestors, or for the days that are to come. All that can be said now is, that we have failed: and that is the common lot of humanity, if the god so wills [*hotan tô theô tauta dokê*]."
97. Thuc. 2.22, 5.26; Isoc. 20.18; Dem. 18.255, 50.1; Dem. *Ex.* 18.
98. Ps.-Aristot. *Ath.* Pol. 28.3
99. Aeschin. 1.93. Cf. 77–78.
100. Is. 8.3; Dem. 57.4. Cf. Dem. 18.57, 57.34; Lyc. 1.23.
101. Isoc. 15.52, trans. Norlin.
102. Isoc. 15.178.
103. Isoc. 15.179. Cf. Dem. 28.23.
104. Din. 1.59, trans. Burtt.
105. Din. 1.105–6; cf. 1.33.
106. Isoc. 20.18, trans. Norlin, modified. Cf. Aeschin. 1.196.
107. Sunstein, *Infotopia*, 16.
108. For a reading of this text as pro-democracy satire, see S. Hornblower, "The *Old Oligarch* (Pseudo-Xenophon's *Athenaion Politeia*) and Thucydides: A Fourth-Century Date for the *Old Oligarch*?," in *Polis and Politics: Studies in Ancient Greek History*, ed. P. Flensted-Jensen, T. H. Nielsen, and L. Rubinstein (Copenhagen: Museum Tusculanum Press, 2000), 363–84.
109. Ps.-Xen. *Ath. Pol.* 1.1.
110. Ps.-Xen. *Ath. Pol.* 1.6–7.
111. Ps.-Xen. *Ath. Pol.* 1.8–9.
112. Ps.-Xen. *Ath. Pol.* 3.11.
113. Aristot. *Pol.* 1310a10, 1309a35–40.
114. Ps.-Aristot. *Ath. Pol.* 41.1.

CHAPTER 2

The Legal Construction of the Fact, between Rhetoric and Roman Law

Nicolas Cornu Thénard

The concept of fact occupies an important place in Western legal thought, in no small part because it helps us to delineate the concept of law. From classical Roman theory to contemporary legal discussions, a fundamental distinction[1] is consistently made that portrays fact as the opposite of law. It has been so central to legal discourse[2] that fact and law have often been understood as offering negative definitions of one another.

This representation is obviously questionable. When considered separately, the respective definitions of fact and law reveal complexities that give rise to diverging opinions. But when these terms are viewed in relation to one another, they are often perceived as two sides of a logical and immutable construction. For civil lawyers, the fact/law distinction is understood as an expression of the more general opposition, defined in Kelsenian terms, between *Sein* (*is*) and *Sollen* (*ought*).[3] The distinction is commonly used in the civil law tradition in this sense in order to explain legal notions and rules, describe the reasoning of judges, or define the competencies of sovereign courts.[4]

In contemporary legal discourse, however, the logic of this opposition is not always respected. As it is common practice—although widely criticized since David Hume—to infer that which *ought* from that which *is*, *law* and *fact* are often coarticulated in a dynamic process in which the precise contours of the legal norm change depending on the specific facts to which the norm is to be applied. The same jurists who present this opposition as obvious and logical willingly propose to subvert it in order to make law dependent on facts. This trend is obviously quite current, not only in juristic discourse, but also in media articles and political declarations dealing with the merits of a legislative text or a judicial decision. It is commonly said that law must be adapted to the facts[5] and that normative texts have to keep in step with the evolution of society, which never stands still. Therefore, a common theme in electoral campaigns is *change*, regardless of its purpose. In France in particular, this pragmatic approach has led to an increase in legislation aimed at providing different rules for different fact patterns—even if these practices make it difficult to guarantee the certainty of law and the public's knowledge of said law. Jurisprudence itself moves in this direction in many ways. In particular, this approach is visible in the contemporary sociology of law, which tries to achieve a better "fit" between law and facts[6]—even if it seems difficult to view these facts independently from legal categories.

This results in two approaches to the law/fact distinction in Continental jurisprudence—a more formalist approach that supports this distinction and a more pragmatic one that calls it into question. Each of them has its own disadvantages. In their rigid insistence on formalist, context-free interpretation of law, jurists have sometimes been blind to the evolution of social practices and to the inefficiencies created by the inflexible application of legal rules. Yet the pragmatic approach, for its part, brings the risk of self-contradiction. On the one hand, we who follow that approach treat the law/fact distinction as one of the structural building blocks of law, one that helps us to understand and explain the concept of law itself. On the other hand, we deny the reality of this distinction in actual legal practice, thereby threatening the coherence of the distinction itself. By requiring law to be adapted to fact, jurists following the pragmatic approach risk making the law itself ever more difficult to discern.

This chapter brings to bear on these debates an analysis of the classical Roman distinction between law and fact. Roman jurists invented this distinction. They were the first to set up a strict terminological opposition between fact (*factum*) and law (*ius*). When they use these terms, however, they do not make the same contradictions as some jurists do today. They remain rigorous, never expressly justifying a particular legal interpretation as an adaptation of *ius* to *factum* or vice versa. This interpretative rigor can only be understood in relation to the special meaning, different from our own, that the Roman jurists give to the law/fact distinction.

As evidenced by their surviving writings in the *Digest* of Justinian, they do not view *factum* and *ius* as abstract conceptual categories that differ from one another in some essential way.[7] Rather, they understand this distinction in terms of two modes of reasoning, two types of argumentation that can be employed to resolve a dispute. In their view, one can choose to discuss a question either as a question of fact (*quaestio facti*) or as a question of law (*quaestio iuris*). However, these two modes of reasoning are strictly distinct from one another. That is why, according to Roman jurists, legal reasoning is always independent of any specific factual scenario. The facts relevant for the formulation of this reasoning are artificial constructs of the law.

The Roman Law/Fact Distinction and the Autonomy of Legal Reasoning

In the language of the Roman jurists, the term *factum* (fact) is used in two contexts, either in relation to the term *ius* (law) or in isolation, without reference to *ius*. The first of these contexts, examined in this section, enables us to draw out the principles of the distinction between fact and law. It shows that use of the words *factum* and *ius* together in the *Digest* is always intended to set them in opposition. The distinction serves both to differentiate between two modes of reasoning—one "factual," the other "legal"—and to make possible a form of legal reasoning that is autonomous from any specific factual considerations.

Principles of the Roman Law/Fact Distinction

The distinction between law and fact as imagined by Roman jurists is peculiar in several key respects.[8] Unlike modern Continental lawyers, the classical jurists use the law/fact opposition for strictly pragmatic purposes, never as a theoretical construct. They never set up an opposition between law (*ius*) and fact (*factum*) in the abstract. Rather, they use the terms *factum* and *ius* mostly in relation to other nouns, in order to make their sense more precise. This use of *factum* and *ius* arises in four legal contexts.[9]

Ignorance of law and fact. One context is the law of mistake, or "ignorance," of law and fact. The jurists use the terms *ius* and *factum* to distinguish between *ignorantia iuris* and *ignorantia facti*. *Ignorantia iuris* is a mistake concerning a matter of law—for example, the norm governing the order of inheritance in the law of succession—that every person is required to know.

Ignorantia facti is ignorance concerning a matter of fact—for example, a party's unawareness of the fact of a decedent's death, which an heir can allege in order to toll the statute of limitations for claim of an inheritance.

Conditions. Another context is the law governing the conditions (*condiciones*) of certain types of legal act (*negotium*). A *condicio iuris* is a legally imposed mandatory precondition for the validity of an act, such as the requirement of certain formalities for the execution of a valid Roman will. A *condicio facti*, by contrast, is a condition imposed by the party or parties that applies only to a specific act, such as a condition that performance under a contract is due only "if Titius has been elected consul."

Actions. A third context is the law governing the forms of action in Roman civil procedure. In this setting, *actiones in ius* are forms of action that turn mainly on questions of law. An example is the *actio ex testamento*, which lies to enforce a testamentary legacy whose terms require the heir under the will to convey certain property to a legatee. *Actiones in factum*, meanwhile, turn mainly on questions of fact and thus require consideration of the specific factual circumstances of a case. An example of an *actio in factum* is the *actio doli*, which lies to recover damages caused by the *dolus malus*, roughly translatable as "fraud," of the defendant. The question of whether the defendant acted *dolo malo* necessarily requires consideration of the particular facts of the case.[10]

Questions of law and fact. The last context is juristic discussion of "questions of law" (*quaestiones iuris*) and "questions of fact" (*quaestiones facti*). This fundamental organizing opposition for discussion of law and fact in the jurists' writing embraces all of the other contexts and thus requires further examination.

When discussing *quaestiones iuris* and *quaestiones facti*, the Roman jurists never suggest that the difference between the two types of question rests on a distinction between fact and value, the Kelsenian "is" (*Sein*) and "ought" (*Sollen*). The Roman jurists' perspective is instead pragmatic. For them, the distinction turns simply on the scope, or degree of abstraction, of the issue under discussion in a given question. The rhetorician Quintilian expresses this idea concisely in a passage of his *Institutio oratoria* (7.1.18).

> *Iuris autem quaestiones solent esse nonnumquam ex aliis atque aliis conflictionibus, facti semper idem spectant.*

> Questions of law can arise sometimes from one controversy, sometimes from another, whereas questions of fact always concern the same one.

A question of law, Quintilian explains, can be general in scope, covering multiple possible factual scenarios, whereas a question of fact is limited to a single specific case. This dividing line between *quaestiones iuris* and *quaestiones facti* is used to demarcate *ius* and *factum* in the other three contexts in which this distinction is made. Whenever the jurists contrast ignorance of fact and ignorance of law, conditions of fact and conditions of law, or even actions *in factum* and actions *in ius*, they always have this same scope-based opposition in mind.

One implication of the Roman understanding of the *ius/factum* opposition is that there is no objective boundary between legal and factual questions, comparable to the boundary between *Sollen* and *Sein* in modern Continental jurisprudence. Either type of *quaestio* can be used to determine both what ought to be and what is. It is thus possible to debate whether a given issue is best resolved through a wide-reaching, general solution, as a question of law, or through a narrow, case-specific solution, as a question of fact. The Roman jurists have no hesitation about opposing one another when such a methodological controversy arises.[11]

Why should they favor one or the other of these approaches? A well-known text[12] by a jurist from the second century, Neratius Priscus, offers one possible explanation (*Dig.* 22.6.2 [Nerat. 5 *membr.*]).

> *In omni parte error in iure non eodem loco quo facti ignorantia haberi debebit, cum ius finitum et possit esse et debeat, facti interpretatio plerumque etiam prudentissimos fallat.*

> Mistake of law should not be treated under the same heading as ignorance of fact in every area, because the law can and must be finite, whereas the interpretation of fact often deceives even the wisest lawyers.

This fragment is the only one in the entire corpus of classical Roman law that seems to consider the respective natures of *factum* and *ius* in relation to one another and in the abstract. In reality, Neratius is contrasting not "law" and "fact" but "law" (*ius*) and "interpretation of fact" (*interpretatio facti*). This opposition serves here a didactic purpose: it is used to explain why mistake of law is treated differently from ignorance of fact. The difference in regimes between the two types of *ignorantia* is conditioned by the different natures of the two fields concerned. *Ignorantia iuris* is sanctioned more harshly than *ignorantia facti* because *ius* is understood to be more knowable than *interpretatio facti*.

From Neratius' perspective, knowledge of the law is obligatory not because the lawmaker has commanded it but because the very nature of *ius* makes knowledge necessary. To be limited is part of the nature and function of law (*ius finitum et possit esse et debeat*). *Ius* thus essentially lends itself to knowledge, for which reason mistake of law is not acceptable. This finiteness of *ius*, which Neratius highlights, serves a pragmatic function, however, rather than a strictly conceptual one. The law is made finite so it may be certain, thereby ensuring that it can be known by all those who are subject to it. Certainty is, indeed, the essential characteristic of *ius* for the Roman jurists,[13] which is why, according to Neratius, the law consists of a specific body of precepts. *Ius* must be *certum* in order to fulfill its function.

Although the approach taken to make law certain can vary according to a jurist's methodological preferences, empirical or dogmatic,[14] the requirement of certainty is universally acknowledged in the Roman jurists' writings. More often than not, this criterion determines which rule is applied or which legal interpretation is used in the language of the jurists; expressions such as *certum est* or *manifestum est* are used very frequently in this context. According to the account given by the jurist Pomponius,[15] certainty is the fundamental motivation that may explain the entire history of Roman law; that is why, in this respect, Giambattista Vico viewed certainty as an essential feature that determined Roman *ius civile*.[16] The same characteristic is also recognized by the Roman rhetoricians, following the example of Quintilian.[17] Ultimately, certainty is the prerequisite for the law to be binding, since only knowledge of *ius certum* is obligatory.[18] Certainty is, in this way, a crucial factor in defining *ius*.

The requirement of certainty implies a distinction, however, between the certain and definite law, on the one hand, and what is uncertain and indefinite, on the other hand. Hence Neratius' maxim concludes that "the interpretation of fact often deceives even the wisest lawyers" (*facti interpretatio plerumque etiam prudentissimos fallat*). Interpretation of facts is deceptive because the uniqueness of each concrete fact makes a process of interpretation both necessary and difficult.[19] A single event is often composed of numerous details that cannot all be discerned or known. It is sometimes a product of a complex sequence of earlier occurrences, and it can appear to have a meaning that it does not really have. Once an event becomes relevant to a dispute, it cannot obviously be assessed in isolation—its significance can only be understood through a process of interpretation. Yet the act of interpretation implies an emphasis on some of the features of an event, as deemed more significant than others. This choice of emphasis sometimes opens the door to arbitrariness.[20] In Neratius' view, the difficulty inherent in interpretation of fact explains why *ignorantia facti* is a valid defense in court. It also justifies the distinction between fact and law itself, because if the law had to be molded to fit the uniqueness of every fact, the law would itself become indefinite and unknowable. Its very existence would thereby be called into question.

Other well-known fragments of the Roman jurists can be understood in the same sense. One example is the observation, by the jurist Julian, that a solution provided by the law must only be applied to a case when the application is obvious (*Dig.* 1.3.10 [Iul. 59 *dig.*]).

> *Neque leges neque senatus consulta ita scribi possunt, ut omnes casus qui quandoque inciderint comprehendantur, sed sufficit ea quae plerumque accidunt contineri.*
>
> Neither statutes nor *senatus consulta* can be written in such a way as to include all of the cases that might arise at any time. It is enough for them to cover those that occur most frequently.

The jurist Paul expresses a similar point of view (*Dig.* 1.3.23 [Paul. 4 *ad Plaut.*]).

> *Minime sunt mutanda, quae interpretationem certam semper habuerunt.*
>
> One must not change rules for which the interpretation has always been certain.

The jurists' perspective is consistent. In their view, the law should not always reflect every aspect of reality. If the law always had to adapt to reality, its expression would be as complex and singular as the endless diversity of specific facts and, as a consequence, would cease to be certain. This consideration justifies the distinction between fact and law per se and consequently determines the role of *quaestiones facti*: their purpose is to resolve conflicts independently from a legal argument.

The Purpose of the *quaestio facti*: Maintaining the Autonomy of Legal Reasoning

To understand the role of the *quaestio facti*, we need to examine more closely the contexts in Roman law in which questions of fact are employed. These contexts can be analyzed in terms of ancient rhetorical theory, particularly the theory invented by the Greek Hermagoras of Temnos that the Latin rhetoricians call *status*.[21] This theory posits that any debate turns on some essential point that may determine the choice of the arguments. That fundamental issue is referred to as the *status*, and several different types of *status* can be distinguished. Although the ancient rhetoricians differed in their classifications of *status*,[22] the classification of Cicero seems to have been especially influential for Roman thought and can thus be used for illustration.

Cicero considers that any controversy in a judicial setting turns on one of three essential questions: *sitne* (whether it is), *quid sit* (what it is), or *quale sit* (how to qualify it);[23] that is, a controversy is about the existence of a contested fact, what name or definition to give to the fact, or what qualities or characteristics the fact should be recognized as having. Thereby three possible lines of inquiry are identified: *conjecture*, *definition*, and *qualification*. Two of these lines—conjecture and qualification—serve as the primary bases for questions of fact in the writings of the Roman jurists.

Conjecture. The first *status*[24]—conjecture—encompasses the simplest forms of *quaestio facti*. In the conjecture framework, the parties to a judicial proceeding debate the existence of a material fact.[25] They discuss the time, place, or participants involved in the event in controversy. One must note that in this kind of *quaestio facti*, the parties are understood to have conflicting positions, and it is likewise understood that there is no absolute evidence that could resolve the question. In this framework, the fact in itself is never obvious, but rather is questioned and discussed.

Qualification.[26] This observation is even more pertinent when *quaestiones facti* concern not the material aspect of a fact, but rather its intentional dimension. When questions of fact relate to someone's intent, they fall under the heading of the qualification *status*. Cases involving donative transfers, for example, are always interpreted as *quaestiones facti* of the qualification type, as some of the writings of the jurist Julian demonstrate.[27] According to the jurist Ulpian, cases involving conditions included in the terms of contracts and other private transactions (*condiciones facti*) are also construed as raising *quaestiones facti* of qualification.[28] When an inquiry of the qualification type is conducted to determine the intent of the parties to a legal transaction, the fact finder must do more than simply determine the existence of a material fact, as in a *quaestio facti* of the conjecture type. The fact finder must necessarily also evaluate or characterize the quality of the factual circumstances. In such cases, the *quaestio facti* concerns both fact and value, both *Sein* and *Sollen*.

A text by Celsus offers a brief example of the qualification type of *quaestio facti* (*Dig.* 24.1.47 [Cels. 1 *dig.*]).

> *Utrum negotium uxoris gerens an officio mariti ductus in rem eius impenderit vir, facti, non iuris est quaestio.*

> Whether a husband has charged expenses to the separate property of his wife while he was managing her business or while fulfilling his duty to her as a husband is a question of fact, not a question of law.

In Celsus' example, a husband has charged certain expenses to his wife's separate property. In principle, the prohibition in Roman law on gifts between spouses renders this act void and requires restitution of any spent property to the wife, since such an expenditure would ordinarily be construed as a gift of property from the wife to her husband. According to the Roman jurists, the prohibition furthers the public policy of protecting conjugal affection from becoming dependent on mutual gifts. The prohibition particularly applies to cases in which the husband spends his wife's separate property in order to fulfill his marital duty to her—that is, to meet her financial needs. For example, if the husband spends the wife's property in order to maintain her dowry,[29] she may demand that he reimburse the amount that has been spent. It often happens, however, that a husband is simply managing the property of his wife. In such cases, he may incur necessary expenses to maintain this property. Any such expenses are chargeable to the wife and are not subject to restitution.[30]

Within that context, Celsus analyzes the issue as a question of fact, not a question of law. The validity of the expenditure from the wife's separate property turns on the intent of the husband. If the expenditure was made for a purpose arising out of the husband's duty, the amount spent must be restored to the wife. But if the expenditure was made as part of the ordinary management of the wife's property, it may be classified as what Roman law calls a *negotiorum gestio*, an act undertaken by an unauthorized agent for the benefit of the principal. In the latter case, the expenditure is valid and not subject to restitution.[31] Celsus therefore rejects a solution that is general in scope, instead classifying the case as a *quaestio facti*. As a consequence, the judge must both find facts, determining what the underlying factual circumstances of the husband's actions were, and characterize those facts, either as a *negotiorum gestio* or as an act undertaken in fulfillment of the husband's duty to his wife. Observation and evaluation appear inseparable here. The judge's assessment of whether the sum must be restored to the spouse or not depends on the concrete circumstances of the individual case.[32]

The case described by Celsus is by no means an isolated example of the use of *quaestiones facti* to arrive at both factual findings and evaluations. The same approach is taken in the law governing private acts (*negotia*) whenever the Roman jurists conclude that the resolution of a case depends on an evaluation of intent. If the jurists conclude that the legal effect of a gift, a will,[33] or a certain type of contract[34] depends on what the donor or testator intended or what the contracting parties agreed to, they frame the issue as a *quaestio facti*.[35] The outcome of this specific inquiry directly determines the solution reached in the case. *Quaestiones facti* are also used in cases involving delictual responsibility,[36] as well as in many cases involving *dolus*.[37] *Dolus* is sanctionable in Roman law only if *malus*—that is, if the device or contrivance used to deceive another manifests malicious intent.[38] To resolve the issue, the decision maker must determine whether the act that was carried out actually deceived anyone and whether, in carrying it out, the author of the act was conscious of the deceit. Such an evaluation can only be achieved in the framework of an examination of the specific case: this *res facti*[39] is examined *ex facto*,[40] in the context of an action *in factum*.

It is clear from all of these examples that the Roman jurists never understand the law/fact opposition as a distinction between two concepts considered in the abstract. They instead use the opposition to contrast two means of resolving conflicts. By framing an issue as a *quaestio facti*, they ensure that the judge's decision can be adapted to the circumstances of a specific case. The solution may therefore vary according to time, place, and the identity of the participants. But since the *quaestio facti* approach is in strict contrast with the *quaestio iuris* method, the solution to the issue can never have general applicability or alter existing legal norms. If one follows the line of reasoning of the Roman jurists, the real facts of a case decided as a *quaestio facti* have no bearing, in any way, on the content of *ius*.

The Artificial Construction of Fact: **Ex iure oritur factum**

The foregoing discussion of contexts in which the Roman jurists discuss law and fact in opposition to each other leaves aside another set of situations in which the term *factum* is used. In those contexts, *factum* appears in isolation, without being placed in contrast with law, and thus no longer describes the same notion as before. There, fact is not set into opposition with law but is instead used to designate a part of the law itself, since each legal norm is constructed on the basis of certain factual assumptions. In those contexts, however, fact no longer describes reality itself. It is, rather, an artificial construction.

How can a law that is allegedly certain be formulated from a material that is supposedly elusive? How can legal science be built on such an unstable foundation without crumbling? In view of the analysis developed by the classical jurists, we must understand that the idea underlying the maxim of the medieval jurist Baldus, *ex facto oritur ius* (from fact arises law),[41] cannot be attributed to the Romans without certain precautions. Left in its raw state, fact cannot give "rise" to law. According to the Romans, in order for facts to serve as the basis for resolving a question of law, they must be certain and objective. Each fact must be constructed as an instance of some general category. Baldus' maxim can thus perhaps be reversed: *ex iure oritur factum*—it is fact that arises from law.

How does this process of construction work? Here again, the ancient rhetorical theory of *status* is helpful for understanding the jurists' thinking. In *status* theory, a fact discussed in the context of a legal argument must be constructed in two stages, two types of the *status* presented above: definition and qualification.

Definition

The term *definition* must be considered here in its literal sense: that of delimiting, containing, opposing the identical to the different.[42] In this sense, any use of a word to group several things under the same category constitutes definition regardless of the explanation given, and this technique is quite common in the writings of the jurists. Definition appears with this meaning not only in the last two books of the *Digest*, where definitions of various legal concepts are grouped and presented together for didactic purposes, but throughout the corpus of surviving juristic texts.[43]

In applying the rhetorical technique of definition, the jurists remain aware of the elusive nature of facts. That awareness explains the peculiar methodological framework in which Roman juristic definitions are established.[44] The circumstances always being singular and different from one another, they can only give rise to a legal reasoning through the intermediary of a *casus* (case).[45]

In a *casus*, the writer abstracts from a concrete fact pattern certain elements that are relevant to a legal analysis. This technique has practical limits, however, since the process of abstraction can never account exhaustively for every possible factual situation to which the law might apply. Two famous passages from the Roman jurists—one by Celsus and the other, previously discussed, from the writing of Julian—grapple with this problem.

> *Ex his, quae forte uno aliquo casu accidere possunt, iura non constituuntur.* (*Dig.* 1.3.4 [Cels. 5 *dig.*])
>
> Legal norms are not established on the basis of occurrences that may happen to arise in one particular case.

> *Neque leges neque senatus consulta ita scribi possunt, ut omnes casus qui quandoque inciderint comprehendantur, sed sufficit ea quae plerumque accidunt contineri.* (*Dig.* 1.3.10 [Iul. 59 *dig.*])
>
> Neither statutes nor *senatus consulta* can be written in such a way as to include all of the cases that might arise at any time. It is enough for them to cover those that occur most frequently.

As Celsus and Julian explain, legal rules cannot pretend to encompass all cases. By extension, they are unable to cover the infinite diversity of unique factual scenarios. This perception gives rise to a mistrust of definitions. The general applicability of the definition[46] is strongly criticized. In this respect, the attitude of the classical jurists is similar to that of the classical rhetoricians, as evidenced by comparing passages written by the rhetorician Quintilian and the jurist Javolenus.[47]

> *Quid quod et uno verbo definitur res eadem . . . et latiore varioque tractatu, ut omnes oratores plerumque fecerunt. Rarissime enim apud eos reperitur illa ex consuetudine philosophorum ducta servitus (est certe servitus) ad certa se verba adstringendi, idque faciendum in libris Ciceronis de oratore vetat M. Antonius. Nam est etiam periculosum, cum, si uno verbo sit erratum, tota causa cecidisse videamur, optimaque est media illa via, qua utitur Cicero pro Caecina, ut res proponatur, verba non periclitentur.* (Quint. *Inst. or.* 7.3.16–17)

> Moreover, a given thing can be defined both by a single word . . . and also in a broader and varied manner, as all the orators have generally done. For the slavery of binding ourselves to certain words (as slavery it indisputably is), which has its origin in the practice of the philosophers, is very seldom found in their own writings, and Marcus Antonius, in Cicero's *De oratore*, forbids this practice. For it is also dangerous, since if we err in a single word, we are likely to lose the whole case. The best course is the middle way that Cicero adopts in his oration *Pro Caecina*, in which the matter is set forth without using words that create a risk of losing.

> *Omnis definitio in iure civili periculosa est: parum est enim, ut non subverti posset.* (*Dig.* 50.17.202 [Iavol. 11 *epist.*])

> Any definition in the civil law is dangerous, since there are not many that cannot be subverted.

Definition is dangerous in civil law, Quintilian and Javolenus both explain, because the diversity of circumstances risks undermining the general applicability and certainty of *ius*. Since facts can always be viewed from many different perspectives, no definition can prevail a priori over the others or claim to cover all factual circumstances. Indeed, any definition that purported to cover all possible factual circumstances would reveal itself to be inadequate as soon as there arose an unexpected fact pattern that the definition could not take into proper account. In such a case, the words (*verba*) of the definition would not be adapted to the underlying reality (*res*) to which it was supposed to apply, and the definition, now revealed to be unreliable, could then be circumvented. The technique of definition, which the jurists use as a means of safeguarding legal predictability and certainty, should thus only be used when that certainty can be preserved intact.

Despite all their mistrust of the dangers of definition, the Roman jurists make extensive use of the technique,[48] both in their law-teaching manuals and in their casuistic (*casus*) writings.[49] For the jurists, the technique of definition has several advantages. It makes it possible to create fixed categories from variable, indefinite material. It also makes it possible to isolate an event and to attach a legal effect to that event.[50]

The function that definition serves in the Roman jurists' reasoning is made clearer by the discussions of *status* theory in the work of the classical rhetoricians.[51] Illustrative is Cicero's statement, in his *De inventione* (1.11), of the purpose of the *status finitionis*.

> *Nominis est controversia, cum de facto convenit et quaeritur, id quod factum est quo nomine appelletur.*
>
> A controversy about definition arises when there is agreement about a fact and the question is what name should be used to describe that which has been done.

The purpose of the *status* of definition,[52] according to Cicero, is to determine the appropriate "name" (*nomen*) with which to describe a given fact. The controversy is not about the reality of a past event, since the parties are already in agreement about the underlying facts. Rather, the controversy is about the name that should be given to this reality. Cicero offers an example of this kind of controversy in the same passage of *De inventione*.[53] Someone has taken a sacred object off of private property; that much is uncontested. The question is one of legal interpretation: does this act constitute theft or sacrilege? To determine to which of the two legal categories the event in question belongs, a discussion about definition is required. The two parties must explain what is covered by each of these categories (theft and sacrilege). By comparing the definitions offered with the event in question, each party makes a case for the name that should be used to describe the event.

As used in these exercises in definition, the term *factum* can thus have a broad range of meanings that extends beyond the usual semantic domain of "fact" in English. In the writings of the jurists, *facta* include, *inter alia*, acts of appointment, delivery, payment, and performance (*datio*); any voluntary action performed in order to manage a business (*gestum*); criminal offenses of various kinds; chance events.[54] Indeed, almost any event or occurrence that is discussed by the jurists is likely to be called a *factum*. When used in those senses, however, the notion of *factum* can no longer be assimilated to the underlying reality that it describes. The artificial, constitutive nature of definition is apparent in several respects. Above all, the word *definition* itself, considered in its literal sense of "demarcation," assumes that determining meaning is equivalent to marking out the boundaries of a piece of agricultural land. In both cases, the process of marking out boundaries changes the observer's perception of the reality. In the case of definition of facts, the technique of definition establishes a *factum* by isolating some event from its context. Yet that context is essential for interpreting the *factum* in the first place. The fact of a theft, for example, can be identified and isolated as a theoretical matter, but one's interpretation of the fact in itself is inseparable from the context in which it took place. A theft committed under necessity or duress will not be evaluated the same way as a theft committed simply out of a desire for gain. In such cases, it can seem artificial to isolate a fact from its immediate context.

The artifice that is inherent to any definition is especially blatant in cases of legal definition. As the Roman law scholar Antonio Carcaterra has shown, the classical jurists' efforts to define legal terms lead them to distinguish special legal meanings of words that differ from the meanings of the same words as they are used in ordinary language.[55] The moment it is defined, a *nomen iuris* acquires an independent signification that takes on coherence within the structure of legal discourse. If superimposed onto ordinary language, it will only move further away from the realities that it claims to describe.

One definition given by the jurist Paul—that of the legal term *restitutio*—offers an example of this process of differentiating a legal definition from the meaning of the same word in ordinary language (*Dig.* 50.16.75 [Paul. 50 *ad ed.*]).

> *Restituere is videtur, qui id restituit, quod habiturus esset actor, si controversia ei facta non esset.*

> A person is viewed as making restitution [*restituere*] when he has restored [*restituit*] what the plaintiff would have had if a cause for controversy had not arisen.

Paul's passage illustrates the creativity and artificiality that are inherent in the process of legal definition. The artifice is apparent partly from Paul's definition itself, which defines the legal term *restitutio* by departing from the meaning of the concept of restitution in ordinary Latin. On a superficial reading of the passage, the jurist appears to set up a definition that lacks logical rigor, since he defines the Latin verb *restituere* in terms of another form of the same verb (*qui id restituit*).[56] In reality, however, Paul is here defining a specifically legal meaning of *restituere* and setting it off from the ordinary meaning of the word. In ordinary language, Latin *restitutio* and its congeners have the sense of returning a thing that one wrongfully possesses. But in Paul's legal language, *restitutio* describes only the fact of restoring something belonging to the plaintiff to the hypothetical state that would have existed had the quarrel between the plaintiff and defendant that led to litigation never taken place. What may look like a flaw of logic is, in reality, a virtue of Paul's definition. By using the ordinary sense of *restituere* in the legal definition of the term, the jurist makes clear that a specifically legal sense of the word must be distinguished from the ordinary sense.

The artifice of legal definition is also apparent from Paul's avoidance of any discussion of concrete factual scenarios. In this respect, the jurists follow the advice of the rhetoricians. As both Cicero and Quintilian explain, a definition must be concise; the brevity of a definition makes it more convincing.[57] Yet this concision is inevitably simplistic. The underlying realities that are being defined always give rise to interpretation. Any definition that purports to synthesize those realities in brief terms is thus, by its very nature, underinclusive. Deciding what to include in the definition necessarily requires the making of creative choices. In both content and form, a legal definition is the product of an exercise of construction.

For all its artificiality, the creative exercise of definition has a remarkable virtue: it makes it possible to construct bounded, fixed legal concepts out of factual circumstances that are inherently elusive. It highlights salient facts on which legal reasoning can rely and that serve as a pattern for interpreting reality.[58] The legal concepts that are constructed through definition can then be used to evaluate new fact patterns.

Qualification

Once a legal concept has been worked out through a process of definition, the third technique of ancient *status* theory—qualification—can be applied to determine the legal consequences of a given set of facts. The Roman sense of qualification is different from the procedure that modern civil lawyers call "qualification"[59] and that common lawyers call the resolution of a mixed question of law and fact. For the classical jurists and rhetoricians, the technique of definition includes both the formulation of a legal category and the use of that category to label—and thus give legal significance to—a particular fact pattern. The technique of qualification, meanwhile, refers to something different.

A passage from Quintilian very well shows the difference between definition and qualification (*Inst. or.* 7.8.2).

> *Sit enim lex: "Venefica capite puniatur." "Saepe se verberanti marito uxor amatorium dedit, eundem repudiavit: per propinquos rogata ut rediret non est reversa: suspendit se maritus. Mulier veneficii rea est." Fortissima est actio dicentis amato-*

rium venenum esse: id erit finitio. Quod si parum valebit, fiet syllogismus, ad quem velut remissa priore contentione veniemus: an proinde puniri debeat ac si virum veneno necasset.

Let us suppose a law that provides: "A poisoner must be punished by death." "A wife who was frequently beaten by her husband gave him an aphrodisiac and abandoned him. Begged by relatives to return, she did not come back; the husband hanged himself. The wife is prosecuted for poisoning." The strongest charge is to claim that the aphrodisiac is a poison: this will be a definition. If this is not effective enough, one will have recourse to syllogism, which we will come to after having given up the first struggle, as it were: should the wife be punished as if she had killed the man by means of a poison?

Quintilian is evoking a stock subject of declamation borrowed from the curriculum used in ancient schools of rhetoric.[60] The applicable legal rule punishes a fact—poisoning—by death. In this case, a specific circumstance gives rise to a controversy: a wife gave her husband an aphrodisiac and left him; then, when she would not come back, the husband hanged himself.

Quintilian proposes two main approaches that the prosecution can take in a case of this type. The first is to use definition: the prosecuting party claims that the aphrodisiac is a poison (*amatorium venenum esse*). In keeping with the account of definition discussed earlier, this approach requires that the party first define the legal category of poison (*venenum*). To do so, the prosecution might use an argument such as the one given by the jurist Gaius:[61] *venenum* can be defined as a substance that alters the natural disposition of the person to whom it is administered. Within this broad definition, there can be good poisons and bad ones. A bad poison is one that has been made, sold, or possessed with the aim of causing death.[62] After this first step, the prosecution must then address whether the circumstances of the case fit into the category thus defined. Here, it might argue that the aphrodisiac did indeed have the effect of altering the natural disposition of the person to whom it had been given and that the change of the husband's natural disposition in Quintilian's hypothetical case had fatal consequences. The love potion so altered the husband's judgment, the prosecution might argue, that he was unable to cope with his wife's leaving him and therefore killed himself. Since the aphrodisiac did, in this particular case, cause the death of the husband, the wife's conduct falls within the legal category of poisoning and, as such, is punishable by death.

The line of reasoning just sketched out is referred to in Continental doctrine as a legal qualification of fact. In the common law tradition, it would be treated as an argument involving a mixed issue of law and fact. But it is presented by Quintilian as a definition. This approach calls for reflection on the essential characteristics of a legal category, with the aim of shedding light on a concrete fact pattern. It makes it possible to identify a specific event with a legal category.

Quintilian's first approach is not the only way for the prosecution to make its case, however. Because it is uncertain whether definition is the most effective trial strategy in this case, Quintilian also offers a second approach. It may happen, he explains, that the defendant's strategy is to offer a different, more precise legal definition of poison. The defense could argue, for example, that a substance cannot constitute a *venenum* unless it is the only cause of death. In the present case, if the wife had not also run off, the husband would not have hanged himself. The aphrodisiac was indeed enough to alter his judgment, but it was certainly not enough to kill him; an *amatorium* (aphrodisiac) seems to differ from a *venenum* (poison) in this respect. If this were the defense's argument, the prosecution might well lose its case if it adopted Quintilian's first approach as its trial strategy.

This is why Quintilian offers a different, second approach. He suggests that the prosecution turn to the use of a syllogism. In his second approach, it would concede that the substance at issue in the case was an *amatorium* and that the category of *amatorium* differed in significant respects from the category of *venenum*. The prosecution would then argue, however, that the circumstances of this particular case tended to bring together the two categories of *amatorium* and *venenum*. The aphrodisiac alone certainly did not bring about the death of the husband, but the aphrodisiac and the wife's abandonment taken together did cause his death. Therefore, although administration of an aphrodisiac and administration of poison differ from one another in important respects, they had the same ultimate consequences in this particular case and should be punished in the same way.

In this second approach, Quintilian is recommending that the prosecution resort to an analogy, a type of argument that, according to the ancient rhetorical literature, belongs to the *status qualitatis*, the technique of qualification.[63] Quintilian's distinction between the first and second approaches to the hypothetical prosecution thus illustrates the contrast between the definition and the qualification in the context of a question of law (*quaestio iuris*), that is, the legal qualification. Definition involves explaining the scope of a category; legal qualification involves the interpretation of a rule.

This form of qualification also requires one further step in the legal construction of fact. In definition, the jurists abstract from material reality in order to define a legal concept, general in scope. A similar, additional process of factual abstraction must also take place in legal qualification. In this context, in deed, the *qualitas* of the situation is not evaluated in respect of a *quaestio facti*, according to the specific circumstances, but within the framework of a *quaestio iuris*. It must therefore be conceived in general terms. Two approaches are taken thus to the legal qualification of facts in Roman theory.

Constitutio iuridicialis absoluta. The first approach, which the rhetoricians call *constitutio iuridicialis absoluta*, is static.[64] The parties concede that a given fact pattern fits within a particular legally relevant category. They nevertheless proceed to debate whether the legal norm that ordinarily applies to the category is properly construed to apply in the given case.

A significant example of this approach is given in the anonymous Latin rhetorical treatise *Rhetorica ad Herennium* (1.24, trans. Caplan, revised).

> *Absoluta est, cum id ipsum, quod factum est, ut aliud nihil foris adsumatur, recte factum esse eam rem dicemus, eiusmodi: mimus quidam nominatim Accium poetam conpellavit in scaena. Cum eo Accius iniuriarum agit. Hic nihil aliud defendit nisi licere nominari eum, cuius nomine scripta dentur agenda.*

> [The *constitutio iuridicialis*] is absolute when we contend that what has been done was right in itself, without our drawing on any extraneous considerations. For example, a certain mime insulted the poet Accius by name on stage. Accius brought against him an action for injury. The player makes no defense except to maintain that it was permissible to name a person under whose name dramas were given to be performed on stage.

In explaining the *constitutio iuridicialis absoluta*, the author of this passage first defines the approach. For the defense, this method of interpretation consists of justifying a fact without resorting to any of the external arguments that the debate might offer. In this approach, the defendant will not invoke a specific circumstance that could explain or excuse his conduct, nor will he try to change the definition applied to the conduct at issue. In essence, the defendant agrees with the plaintiff that the fact pattern at issue falls under a particular legal category, but he offers a contrary interpretation of the legal rule that applies to that category.

The example given by the *Rhetorica ad Herennium* is significant on this point. A mime shouted at a poet on stage; consequently, the poet brings an action for injury against him. The mime disputes neither the alleged fact nor the definition that it is given as such: he acknowledges having committed the act in question and accepts that this act is described by the term *conpellatio*. He did shout at Accius in public. But he disputes the interpretation of the rule put forward by Accius. For Accius, the defendant's *conpellatio* makes him liable under the applicable law governing actions for injury. But according to the defendant, Accius' interpretation of the law is mistaken. In the defendant's opinion, a legal rule specifically makes provision for the *conpellatio* involved here. The law expressly permits shouting at someone from the stage, provided that the person being shouted at is the writer of plays put on in public. Since this condition is met in this case, the mimic argues that he should not be convicted. The *constitutio iuridicialis absoluta* is comparable, in this way, to an affirmative defense. It rests on a strict interpretation of the law, applied to a factual scenario for which a legal rule makes express provision.

Constitutio negotialis. Sometimes the jurists apply the technique of legal qualification even to a fact that falls outside the natural domain of application of a legal rule. In such cases, the *qualitas* of the fact is established via a second approach that the rhetoricians call a *constitutio negotialis*.[65] Like *constitutio iuridicialis absoluta, constitutio negotialis* involves an assessment of the "quality" of a fact that has already undergone definition. The parties to a legal controversy are thus in agreement that a given event or factual scenario can be labeled with a particular legally relevant category (e.g., "theft," "poison"), but they disagree about the qualification of the fact thus defined—that is, about whether the legal rule covering that category (e.g., a legal rule punishing poisoning) properly applies to the fact at issue in their controversy. Like a *constitutio iuridicialis absoluta*, a *constitutio negotialis* is framed in the form of a *quaestio iuris*, a question of law, not a question of fact. But in this second approach, unlike in the *constitutio iuridicialis absoluta* approach, a party makes an argument in favor of extending the interpretation of a legal rule beyond its current domain of application, to cover an unforeseen factual scenario.[66] Often, the finite character of *ius* and the impossibility of framing a legal rule that encompasses every possible case oblige the jurists to devise new interpretations of existing legal rules. Clearly, this form of interpretation arouses most of the Roman jurists' reflections,[67] and it can follow two possible routes.

One route is to use an analogy. A party will compare two *facta* that have distinct but relatively similar definitions—such as giving an *amatorium* and giving a *venenum* in Quintilian's example—and will argue that the similarity between the two *facta* justifies the application of a rule covering one category to the other category as well.[68] Put another way, where the law is silent, analogy is employed to extend the scope of legal construal, relying on the so-called spirit of a legal rule. In the classical rhetorical tradition, such analogies take the form of a syllogism called a *ratiocinatio* or *collectio*.[69] In Quintilian's case of the wife who poisoned her husband, the analogy involved application of a rule prohibiting the fact of poisoning to the fact of administering an aphrodisiac to someone and then abandoning him.

Analogical reasoning of this type is very frequently used by the Roman jurists to argue for the appropriateness of a particular interpretation of a legal rule, and it has been the subject of much discussion in modern scholarship.[70] Such reasoning justifies, for example, the Roman legal rule invalidating any gift in contemplation of death (*donatio mortis causa*) made by an insolvent person. The jurists justify that rule by drawing an analogy to another one, invalidating any testamentary bequest made by an insolvent testator. Because gifts made *mortis causa* "take on the likeness of bequests" (*legatorum instar optinent*), such gifts should likewise be held invalid.[71] Similar reasoning also justifies the rule that the betrothal of a daughter who is under the legal power of her father is valid only if the daughter has given her consent. The rule is justified by an analogy with marriage. Since "betrothal, like marriage, is made effective by the consent of the contracting parties," a daughter-in-power must also consent to her betrothal.[72] In these and many other examples of such argument in the jurists' writing, legal reasoning is once again distanced from reality. To resolve all of these cases, a given event is first defined as a particular *factum*, and the legal consequences of that *factum* are then determined by means of qualification; the *factum* is analogized to another *factum*, and a legal rule that usually applies only to the second *factum* is then extended to apply to the first *factum*.

The second route that *constitutio negotialis* can take—legal fiction—requires even more creativity on the part of the jurists. In legal fiction, as in analogy, a rule established for one fact is applied to another fact. Both techniques, legal fiction and analogy, extend the scope of application of an existing rule without developing a new category of *factum*, thus preserving legal certainty and avoiding the excessive multiplication of legal categories. In this second route, however, the two facts are not similar at all. On the contrary, the qualification is made with the certainty that the fact qualified is obviously different from the fact foreseen by the law: the legal fiction presupposes the certainty of its own falsehood.[73]

This technique is very frequently employed by the Roman jurists, and many of its uses have been well studied by modern scholars.[74] One legal fiction, for example, holds that a Roman citizen who has been captured by the enemy is deemed to be dead.[75] Another treats the person who has fraudulently transferred property to a third party as if he were still in possession of that property.[76] One of these fictions provides an especially good illustration of the autonomy of Roman legal reasoning from factual reality: it is the fiction that "a child in utero is treated exactly as if the child were already born" (*qui in utero est perinde ac si in rebus humanis esset custoditur*).[77] Like other Roman legal fictions, this one is motivated by a persuasive purpose. It addresses the uncertainty created by the period of pregnancy, up until the potential birth of an heir. When a man dies while his wife is pregnant, the rights of all of his heirs remain uncertain until the child either is or is not born alive.[78] To avoid this uncertainty, the fiction establishes a qualification by substituting one fact for another. In this case, it sets up an evidently false fact and deals with succession accordingly, proceeding as if the child in utero, should it come into the world at the end of the pregnancy, were already born during this period.

Legal fiction thus takes one final step in the artificial construction of fact. As an instrument of legal qualification, it makes it possible to evaluate a situation without having to take into account the material reality of any specific case. Nor does this qualification depend on scientific representations of the reality. With regards to the child in utero, the definition of the beginning of existence[79] was a subject of debate in ancient medical and philosophical literature.[80] The fiction of the unborn child allows one to qualify this situation without having to enter the debate. Moreover, material reality is openly bracketed and denied, since a child in utero is considered to be already born only by virtue of legal interpretation. The fiction allows jurists to resolve cases on the basis of completely artificial "facts"—as they do here in the case of the posthumous child.

Conclusion

Of course, the Roman jurists' creativity is not infinite and always has in view the practical objective of reaching a convincing solution for a particular case. Yet their reasoning in these and other examples also sheds light on the broader aims of jurisprudence and the methods used to achieve those aims. The vocation of jurisprudence is not literally to adapt the law to the facts. As artificial constructs of the law, facts are, by definition, not identical to the underlying reality that they represent. The law cannot be adapted to an object that the law itself has built. The primary purpose of jurisprudence is also not to construct a representation of the world[81] (though some recent scholarship suggests this),[82] much less to exhaustively map every possible factual scenario onto an appropriate legal rule.[83] Such an enterprise can only be in vain, as Jorge Luis Borges shows in his short story "Etcétera": unless we alter their nature, neither of these two elements, the map or the object, can be reduced to the other.[84]

The essential vocation of jurisprudence is, rather, to resolve disputes. To fulfill this vocation, jurists must always artificially isolate and abstract away from the facts of specific cases, in order to reach decisions that can be justified in terms of generalizable legal principles. Such legal principles have many sources, and every interpretation in this respect can express moral, political, social, or religious orientations. Much the same could also be said about the interpretation of fact. But legal reasoning in itself is autonomous from fact. The terms in which it is formulated and the lines of argument it follows are conceived precisely to avoid consideration of whether the facts to which a legal norm is being applied are or are not "reality" or the "truth." It is always possible to put aside this mode of strictly legal reasoning and to evaluate each unique factual scenario separately and on its own terms, albeit at the risk of producing inconsistent and sometimes arbitrary interpretations. This is precisely what the Romans' *quaestio facti* framework does. The reflections of the Roman jurists make clear, however, that as soon as one opts for a mode of reasoning that relies on generalizable legal principles, some use of artificial construction of fact necessarily follows. Such reasoning aims less at finding the factual "truth" behind a dispute and more at reaching predictable legal decisions.

Notes

I want to thank Clifford Ando and William Sullivan for their help in the translation of this chapter.

1. On the foundations of this distinction, see V.-Al. Georgescu, "L'opposition entre '*ius*' et '*factum*' en droit romain et en droit moderne: Contribution à l'étude des styles de la pensée juridique," in *Scritti in onore di C. Ferrini pubblicati in occasione della sua beatificazione* (Milan: Soc. ed. "Vita e pensiero," 1948), 3:144–65; N. Cornu Thénard, "La notion de fait dans la jurisprudence classique: Étude sur les principes de la distinction

entre fait et droit" (PhD diss., Université Paris II, 2011). For contemporary formulations of the distinction, see, in particular, G. Marty, *La distinction du fait et du droit: Essai sur le pouvoir de contrôle de la Cour de cassation sur les juges du fait* (Paris: Sirey, 1929); *Le fait et le droit: Études de logique juridique*, Travaux du Centre national de recherches de logique (Brussels: Bruylant, 1961); K. Olivecrona, "Legal Language and Reality," in *Essays in Jurisprudence in Honor of Roscoe Pound* (Indianapolis: R. A. Newman, 1962), 151–91; L. Husson, "Le fait et le droit," in *Nouvelles études sur la pensée juridique* (Paris: Dalloz, 1974), 145–60; M. Rotondi, "Considérations en 'fait' et en 'droit,'" *Revue trimestrielle de droit civil*, 1977, 1–16; T. Ivainer, *L'interprétation des faits en droit: Essai de mise en perspective cybernétique des "lumières du magistrat"* (Paris: LGDJ, 1988); O. Pfersmann, s.v. *Fait*, in *Dictionnaire de la culture juridique* (Paris: PUF, 2003), 695–98; G. Levi, *Fatto e diritto* (Milan: Giuffrè, 2002).

2. This is at least so in Western legal culture: see C. Geertz, "Civilisations et savoir: Fait et droit en perspective comparée," in *Savoir local, savoir global: Les lieux du savoir*, trans. D. Paulme, 3rd ed. (Paris: PUF, 2002), 207–90.

3. In this vein, J. Rivero writes that "pour le philosophe du sens commun . . . , la distinction est si évidente qu'elle ne soulève pas de problèmes: le droit relève de la catégorie du normatif: il dit ce qui doit être; le fait, c'est ce qui est; entre le domaine du *sollen* et le domaine du *sein*, il ne saurait y avoir de confusion" ("La distinction du droit et du fait dans la jurisprudence du Conseil d'État français," in *Le fait et le droit*, 130). L. Husson explains, for his part, that the opposition between fact and law can be defined as "celle de ce qui est constaté et de ce qui est prescrit, ou, pour employer les verbes allemands, comme celle du *sein* et du *sollen*" ("Le fait et le droit," in *Nouvelles études sur la pensée juridique* [Paris: Dalloz, 1974], 145–60). In the same way, for J. Carbonnier: "c'est l'opposition même de l'être au devoir-être" (*Sociologie juridique*, Paris: PUF, 1994, 286).

4. It is commonly said, in this regard, that the French *Cour de cassation* can only judge the law, whereas the courts of the first and second instances judge both law and fact. In reality, although this presentation is seductive from a didactic point of view, it is erroneous: see N. Cornu Thénard, "Fait et droit dans la répartition des compétences juridictionnelles," *Tribonien* 3 (2019): 6–26.

5. On the myth of adapting law to fact, see Ch. Attias and D. Linotte, "Le mythe de l'adaptation du droit au fait," *Recueil Dalloz et Sirey de doctrine, de jurisprudence et de législation*, 1977, 251–58.

6. On these doctrines and their methodological specificities, see, in particular, J. Carbonnier, *Sociologie juridique*, 80–149; A.-J. Arnaud, *Critique de la raison juridique*, vol. 1 (Paris: LGDJ, 1981).

7. Understood as such, the distinction between law and fact is obviously a myth, as shown by R. J. Allen and M. S. Pardo in "The Myth of the Law-Fact Distinction," *Northwestern University Law Review* 97 (2003): 1769–1807.

8. For more detail, see Cornu Thénard, "La notion de fait," 28–169, the main conclusions of which are briefly summarized here.

9. See Cornu Thénard, "La notion de fait," 28–169.

10. On the differentiation of actions turning mainly on questions of law from those turning mainly on questions of fact, cf. Cornu Thénard, "La notion de fait," 398–487.

11. See N. Cornu Thénard, "Le duel entre fait et droit chez les juristes classiques," in *Carmina iuris: Mélanges en l'honneur de Michel Humbert*, ed. E. Chevreau, D. Kremer, and A. Laquerrière-Lacroix (Paris: De Boccard, 2012), 191–205.

12. On this fragment, see, in particular, V. Scarano Ussani, *Valori e storia nella cultura giuridica fra Nerva e Adriano: Studi su Nerazio e Celso* (Naples: Jovene, 1979); Scarano Ussani, *Empiria e dogmi: La scuola proculiana fra Nerva e Adriano* (Turin: Giappichelli, 1989); A. M. Honoré, "A Study of Neratius and a Reflection on Method," *Tijdschrift voor Rechtsgeschiedenis* 43 (1975): 223–40; F. Casavola, "Cultura e scienza giuridica nel secondo secolo d. C.: Il senso del passato," in *Aufstieg und Niedergang der römischen Welt* (Berlin: de Gruyter, 1976), 2.15:131–75; A. Carcaterra, "*Facti interpretatio* nella epistemologia di Nerazio (D. 22.6.2)," *Bullettino dell'Istituto di diritto romano* 84 (1981): 35–57; Carcaterra, "'*Ius finitum*' e '*facti interpretatio*' nella epistemologia di Nerazio Prisco (D. 22.6.2)," in *Studi A. Biscardi* (Milan: Cisalpino, 1984), 5:405–36; L. C. Winkel, *Error iuris nocet* (Zutphen: Terra, 1985), 43–53, 82–83; S. Nappi, "*Ius finitum*," *Labeo* 43 (1997): 30–69.

13. For this reading of Neratius, see Scarano Ussani, *Empiria e dogmi*, 9; Casavola, "Cultura e scienza giuridica," 162–63.

14. The empirical approach prioritizes predictability of legal outcomes, whereas the dogmatic approach prioritizes the stability of doctrine. See Scarano Ussani, *Empiria e dogmi*; A. Burdese, "La certezza del diritto nell'esperienza di Roma antica," in *Miscellanea Romanistica* (Madrid: Fund. "Ursino Alvarez," 1994), 1–11; Cornu Thénard, "Le duel."

15. *Dig.* 1.2.2 pr.–10 (Pomp. *l.s. enchir.*). For discussion of these fragments and others that point to a requirement of legal certainty in Roman jurisprudence, see V. Scarano Ussani, *L'utilità e la certezza: Compiti e modelli del sapere giuridico in Salvio Giuliano* (Milan: Giuffrè, 1986), 81–104; M. Bretone, *Tecniche e ideologie dei giuristi romani* (Naples: EDI, 1971), 142–44. For more general reflections on legal certainty in Roman law, see A. Torrent, *Conceptos fundamentales del ordinamento jurídico romano* (Salamanca: Graf. Europa, 1973), 125–41; *La certezza del diritto nell'esperienza giuridica romana*, ed. M. Sargenti and G. Luraschi (Padua: CEDAM, 1987); Burdese, "La certezza del diritto"; T. Giaro, *Römische Rechtswahrheiten: Ein Gedankenexperiment* (Frankfurt am Main: Klostermann, 2007).

16. G. Vico, *De universi iuris uno principio et fine uno* (Naples: Mosca, 1720), 117.4, 128.2, 180.

17. Explaining that proof must be based on inputs that are certain, Quintilian lists the

sources of law among the things that can be treated as certain (*Inst. or.* 5.10.11–13): *Ergo cum sit argumentum ratio probationem praestans, qua colligitur aliud per aliud, et quae quod est dubium per id quod dubium non est confirmat, necesse est esse aliquid in causa quod probatione non egeat. . . . Pro certis autem habemus primum quae sensibus percipiuntur, ut quae videmus audimus, qualia sunt signa; deinde ea <in> quae communi opinione consensum est, deos esse, praestandam pietatem parentibus, praeterea quae legibus cauta sunt, quae persuasione etiam si non omnium hominum, eius tamen civitatis aut gentis in qua res agitur in mores recepta sunt, ut pleraque in iure non legibus sed moribus constant.*

18. *Dig.* 22.6.9.3 (Paul. *l.s. de iuris et facti ign.*). On the evolution of this principle in the thought of Labeo and Paul, who discuss the possibility of consulting a jurist on the law, see P. Cerami, "*Ignorantia iuris*," *Seminarios complutenses de derecho romano* 4 (1992): 57–85.

19. As stated by Carcaterra ("*Facti interpretatio*" [1981]), deceptive is not the fact itself but its interpretation.

20. See J. Parain-Vial, *La nature du fait dans les sciences humaines* (Paris: PUF, 1966). For an argument that the defects revealed by Neratius proceed from inductive reasoning used in matters of *interpretatio facti*, see Carcaterra, "*Facti interpretatio.*"

21. On this theory, see, in particular, L. Calboli Montefusco, *La dottrina degli "status" nella retorica greca e romana* (Hildesheim: Olms-Weidmann, 1986); Calboli Montefusco, "Logica, retorica e giurisprudenza nella doctrina degli *status*," in *Per la storia del pensiero giuridico romano*, ed. D. Mantovani (Turin: Giappichelli, 1996), 209–28; H. Lausberg, *Handbook of Literary Rhetoric: A Foundation for Literary Studies*, trans. M. T. Bliss, A. Jansen, and D. E. Orton (Boston: Brill, 1998), 122–52. On its influence on civil procedure and Roman legal science, see J. Stroux, "Summum ius summa iniuria: Un capitolo concernente la storia della *interpretatio iuris*," trans. G. Funaioli, *Annali del seminario giuridico della R. Università di Palermo* 12 (1929): 639–91; A. Steinwenter, "Rhetorik und römischer Zivilprozeß," *SZ-RA* 65 (1947): 69–120; E. Meyer, "Die Quaestionen der Rhetorik und die Anfänge juristischer Methodenlehre," *SZ-RA* 68 (1951): 30–73; J. Santa Cruz Teijero, "Der Einfluß der rhetorischen Theorie der Status auf die Auslegung der Gesetze und Rechtsgeschäfte," *SZ-RA* 75 (1958): 91–115; U. Wesel, *Rhetorische Statuslehre und Gesetzauslegung der römischen Juristen* (Cologne: C. Heymann, 1967); B. Vonglis, *La lettre et l'esprit de la loi dans la jurisprudence classique et la rhétorique* (Paris: Sirey, 1968); U. Babusiaux, *Papinians quaestiones: Zur rhetorischen Methode eines spätklassischen Juristen* (Munich: C. H. Beck, 2011), 21–61.

22. On the different classifications to which this theory gave rise, see Calboli Montefusco, *La dottrina degli "status,"* 197–206; Lausberg, *Handbook of Literary Rhetoric*, 42–97. See also the diagrams in J. Cousin, *Institution oratoire: Livres II-III* (Paris: Belles Lettres, 2003), 122–25.

23. Cic. *Or.* 45: *Nam quoniam, quicquid est quod in controversia aut in contentione*

versetur, in eo aut sitne aut quid sit aut quale sit quaeritur: sitne, signis; quid sit, definitionibus; quale sit, recti pravique partibus. On this tripartite classification, see also Cic. *De orat.* 1.139, 2.104, 2.113, 3.70; *Part. orat.* 33.62.101; *Top.* 82.92. See also Quint. *Inst. or.* 3.5.6, 3.6.44, 3.6.80–82.

24. On the use of *quaestiones facti* in matters of conjecture, see Cornu Thénard, "La notion de fait," 106–12.

25. A definition of the *status coniecturae* is given in the *Rhetorica ad Herennium* (1.18): *Hic quoniam coniectura verum quaeritur, de facto erit controversia et ex eo constitutio causae coniecturalis nominatur.*

26. On the use of the *status* of qualification in *quaestiones facti*, see Cornu Thénard, "La notion de fait," 326–487.

27. *Dig.* 39.6.13.1 (Iul. 17 *dig.*): *Marcellus notat: in mortis causa donationibus etiam facti quaestiones sunt. Nam et sic potest donari, ut omnimodo ex ea valetudine donatore mortuo res non reddatur: et ut reddatur, etiamsi prior ex eadem valetudine donator decesserit, si tamen mutata voluntate restitui sibi voluerit. Sed et sic donari potest, ut non aliter reddatur, quam si prior ille qui acceperit decesserit. Sic quoque potest donari mortis causa, ut nullo casu sit eius repetitio, id est nec si convaluerit quidem donator*; 39.5.2.7 (Iul. 60 *dig.*): *Titio decem donavi ea condicione, ut inde Stichum sibi emeret: quaero, cum homo antequam emeretur mortuus sit, an aliqua actione decem recipiam. Respondi: facti magis quam iuris quaestio est: nam si decem Titio in hoc dedi, ut Stichum emeret, aliter non daturus, mortuo Sticho condictione repetam: si vero alias quoque donaturus Titio decem, quia interim Stichum emere proposuerat, dixerim in hoc me dare, ut Stichum emeret, causa magis donationis quam condicio dandae pecuniae existimari debebit et mortuo Sticho pecunia apud Titium remanebit.* On these texts, see Cornu Thénard, "La notion de fait," 111–12, 134–36.

28. *Dig.* 40.4.13.1 (Ulp. 5 *disp.*): *Idem quaeri potest et si fabris duobus vel pictoribus, si membrum depinxissent vel si fabricassent navem, quid adscriptum sit: nam voluntatis erit quaestio, num alteri alterius facti condicionem iunxerit.*

29. Roman law required the husband to make whatever investments were required to maintain the value of his wife's dowry at his own personal expense. See *Dig.* 25.1.15 (Nerat. 2 *membr.*).

30. The same applies to *impensae necessariae*, expenses whose omission would have reduced the value of the dowry (*Dig.* 25.1.14 pr. [Ulp. 5 *reg.*]).

31. That Celsus here has precisely the *negotiorum gestio* in view explains his analysis of this case. See O. Lenel, *Palingenesia iuris civilis* (Leipzig: Tauchnitz, 1889), 1:129.

32. Celsus lays down guidelines to follow in the *interpretatio facti*, and he suggests a link between observation and evaluation, by setting forth several objective indicia from which the subjective intent of the husband can be inferred (*Dig.* 24.1.47 *in fine*: . . . *coniectura eius rei ex modo et ex genere impensae non difficilis est*).

33. For a case in which the interpretation of a clause imposing a condition precedent

to the appointment of an heir is framed as a *quaestio facti*, see *Dig.* 28.5.15.1 (Ulp. 7 *ad Sab.*). The examination, within this framework, of the intent of the testator determines the person on whom the testator's property will devolve. Cf. also the discussion of a testamentary guardianship provision at *Dig.* 50.16.122 (Pomp. 8 *ad Q. Muc.*).

34. For a case in which the maturity date of an obligation is framed as a *quaestio facti*, see *Dig.* 45.1.41 pr (Ulp. 50 *ad Sab.*). The question of the meaning of a stipulatory contract is framed as a *quaestio facti* in *Dig.* 45.1.94 (Marcel. 3 *dig.*).

35. See F. Pringsheim, "*Id quod actum est*," *SZ-RA* 78 (1961): 1–91; U. Babusiaux, *Id quod actum est: Zur Ermittlung des Parteiwillens im klassischen römischen Zivilprozess* (Munich: C. H. Beck, 2006).

36. *Dig.* 44.7.52.8 (Modest. 2 *reg.*): *Ex peccato obligamur, cum in facto quaestionis summa constitit.*

37. For Labeo's classical definition of *dolus*, see *Dig.* 4.3.1.2 (Ulp. 11 *ad ed.*).

38. On the legal definition of *dolus malus*, which presupposes an inquiry into intent, see A. Carcaterra, *Dolus bonus / Dolus malus: Esegesi di D.4.3.1.2–3* (Naples: Jovene, 1970).

39. *Dig.* 6.1.52 (Iul. 55 *dig.*): *Cum autem fundi possessor ante litem contestatam dolo malo fundum possidere desiit, heredes eius in rem quidem actionem suscipere cogendi non sunt, sed in factum actio adversus eos reddi debebit, per quam restituere cogantur, quanto locupletes ex ea re facti fuerunt.*

40. *Dig.* 44.4.1.2 (Paul. 71 *ad ed.*): *Sed an dolo quid factum sit, ex facto intellegitur.*

41. On this maxim's origin, see L. Prosdocimi, "'*Ex facto oritur ius*': Breve nota di diritto medievale," in *Studi senesi in memoria di Ottorino Vannini* (Milan: Giuffrè, 1957), 802–13.

42. Aristot. *Top.* 1.5.102a.

43. See especially R. Martini, *Le definizioni dei giuristi romani* (Milan: Giuffrè, 1966), 135–366.

44. On this well-known aspect of the Roman jurists' method, see F. Schulz, *Prinzipien des römischen Rechts* (Munich: Duncker & Humblot, 1934), 27–44; Schulz, *History of Roman Legal Science* (Oxford: Clarendon Press, 1946), 119–277. See also articles by F. Gallo, G. Grosso, and L. Lantella, under the title "La concretezza della giurisprudenza romana," in *Index* 5 (1974–75): 1–37; B. Schmidlin, *Die römischen Rechtsregeln* (Cologne: Böhlau Verlag, 1970), 143–62; L. Vacca, *Contributo allo studio del metodo casistico nel diritto romano* (Milan: Giuffrè, 1976); M. Kaser, "Zur Methode der römischen Rechtsfindung," in *Ausgewählte Schriften* (Naples: Jovene, 1976), 1:3–83.

45. On the relations between *res facti* and *casus* in the Roman jurists, see Cornu Thénard, "La notion de fait," 174–82.

46. Quint. *Inst. or.* 3.5.10: *Nam finitione quidem comprendi nihil non in universum certum erit.*

47. See F. Stella Maranca, "Le *regulae iuris* e la *definitio in iure civili*," in *Recueil F. Gény* (Paris: Sirey, 1934), 2:91–127; Martini, *Le definizioni*, 12–60, 367–403.

48. See M. Villey, *Recherches sur la littérature didactique en droit romain* (Paris: Domat-Montchrestien, 1945), followed by Martini (*Le definizioni*, 1–14) and A. Carcaterra (*Le definizioni dei giuristi romani: Metodo, mezzi e fini* [Naples, 1966], 23–38).

49. R. Martini's systematic study reveals, in this regard, the extent of the domain to which these definitions apply and the diversity of texts in which they figure.

50. When used in this context, the term *factum* bears comparison to what contemporary Continental doctrine calls "juridical fact." The concept is traditionally defined as "any fact to which the law attaches a legal consequence which was not necessarily sought by the author of the fact" (G. Cornu, *Vocabulaire juridique*, 11th ed. [Paris: PUF, 2016], 449).

51. On the influence of rhetoric on the framing of definitions by the jurists, see D. Behrens, "Begriff und Definition in den Quellen," *SZ-RA* 74 (1957): 352–63; Martini, *Le definizioni*, especially 15–60, 367–403.

52. On this *status*, see Quint. *Inst. or.* 7.3 (*de finitione*); Cic. *Inv.* 1.10–11; Cic. *Part. or.* 123–28; Lausberg, *Handbook of Literary Rhetoric*, 70–72; Calboli Montefusco, *La dottrina degli "status,"* 77–92.

53. Cic. *Inv.* 1.11: *Quare in eiusmodi generibus definienda res erit verbis et breviter describenda, ut, si quis sacrum ex privato subripuerit, utrum fur an sacrilegus sit iudicandus; nam id cum quaeritur, necesse erit definire utrumque, quid sit fur, quid sacrilegus, et sua descriptione ostendere alio nomine illam rem, de qua agitur, appellare oportere atque adversarii dicunt.*

54. For a typology of *factum* in the classical Roman jurists' thought, see Cornu Thénard, "La notion de fait," 208–59.

55. Carcaterra, *Le definizioni*, 117–68.

56. The supposed lack of logical rigor in Roman jurists' definitions has sometimes been criticized by modern scholars. See, e.g., Schulz, *Prinzipien*, 30–32.

57. Cic. *Inv.* 1.11: *Quare in eiusmodi generibus definienda res erit verbis et breviter describenda*; *Inv.* 2.53–55: *Primus ergo accusatoris locus est eius nominis, cuius de vi quaeritur, brevis et aperta et ex opinione hominum definitio. . . . Deinde defensoris primus locus est item nominis brevis et aperta et ex opinione hominum descriptio*; *De or.* 1.42.189: *est enim definitio rerum earum, quae sunt eius rei propriae, quam definire volumus, brevis et circumscripta quaedam explicatio*; *Orat.* 33.116: *est definitio oratio, quae quid sit id de quo agitur ostendit quam brevissime.* A similar observation can be found in *Rhet. Her.* 4.35: *Definitio est, quae rei alicuius proprias amplectitur potestates breviter et absolute.* Cf. also Quint. *Inst. or.* 7.3.2: *Finitio igitur est rei propositae propria et dilucida et breviter comprensa verbis enuntiatio.*

58. See C. Ando, *Roman Social Imaginaries: Language and Thought in Contexts of Empire* (Toronto: University of Toronto Press, 2012), 29–51.

59. E.g., G. Cornu's *Vocabulaire juridique* (837) defines qualification as "the intellectual operation of legal analysis, an essential tool of legal thought, consisting of taking into consideration the element that must be qualified (raw fact, act, rule, etc.) and enter-

ing it into a preexisting legal category (from which results, by attachment, the legal system applicable to it) by recognizing in it the essential characteristics of the category to which it is attached." The influence of legal positivism seems to explain the confusion between definition and qualification. Following this doctrine, an event can only be legally grasped if positive law gives it a definition, and positive law is presented as the exclusive source of legal qualification. In these conditions, since entering a concrete element into a category suffices to determine its qualification, the role of the interpreter is limited to an effort at definition.

60. Jean Cousin draws a comparison between this passage and *Declam. Min.* 350 (*Institution oratoire: Livres VI–VII* [Paris: Belles Lettres, 1977], 235–36).

61. *Dig.* 50.16.236.pr. (Gai. 4 *ad l. XII tab.*): *Qui "venenum" dicit, adicere debet, utrum malum an bonum: nam et medicamenta venena sunt, quia eo nomine omne continetur, quod adhibitum naturam eius, cui adhibitum esset, mutat. Cum id quod nos venenum appellamus, graeci* φάρμακον *dicunt, apud illos quoque tam medicamenta quam quae nocent, hoc nomine continentur: unde adiectione alterius nomine distinctio fit. Admonet nos summus apud eos poetarum Homerus: nam sic ait:* φάρμακα, πολλὰ μὲν ἐσθλὰ μεμιγμένα, πολλὰ δὲ λυγρά.

62. *Dig.* 48.8.3 pr. (Marcian. 14 *inst.*): *Eiusdem legis corneliae de sicariis et veneficis capite quinto, qui venenum necandi hominis causa fecerit vel vendiderit vel habuerit, plectitur.*

63. The function of this *status* is described by the rhetorians: *Hoc in genere, in quo quale sit quaeritur, [ex controversia] iure et recte necne actum sit quaeri solet* (Cic. *Part. or.* 43); *Nam et qualis sit cuiusque rei natura et quae forma quaeritur* (Quint. *Inst. or.* 7.4.1). On the *status qualitatis*, see Calboli Montefusco, *La dottrina degli "status,"* 93–138; Lausberg, *Handbook of Literary Rhetoric*, 72–82. This *status* is sometimes called *constitutio generalis* by Cicero, as at *Inv.* 2.62: *Cum et facto et facti nomine concesso neque ulla actionis inlata controversia vis et natura et genus ipsius negotii quaeritur, constitutionem generalem appellamus.* But the expressions are equivalent; see Calboli Montefusco, *La dottrina degli "status,"* 93–94.

64. On the *constitutio iuridicialis absoluta*, see Montefusco, *La dottrina degli "status,"* 108–13.

65. Cic. *Inv.* 2.62: *Negotialis est, quae in ipso negotio iuris civilis habet implicatam controversiam.* For a more in-depth analysis of the meaning and scope of this *constitutio negotialis*, see Calboli Montefusco, *La dottrina degli "status,"* 99–105; Cornu Thénard, "La notion de fait," 267–72.

66. Cic. *Inv.* 2.69: *Absoluta est, quae ipsa in se, non ut negotialis implicite et abscondite, sed patentius et expeditius recti et non recti quaestionem continet* ("The *constitutio iuridicialis absoluta* is that which embraces the determination of right and wrong more clearly and openly, not as in the *negotialis*, less openly and more obscurely").

67. Cic. *Inv.* 1.14: *Haec ergo constitutio, quam generalem nominamus, partes videtur nobis duas habere, iuridicialem et negotialem. . . . negotialis, in qua, quid iuris ex civili more et aequitate sit, consideratur; cui diligentiae praeesse apud nos iure consulti existimantur.*

68. On analogy, see, in particular, Ch. Perelman and L. Olbrechts-Tyteca, *Traité de l'argumentation*, 6th ed. (Brussels: Université de Bruxelles, 2008), 499–549; S. Brewer, "Exemplary Reasoning: Semantics, Pragmatics, and the Rational Force of Legal Argument by Analogy," *Harvard Law Review* 109, no. 5 (1996): 923–1028. On the use of analogy in Roman law, see C. Vlahos, "La préposition Pro dans le discours de la jurisprudence classique: Un outil linguistique au service de *l'ars boni et aequi*" (PhD diss., Université Paris II, 2002), 102–60; C. Ando, "Exemplum, Analogy, and Precedent in Roman Law," in *Between Exemplarity and Singularity: Literature, Philosophy, Law*, ed. M. Lowrie and S. Lüdemann (New York: Routledge, 2015), 111–22.

69. Quintilian presents syllogism as one *status* of several law-specific ones (along with *scriptum et voluntas*, *leges contrariae*, and *ambiguitas*). But syllogism, or *collectio*, is essentially a form of qualification, as Quintilian himself implies when he relates the three "rational" categories of *status* (*coniectura*, *finitio*, *qualitas*) to the various "legal" categories (*scriptum et voluntas*, *leges contrariae*, *collectio*, *ambiguitas*). Cf. Quint. *Inst. or.* 3.6.88: *Sic nascuntur haec velut simulacra ex illis tribus, interim simplicia, interim et mixta, propriam tamen faciem ostendentia, ut scripti et voluntatis, quae sine dubio aut qualitate aut coniectura continentur, et sillogismos, qui est maxime qualitatis.*

70. See, in particular, Vlahos, "La préposition Pro," 102–60; M. Humbert, "Équité et raison naturelle dans les oeuvres de Celse et de Julien," in *Testi e problemi del giusnaturalismo romano*, ed. D. Mantovani and A. Schiavone (Pavia: IUSS Press, 2007), 419–73; Cornu Thénard, "La notion de fait," 273–82; Ando, "Exemplum, Analogy, and Precedent in Roman Law."

71. *Dig.* 39.6.17 (Iul. 47 *dig.*): *Etsi debitor consilium creditorum fraudandorum non habuisset, avelli res mortis causa ab eo donata debet. Nam cum legata ex testamento eius, qui solvendo non fuit, omnimodo inutilia sint, possunt videri etiam donationes mortis causa factae rescindi debere, quia legatorum instar optinent.*

72. *Dig.* 23.1.11 (Iul. 16 *dig.*): *Sponsalia sicut nuptiae consensu contrahentium fiunt: et ideo sicut nuptiis, ita sponsalibus filiam familias consentire oportet.*

73. In this connection, Y. Thomas distinguishes legal fiction from presumption. Whereas legal fiction asserts something that is definitely false, presumption depends simply on the *incertitude du vrai*. See Y. Thomas, "*Fictio legis*: L'empire de la fiction romaine et ses limites médiévales," *Droits* 21 (1995): 17–63.

74. See, in particular, R. Dekkers, *La fiction juridique: Étude de droit romain et de droit comparé* (Paris: Sirey, 1935); F. Todescan, *Diritto e realtà: Storia e teoria della fictio iuris* (Padua: CEDAM, 1979); Thomas, "*Fictio legis*"; E. Bianchi, *Fictio iuris: Ricerche sulla finzione in diritto romano dal periodo arcaico all'epoca augustea* (Padua: CEDAM, 1997); Vlahos, "La préposition Pro," 65–99; Humbert, "Équité et raison naturelle"; Cornu Thénard, "La notion de fait," 297–324; C. Ando, *Law, Language, and Empire in the Roman Tradition* (Philadelphia: University of Pennsylvania Press, 2011), 1–18, 115–31; Ando, "Fact, Fiction, and Social Reality in Roman Law," in *Legal Fictions in Theory and Practice*, ed. M. del Mar and W. Twining (Boston: Springer, 2015), 295–323.

75. *Dig.* 49.15.18 (Ulp. 35 *ad Sab.*): *In omnibus partibus iuris is, qui reversus non est ab hostibus, quasi tunc decessisse videtur, cum captus est.* The case of the captive has given rise to an abundant literature. For discussion of recent work, see L. D'Amati, *Civis ab hostibus captus: Profili del regime classico* (Milan: Giuffrè, 2004).

76. *Dig.* 50.17.131 (Paul. 22 *ad ed.*): *Qui dolo desierit possidere, pro possidente damnatur, quia pro possessione dolus est.*

77. *Dig.* 1.5.7. (Paul *l.s. de port. q. lib. dam. conc.*): *Qui in utero est, perinde ac si in rebus humanis esset custoditur, quotiens de commodis ipsius partus quaeritur: quamquam alii antequam nascatur nequaquam prosit.* Paul's expression is repeatedly mentioned by classical jurists (*Dig.* 1.5.26, 37.9.77.pr., 38.16.7, 50.16.231). On this fiction, see, in particular, Y. Thomas, "L'enfant à naître et l' 'héritier sien': Sujet de pouvoir et sujet de vie en droit romain," *Annales* 62, no. 1 (2007): 29–68.

78. Not being *in rerum natura* at the moment of death, the infant should not, in principle, succeed the father; however, the Law of the Twelve Tables makes the child in utero eligible to inherit if the child is ultimately born alive (*Dig.* 38.16.3.9 [Ulp. 14 *ad Sab.*]: *Utique et ex lege duodecim tabularum ad legitimam hereditatem is qui in utero fuit admittitur, si fuerit editus*). Under these circumstances, there is a risk that the distribution of the father's property will have to be done twice, immediately after the father's death and then again once the child in utero either is or is not born alive. The fiction responds to this uncertainty by suspending distribution of the decedent's property until the day of the posthumous child's birth.

79. The logic of the fiction helps to explain the idea that underlies this rule. A legal fiction always asserts something that is openly contrary to reality. Here, the fiction is that a child in utero is a child *in rebus humanis*. This fiction suggests that, in the eyes of the law, a child in utero is not, in reality, human; it is not yet part of the *res humanae*. Cf. *Dig.* 37.9.7 pr. (Ulp. 47 *ad ed.*): *Ubicumque ab intestato admittitur quis, illic et venter admittitur, scilicet si talis fuerit is qui in utero est, ut, si in rebus humanis esset, bonorum possessionem petere posset.*

80. See J. Roussier, "La durée normale de la grossesse," in *Droits de l'Antiquité et sociologie juridique: Mélanges Henri Lévy-Bruhl* (Paris: Sirey, 1959), 245–56; E. Nardi, *Procurato aborto nel mondo greco romano* (Milan, Giuffrè, 1971).

81. Even though this construction is, of course, a consequence of Roman jurists' definitions and qualifications.

82. See, e.g., the discussions about the legal status of animals or robots in France, which often reveal that their primary focus is to modify a subject's situation in the legal representation of the world.

83. As Claudia Moatti has shown for Roman social status in particular, the vocation of law is not to confine reality within a supposedly exhaustive logical order. See C. Moatti, "Reconnaissance et identification des personnes dans la Rome antique," in *Identification des personnes: Génèse d'un travail d'État*, ed. G. Noiriel (Paris: Belin, 2007), 27–55; Moatti, "Les erreurs de statut et l'idée de liberté dans l'espace judiciaire romain

impérial jusqu'au III^{è} siècle," in *Recht haben und Recht bekommen im Imperium Romanum: Das Gerichtswesen der Römischen Kaiserzeit und seine dokumentarische Evidenz*, ed. R. Haensch (Warsaw: University of Warsaw, 2016), 523–59.

84. J.-L. Borges ("Etcétera," in *Historia universal de la infamia*, 2nd ed. (Buenos Aires: Tor, 1954). The idea of creating such a map, in an absurd format, was initially conceived by L. Carroll, in *Sylvie and Bruno Concluded* (London: Macmillan, 1893), chap. 11.

CHAPTER 3

Legal Knowledge in Gortyn

Debt Bondage and the Liability of Slaves in Gortynian Law

David M. Lewis

According to Plato (*Leg.* 625a), Crete was renowned for its laws, a claim backed up by an extraordinary profusion of inscribed law across the central part of the island, especially in Gortyn. Despite these epigraphic riches, much debate surrounds the practice of law in the Cretan cities. Should we model the use of Gortyn's written laws on "code" law from the Near East and view it as inaccessible to the average citizen?[1] How widely disseminated among the citizenry of poleis like Gortyn was literacy and legal knowledge? My particular focus in this chapter is the degree to which written rules at Gortyn depended on the legal knowledge of the reader. Did those responsible for enacting written laws at Gortyn assume ignorance on behalf of the reader and therefore go into great detail on every point of a given law? Or did they assume a fair degree of knowledge of basic legal principles, allowing written enactments to skip over points of detail that were too obvious to require chiseling onto stone? Questions about the nature of statutory language and the nature of the interpretive community it was presumed to address bear on issues of hermeneutics at the heart of modern approaches to just these sources. A full study of this problem is beyond the scope of this chapter; instead, I here present a case study: the question of who was held liable when a slave committed an infraction against a third party.

This case study begins with a rather tersely expressed set of rules in column

II (lines 1–10) of the so-called Great Code of Gortyn (*IC* IV **72**).[2] These rules set out various scenarios relating to sexual violence, with differing fines based on the relative status of the perpetrator and victim.

> αἴ κα τὸν ἐλεύθερον ἒ τὰν ἐλευθέραν κάρτει οἴπει, ἑκατὸν στατε͂ρανς καταστασεῖ· αἰ δέ κ' ἀπεταίρο, δέκα· αἰ δέ κ' ὀ δο͂λος τὸν ἐλεύθερον ἒ τὰν ἐλευθέραν, διπλεῖ καταστασεῖ· αἰ δέ κ' ἐλεύθερος ϝοικέα ἒ ϝοικέαν, πέντε δαρκνάνς· αἰ δέ κα ϝοικεὺς ϝοικέα ἒ ϝοικέαν, π[έν]τε στατε͂ρανς.
>
> If someone rapes a free man or woman, he will pay a hundred staters. If an *apetairos*, ten. If a male slave (*dolos*) (rapes) a free man or woman, he will pay double. If a free man (rapes) a male slave (*woikeus*) or a female slave (*woikea*), five drachmas. And if a male slave (*woikeus*) (rapes) a male slave (*woikeus*) or a female slave (*woikea*), five staters.

A straightforward reading of this passage suggests that slaves[3] are held liable for rape in the same way as free persons: in line 7, the *dolos* is literally required to pay (καταστασεῖ) the fine, and other instances are set out through ellipsis in the subsequent lines.[4]

We seem to be dealing with an open and shut case: slaves at Gortyn (unlike at Athens) were held legally liable for their infractions, at least those of a sexual nature, and they, not their owners, were required to pay any fines exacted for the offense. That view was put forward by R. Dareste in *Recueil des inscriptions juridiques grecques* in the late nineteenth century, was endorsed by A. Kränzlein in 1963, and has recently been endorsed by M. Gagarin and J. K. Davies.[5] Others, though, have dissented. For instance, M. I. Finley wrote that "some scholars believe they [sc., Gortynian slaves] also possessed money, but there is no evidence, and surely they did not possess the quantities required to meet the statutory fines (reaching 200 staters for a *doulos* who rapes a free man or woman)."[6] Despite Finley's assertion that there is no evidence for slaves owning money, a literal reading of the above passage suggests the opposite; at any rate, Finley cites no evidence to support his view, and one suspects that his position is based on aprioristic assumptions about the amount of wealth slaves could accumulate in the Greek world.

I have recently argued a similar (though not identical) line to Finley's: that Gortynian slaves had no legal rights and that the evidence adduced for such putative "rights" really shows nothing more than that slaves could possess property and form de facto "marriage" unions with other slaves.[7] More recently still, Gagarin has objected to my approach, writing, "Much of his argument rests on speculation about what (he claims) the texts 'mean,' which in many cases is not the same as what they 'say.'"[8] In other words, aprioristic assumptions about what "must be the case"—based on views on how slavery works in other places—distort a straightforward reading of the law. In what follows, I will show that my position is not simply based on aprioristic assumptions and speculation: other Gortynian laws contemporary to the one cited above show that Finley's view (that slaves did not pay the fines for their own infractions—or at least were not the legally responsible party) was correct.

In this chapter, I first assess Gagarin's method of taking the text at face value, highlighting both that method's strengths and its weaknesses. I then focus on a set of laws on debt bondage, which show that the text on sexual violence quoted above does not tell the whole story and that there are compelling, evidence-based reasons for rejecting Gagarin's view that slaves were liable to pay fines for their sexual transgressions. The chapter ends with some reflections on method, further suggestions about how the possession of goods by slaves may have worked in practice, and some tentative conclusions about the dissemination of legal knowledge among the Gortynians.

Reading Gortyn's Laws Literally

A literal reading of Gortyn's laws can score some signal successes, as revealed by the recent debate between Gagarin and Alberto Maffi over the legal position of Gortynian women.[9] On Maffi's view, the laws describing capacities of Gortynian women to own and manage property mask a harsher reality: a male guardian, like an éminence grise, stands in the background, controlling the woman's actions and severely limiting her choices. Maffi's version of the Gortynian woman thus emerges as a puppet of her guardian and, in legal terms, is not greatly different from her Athenian counterpart. Gagarin has rightly objected to this approach, on the grounds that Maffi's view is conditioned by assumptions—about how women "must have been" treated in the ancient world—that are based on an extrapolation of the legal position of women in Athens and Rome. He convincingly shows that a more natural reading of the text—one that is not coloured by a priori assumptions and does not insert a domineering Athenian-style *kyrios* into a Cretan context on the basis of no evidence at all—reveals that Gortynian women did enjoy various legal rights over property, rights that Athenian women of the same era did not enjoy.

A remarkable recent essay by Alain Bresson has brought this difference into sharper relief.[10] The legal regulation of women's property in the Greek world took a diversity of forms, and it was far from the case that each polis replicated the Athenian approach in carbon copy. Athens stood at one end of a quite diverse spectrum, heavily restricting the legal rights of women.[11] At the other end of that spectrum stood Sparta: as Aristotle (*Pol.* 1269b–1270a) pointed out, citizen women were wholly unregulated in Spartan law, and in Aristotle's view, Lycurgus had committed a major error in only legislating for half of the population. This error on the part of Lycurgus provided Spartan women with ample scope to accumulate property, to the point where they owned some two-fifths of the land in Sparta in Aristotle's own day and came to acquire even more by the third century. Women in Gortyn stood somewhere between these extremes. Though they were not as harshly treated by the law as Athenian women, numerous regulations limited the amount of property that Gortynian women could attain and pushed them towards marriages with close kin if they wanted to preserve the limited level of wealth that they already had. The Gortynians and Athenians had anticipated the destabilizing effects that nonregulation of female property could have and had taken careful (but different) measures to rein in this potentially freewheeling variable.[12]

Gagarin's approach is a useful tool for challenging any reading of Gortynian law that depends on assumptions—about "what must have been the case"—that do not derive from the text itself but are prior beliefs of the historian who approaches it. Gagarin's description of his method reveals its obvious strengths: "First, in interpreting the Gortyn laws, I begin with what the text says and try to understand it in itself. Then if necessary, I look to other laws from Gortyn, and occasionally to laws from other Cretan cities, for help. Only then, if necessary, do I take into consideration how Athenian law or Roman law (or some other system) may have treated a similar situation."[13] A mechanical application of Gagarin's approach (especially of step 1) can, however, lead to difficulties.

Another passage on which Gagarin and Maffi have disagreed is **72** III 40–44.

αἴ κα ϝοικέος ϝοικέα κριθει δοõ ἒ ἀποθανόντος, τὰ ϝὰ αὐτᾶς ἔκεν· ἄλλο δ' αἴ τι πέροι, ἔνδικον ἔμεν.

> If a female slave (*woikea*) is separated from her slave (*woikeus*) husband either while he is living or by his death, she is to have her own things, but if she should carry away anything else, it is a matter for trial.

On Maffi's view, this slave couple belongs to different owners, and the aim of the law is not to protect the slaves' rights (which do not exist) but to split, fifty-fifty, the property that they have accumulated during their time together—property that really belongs to their respective owners.[14] Gagarin, again using the plain meaning of the text to support his view, objects, "But if this is what the law means, we must ask first, why does it not say explicitly that the serfs [*sic*] belong to different owners; second, why does it not speak of 'her owner's things' rather than 'her own things'; and third, why does the law not direct the serf woman's owner to claim his property rather than letting the serf woman claim it?"[15]

Here, Gagarin assumes that all the information required to make sense of the law (both by ancient and modern readers) must be written on the stone, including all the details spelling out the legal position of the respective parties. On his view, if the slaves belong to different owners, that would have been indicated in the text. But another section of the Great Code shows that this assumption is unwarranted. In **72** III 52–IV 23, we find a set of rules describing the ownership of children born to a *woikeus* and a *woikea*. If the child is born when the parents are separated, it belongs to the owner of the *woikeus* (III 52–55). However, if that owner does not want the child, the owner of the *woikea* gains ownership of it (IV 1–3). If the separated couple remarry within a year, ownership of the child reverts back to the owner of the *woikeus* (IV 3–6). As Gagarin rightly notes in his recent commentary on the text, "the rules only matter for serf [*sic*] couples belonging to different masters."[16] But a glance at this section of the text shows no introduction explaining that the *woikeus* and *woikea* belong to different owners, which is exactly what Gagarin has claimed must be the case at **72** III 40–44 for Maffi's view to be correct. There is an inconsistency in Gagarin's reasoning here.

There is a simple answer to this problem: *pace* Gagarin, the text does not always spell out in full the legal positions of the respective parties; rather, it depends to varying degrees on the contextual knowledge of the Gortynian reader. That can be proven for **72** III 52–IV 23 (the aforementioned law on the ownership of slave children), but it can only remain a possible interpretation for **72** III 40–44 (the law, quoted above, on the division of the possessions of a slave couple), which could potentially bear either Gagarin's or Maffi's interpretation. Nonetheless, Gagarin's objections to Maffi's interpretation of this text have no force, because they depend on the assumption that the inscription's reader is presumed to have no contextual knowledge, a view that can be disproven from other parts of the Great Code.

Debt Bondage Laws and the Liability of Slaves

Gagarin is right that we should approach Gortyn's laws without prior assumptions—about how things "must have worked"—extrapolated from other times and places. As he also demonstrates, paying close attention to what the text says can often lead to convincing solutions. Nevertheless, Gagarin's approach—which assumes that all the information required to make sense of Gortyn's laws is written on the stone and which mechanically applies the principle that the text must always have a plain and obvious meaning—can lead to false conclusions. Clearly, making sense of these laws in their original context required, first, the text of the law and, second, the contextual knowledge about Gortynian society presumed of the reader.[17] While the text is on the whole very well preserved, the latter knowledge died out with the Gortynians themselves. Does this mean that we simply cannot comprehend these laws?

The majority of Gortyn's laws are expressed clearly enough to be intelligible to outsiders (e.g., modern scholars), although the collective *klaros* referred to in **72** V 27 remains, for now, an unsolved riddle, despite valiant attempts to explain it.[18] For the interpretation of texts that are neither easily understood nor insolubly baffling, headway can be made by comparing other parts of Gortyn's law that deal with the same problem and by distilling legal principles when these other texts are more explicit or forthcoming in their meaning. For the question of the liability of slaves, I turn to a Gortynian inscription roughly contemporary to the Great Code, *IC* IV **47**, to illustrate this method.

Like the rules for the division of the property of slave spouses due to divorce or the death of one spouse, which are modeled on the regulations for the divorce of free persons (**72** II 45–III 16), the rules found in **47** for slaves held in debt bondage[19] are modeled on rules regulating free persons held in debt bondage, found in column V of the so-called Little Code, *IC* IV **41** (lines 4–17):[20]

> αἰ δέ κα κελομένο ὄι κα παρῆι ϝεργάδδηται ἢ πέρηι, ἄπατον ἤμην. αἰ δὲ πονίοι μὴ κελομένο, τὸν δικασστὰν ὀμνύντα κρίνεν, αἰ μὲ ἀποπονίοι μαίτυρς. *vac.*

ἀλλότριον δ' αἴ τί κ' ἀδικέσει ὁ κατακείμενος, αὐτὸν ἀτῆθαι. αἰ δέ κα μὲ ἔκηι ὀπõ καταστασεῖ, ὁ νικάσανς κ' ὁ καταθέμενος [—]

And if on the orders of the one to whom he belongs (viz., his temporary master) he (viz., the debt bondsman) has done or taken something, he is not liable. But if (the temporary master) should affirm that he did not so order, the judge is to swear an oath and decide, unless a witness testifies. *vac.* And if the debt bondsman wrongs another, then he himself is to be liable. And if he does not have the means to pay, the person who won his case and the temporary master [—]

The regulations break off but pick up again in column VI (lines 1–17):

[—]ẹιο[*c.* 4 πλί] οδ δὲ μή. *vac.* αἰ δέ τις [τ]ὸν κατακείμενον ἀδικήσει, ὁ καταθέμενος μολησεῖ καὶ πρακσῆται τὰς τιμὰνς ἇι ἐλευθέρο, κ' ὅτι κ' ἐσπράκσεται τὰνν ἡμίναν ἔκεν τὸν κατακείμενον, τὰν δὲ τὸν καταθέμενον. αἰ δέ κ' ὁ καταθέμενος μὴ λῆι μολῆν, ἤ κ' ἀποδõι τὸ ὀπήλομα αὐτὸς μολήτο. αἰ δέ τί κ' ὁ κατακεί[μενος—]

[—] but not [more]. *vac.* But if someone wrongs the debt bondsman, the temporary master shall bring suit and shall exact the penalties as for a free person, and whatever penalty he exacts, the debt bondsman is to have one half and the temporary master the other; and if the temporary master does not wish to bring suit, let him (viz., the debt bondsman) bring suit himself when he has discharged his debt; and if the debt bondsman [—]

Though the text breaks off once more, we can see two scenarios in which the law clarifies the rights and duties of legally free persons held in debt bondage. In the first scenario, the law addresses what happens if the debt bondsman commits an offense. Depending on specifics (i.e., the person who set in motion the chain of events that led to the offense), either the debt bondsman himself or his temporary master can be held liable. The second scenario addresses what happens if a third party harms the debt bondsman. Two avenues are open: if the temporary master initiates an action against the offender and wins, he splits the damages fifty-fifty with the debt bondsman, and the damages are assessed at the level for free persons. If he does not wish to initiate an action, the debt bondsman must wait until he has paid off his debt before proceeding against the offender. Although the text is missing after that point, it is likely that, in this event, the law allows the bondsman to keep his winnings to himself (cf. below).

The laws on slaves held in debt bondage in **47** deal with a different scenario: presumably, one free man owes a debt to another, but instead of becoming the creditor's debt bondsman, the debtor sends one of his slaves in his place, to reside with and work for the creditor until the obligation is fully paid. It is vital to recognize that the slave serving in debt bondage is still the property of the debtor; the debtor has instructed the slave to work for his creditor until the debt is repaid.[21] At **47** A 1–8, the law reads,

> [?] κατακείμενος αἰ κ' ἀδικήσει δõλος ἢ δόλα, ὅτι μέν κ[α κατα]θ̣εμένο κελομένο ἀμάρτηι τõι καταθεμένοι τὰν δίκαν ἤμην, ὅτι δὲ κ' αὐτὸς πρὸ ϝιαυτõ τõι ἀρκαίοι πάσται τὰν δίκαν ἤμην τõι δὲ καταθεμένοι μή.
>
> If a slave debt bondsman or a slave debt bondswoman wrongs (someone), in that he does wrong on the orders of his temporary master, the case is to be brought against the temporary master, but in that he himself (does wrong) on his own, the case is to be brought against his original owner and not his temporary master.

Just like the rules for free debt bondsmen, those for enslaved debt bondsmen deal first with the eventuality of an offense by the bondsman. But as we can see, no matter who set in motion the chain of events that led to the offense, the person held legally liable is never the slave: it is either the slave's owner or the owner's creditor (viz., the slave's temporary master). There thus exists a clear difference in rules regarding the liability of the bondsmen, depending on their legal status as either a free person or somebody's slave. At **47** A 10–16, we find further rules:

> αἰ δέ κα τὸν κατακείμενον ἀδικήσει ἄλλος, αἰ μέν κ' ἀνπότεροι μολίοντες νικάσοντι, τὰν ἡμίναν ϝεκάτερος ἐκσίοντι· αἰ δέ κ' ὀ ἄτερος μὴ λῆι, ὀ ἄτερος μολίον αἴ κα νικάσει αὐτὸς ἐκσεῖ.
>
> But if someone else wrongs the (slave) debt bondsman, if both (viz., the original owner and the temporary master) bring suit and win, they shall each have half (of the penalty). And if one of them does not wish (to bring suit), if the other brings suit and wins, he shall have the penalty (himself).

Just like the rules in **41** V, this law turns, in the second instance, to a situation in which the bondsman is the victim of an offense. But in the rules of **47**, unlike in those of **41**, the fact that the bondsman is a slave (and thus the property of his owner) means that he is not the legal recipient of the fine.

For the purpose of the present case study, these rules very clearly illustrate two principles: (1) slaves were not held legally liable for offenses they committed; (2) slaves had no right to any damages awarded in a trial concerning offenses committed against them by third parties. These are not original points. Stefan Link made the former point in 1994,[22] whilst the latter goes back further, to Detlef Lotze in 1959.[23] This illustration brings the present analysis full circle, to the text with which we began, **72** II 1–10. Can we reconcile these texts that seem to show contradictory principles at work?

The first and most unlikely reconciliation is that the Gortynians were inconsistent, enacting a law in which slaves were held liable for their offenses and, at a later date (but not much later: Jeffrey[24] dated **41** and **47** to ca. 500–450, **72** to ca. 450), enacting a law (as part of the Great Code) in which the opposite principle prevailed. That view is confounded by another section of the Great Code, VII 10–15.

> α[ἴ] κ' ἐκς ἀγορᾶς πρ[ι]ά̣μενος δõλον μὲ περαιόσει τᾶν ϝεκσέκοντ' ἀμερᾶν, αἴ τινά κα πρόθ' ἀδικέκει ἒ ὕστερον, τõι πεπαμένοι ἔνδικον ἔμεν.
>
> If someone has bought a slave (*dolos*) from the agora and has not terminated (the purchase) within sixty days, if (the slave) has done wrong to anyone before or after (the purchase), litigation is to be conducted against the one who acquired him.

How can this rule stand if the slaves mentioned at II 1–10 are liable to pay fines in the event that they commit sexual violence? Surely ἀδικέκει covers sexual violence too? It is one thing to argue for inconsistency between Gortynian legal inscriptions of slightly different periods, but to argue for it within the same document requires the belief that the Gortynians were remarkably incompetent.

A second, far more satisfactory possibility for reconciling the texts in question is that the individuals who drafted the code sometimes worked in a kind of shorthand and did not spell out the true legal position of parties when it was perfectly obvious to the (Gortynian) reader what those positions were. The text of **72** II 1–10, then, said (in shorthand) that a slave had to pay such-and-such a fine if he were to rape this or that person, but it did not go to the length of pointing out that the slave's owner was really the one who was legally liable, because this was so obvious to a Gortynian reader that it would have been a waste of the lawgiver's time to go to the trouble of pointing it out. (The main point of this section of the text is simply to itemize the appropriate level of the fine, depending on the statuses of the perpetrator and victim.) This view fits far more neatly with what we know about Gortynian law.

Four points support the shorthand view. First, this particular section of the Great Code is the sloppiest in composition, mixing together the two Gortynian slave words *dolos* and *woikeus*, using inconsistent vocabulary for the offense, meandering through the different scenarios wherein this or that person is the offender or victim, and imposing fines in both drachmas and staters rather than converting them all to drachmas. J. K. Davies has, understandably, called it "rather a mess" in contrast with the more elegantly composed section on adoption.[25] Second, the idea of a shorthand approach that sometimes fails to elaborate on the detailed legal positions of the various parties ties in neatly with the rules on the ownership of slave children at **72** III 52–IV 23. Those rules, as we have seen, do not bother to alert the reader to the fact that the slaves comprising the couple belong to different owners, even though the law is only intelligible on that assumption. Third, the shorthand view harmonizes with the rule at **72** VII 10–15 rather than contradicting it. Fourth, it lends credence to the position taken by Link, Maffi, and myself on the division of the possessions of slave spouses as regulated at **72** III 40–44.

Conclusion

Doubts about a "literal" meaning of some of Gortyn's laws (viz., a mechanical approach whereby what a law says and what a law means must always be identical) can thus be legitimately held on grounds other than speculation.[26] We may have lost the contextual knowledge presumed of the Gortynian reader, but at least part of that knowledge can be reverse engineered from other, clearer sections of legislation that deal with similar legal issues. Such a procedure depends on the assumption that the Gortynians had a consistent set of legal principles, allowing inference from one text to another. While total logical coherence is perhaps too much to expect, Gortyn's laws are certainly more coherent than first meets the eye.[27]

Reconstructing the position on slaves that was institutionalized by the polis—that is, how the law viewed them—is quite different from reconstructing Gortynian slavery in all its complexity. The latter task is certainly not practicable, at least not fully, in the absence of extra-epigraphic evidence, though details in the laws themselves hint at complex background dynamics that sometimes threw up legal problems requiring clarification.[28] The issue of slaves and the possession of money is one such issue. If the position of the law is clear—that slaves had no ownership rights—it does not follow that they had no de facto access to coined money or could not amass money and possessions with the consent of their owners. Literary sources on classical Crete may provide some useful insights here: Aristotle (*Pol.* 1272a19) notes the *phoros* paid towards the public messes by the *perioikoi*, a word he uses for those he elsewhere calls *klarotai* (fr. 586 Rose = fr. 603.1–2 Gigon), a term that is also used by Ephorus (*FGrHist* 70 F 29) for Cretan slaves. Dosiadas (*FGrHist* 458 F 2), writing of the messes at Lyktos, is more specific: the slaves (*douloi*) contribute an Aeginetan stater per capita to the messes (though Dosiadas does not indicate how often this payment was made). This report implies that slaves at Lyktos were expected to possess coined money, even if in small amounts, and were probably free to engage in (some) market exchange.[29] This interpretation is consonant with the details provided in Gortyn's laws, which show, for example, slave couples amassing goods together and slave herdsmen managing—pretty much independently—significant numbers of animals.[30]

When Aristotle wrote (*Pol.* 1264a17–24) that the Cretans let their slaves have the same things as free men, save the right to bear arms and attend the gymnasium, he was likely describing a system whose social institutions—like some of the laws we have looked at in this chapter—were modeled on those for the free populace. That would hardly be unique, for a similar approach was followed in the US South, and the parallel shows that we need not interpret Aristotle's statement as evidence for a benign attitude towards slaves on Crete. Nonetheless, what emerges from the evidence is a picture of a slave population whose masters did not pry into every aspect of their lives. These slaves dwelt mostly in family groups[31] and seem to have managed a good deal of property themselves.

From the position of the law, all property belonged to slaves' owners. But in practice, it is likely that owners rarely intervened in the possessions of their slaves, other than in such scenarios as when a slave couple belonging to different owners split up or when a person's estate was divided among heirs. What happened when a slave committed an offense? Admittedly, I am engaging in pure conjecture, but it is probable that a master faced with a fine of two hundred staters because his slave had raped a citizen would have asset-stripped every possession in that slave's keeping to help meet the expense of the fine. Finley was likely correct in thinking that no slave had amassed enough money to pay such a fine in full, meaning that the master would have had to make up the balance. Perhaps a cash-strapped owner might even have sold the slave if necessity required it. But if the slave raped someone else's slave (perhaps a more frequent occurrence), the fine was far less: five staters. Slaves could conceivably have possessed such an amount of money, and even if legal liability lay with the slave's owner, it is likely that the owner normally would have compelled the slave to surrender savings to pay such a fine.[32] The clear position of the law may mask a situation of rather greater complexity in terms of the practicalities of how the fine was actually paid (viz., from the property possessed by the slave, from a combination of that and the master's own savings if the fine were large, or from selling the slave), which is not to say that the legal positions of the parties were blurred. Situational complexity could considerably help to explain why the language on paying fines in column II of the Great Code is less precise than a lawyer might wish.

Where does this leave the problem with which this chapter began, the dissemination of legal knowledge among the citizenry? As Gagarin has cogently shown in *Writing Greek Law*, the idea that literacy in Crete was restricted to a small scribal class is untenable: Gortyn's laws were prominently displayed and meant to be read by the citizenry.[33] The idea that basic literacy was a mystical skill monopolized by a narrow scribal class, as Whitley has argued, overestimates the technical challenges that confront those wishing to learn an alphabetic script.[34] Gagarin's view of the accessibility of Gortynian law indeed dovetails with Ephorus' observation (*FGrHist* 70 F 149 *ap.* Str. 10.4.20) that literacy was a formally mandated part of the upbringing of Cretan citizen boys.[35] Yet by studying how the Gortynians encoded legal rules on stone and by paying attention to what they left out, we can proceed beyond the assumption that Gortynian citizens encountered written law cold, as it were, relying on the text alone to figure out the solution to whatever legal problem faced them. These laws function by assuming a certain basic knowledge of broad legal principles. Through studying what these laws leave out, we can gain two things: first, some sense of what level of basic legal knowledge was held by Gortynian citizens; and second, a more refined methodology with which we can interpret Gortyn's laws today.

Appendix: The Exposure of Slave Children

This chapter has focused on the issue of liability in the rules on sexual violence mentioned in **72** II. A similar problem involves a rule Davies has taken as evidence that slaves were liable to pay fines, recorded at **72** IV 8–14 (see n. 5 in the present study).

> γυνὰ κερεύονσ' αἰ ἀποβάλοι παιδίον πρὶν ἐπελεῦσαι κατὰ τὰ ἐγραμμένα, ἐλευθέρο μὲν καταστασεῖ πεντέκοντα στατε̃ρανς, δόλο πέντε καὶ ϝίκατι, αἴ κα νικαθε̃ι.
>
> If a woman separated (by divorce) should dispose of her child before bringing it in accordance with what is written, if she is convicted (she) will pay fifty staters for a free (child), twenty-five for a slave.

This rule, just like the rules on sexual violence in **72** II, uses the verb καταστασεῖ to order the payment of a fine, seemingly for free persons and slaves alike.[36] Taken in isolation, though, **72** IV 8–14 seems to confound the line taken in the present analysis. To put it bluntly, if a slave owner were liable for the misdeeds of his slave and if one such misdeed was the unauthorized exposure of the slave's child (who was the owner's property), the owner would end up suing himself for the damages.

A straightforward solution to the problem **72** IV 8–14 seems to present is available when we look at the context in which this rule is embedded: the lengthy set of rules in columns III–IV (noted above) that Gagarin has cogently argued "only matter for serf [*sic*] couples belonging to different masters."[37] To be more precise, the rule under consideration falls between the rules apportioning the slave child to either the male slave's owner or the female slave's owner—depending on whether or not the former wishes to assume title over the child (**72** III 52–55, IV 1–6)—and the rule on who owns the child if the female slave conceives outside a slave "marriage" arrangement (**72** IV 18–23). To make sense of this rule on exposure, we must recall that in a normal slave "marriage" arrangement in which the couple belonged separately to different owners, ownership of the couple's child lies with the owner of the male slave, not the owner of the female slave (**72** III 52–55). Our rule on exposure seems to envisage a scenario where the female slave exposes her child—who belongs to her husband's owner—without permission. This creates an offense that generates a legal requirement for compensation, since she has deprived a free person, who is not her owner, of his human property. (If the child belonged to her owner, the law did not need to intervene, for he could presumably punish her as he saw fit.) That this rule is embedded in a lengthier section of rules assuming separate owners of the slaves and apportioning first call on the ownership of the child to the male slave's owner makes this regulation intelligible. Such an interpretation harmonizes with the general approach pursued in this chapter, and the explanation I have adumbrated above regarding the use of καταστασεῖ as a kind of shorthand in **72** II can be extended to this instance.

Notes

I thank Clifford Ando for the invitation to speak at the conference from which this volume derives, for an incisive methodological observation that has subsequently made my assumptions clearer to the reader, and for editorial advice that has improved this chapter. I also thank Edward Harris and Mirko Canevaro, who read the essay in draft form and offered valuable criticism and suggestions.

1. That approach is suggested by James Whitley in "Cretan Laws and Cretan Literacy," *American Journal of Archaeology* 101 (1997): 635–61.

2. Translations of the Gortyn code herein follow an excellent new collection of Cretan laws, *The Laws of Ancient Crete, c. 650–400 BCE*, ed. Michael Gagarin and Paula Perlman (Oxford: Oxford University Press, 2016), with occasional minor alterations. For an overview of the dossier of Gortynian law, see John K. Davies, "Deconstructing Gortyn: When Is a Code a Code?," in *Greek Law in Its Political Setting*, ed. Lin Foxhall and Andrew Lewis (Oxford: Oxford University Press, 1996), 33–56. For an introduction to the law's contents, see John K. Davies, "The Gortyn Laws," in *The Cambridge Companion to Ancient Greek Law*, ed. Michael Gagarin and David Cohen (Cambridge: Cambridge University Press, 2005), 305–27. In this chapter, I employ the term *code* for purely conventional reasons, and I follow Davies in printing the numbers in *IC* IV in bold for the sake of brevity and neatness of exposition.

3. I here follow the view that *dolos* and *woikeus*—like *doulos* and *oiketes* in Attic Greek—are two terms for a single slave status: see Justus Hermann Lipsius, *Zum Recht von Gortyns*, Abhandlungen der Philologisch-Historischen Klasse der Königlich-Sächsischen Gesellschaft der Wissenschaften, 27, no. 11 (Leipzig: B. G. Teubner Verlag, 1909), 397–99; Moses I. Finley, *Economy and Society in Ancient Greece*, ed. Brent Shaw and Richard Saller (London: Pelican, 1981), 135–37; Alberto Maffi, *Il diritto di famiglia nel Codice di Gortina* (Milan: CUEM, 1997): 120–21; Stefan Link, "Dolos und Woikeus im Recht von Gortyn," *Dike* 4 (2001): 87–112; Karen Kristensen, "Gortynian Debt Bondage: Some New Considerations on *IC* IV 41 IV–VII, 47 and 72 I.56–II.2, X.25–32," *ZPE* 149 (2004): 73–79, at 73. For the time being, that Michael Gagarin treats them as

two different statuses ("slave" and "serf") does not require me to alter my line of argumentation; see Gagarin, "Serfs and Slaves at Gortyn," *Zeitschrift der Savigny-Stiftung für Rechtsgeschichte: Romanistische Abteilung* 127 (2010): 14–31.

4. On the verb, see, though, the comments of Stefan Link in *Das griechische Kreta* (Stuttgart: Franz Steiner Verlag, 1994), 36n124.

5. Cf. Rodolphe-Madeleine Cléophas Dareste, Bernard Haussoullier, and Theodore Reinach, *Recueil des inscriptions juridiques grecques* (Paris, 1891), 1:425: "C'est sur son pécule qu'il paiera les amendes qui peuvent lui être infligées en cas de viol, par exemple"; Arnold Kränzlein, *Eigentum und Besitz im griechischen Recht* (Berlin: Duncker und Humblot Verlag, 1963), 43: "Da aber an der Fähigkeit der ϝοικέες, Eigentum an Mobilien zu haben, auf Grund anderer Stellen des Gesetzes nicht zu zweifeln ist, können wir unbedenklich mit der herrschenden Meinung annehmen, daß die Unfreien die Buße selbst bezahlen mußten, sie ihnen umgekehrt aber auch selbst zugutekam, wenn das Verbrechen an ihnen begangen worden war"; Gagarin, "Serfs and Slaves," 26: "The rules setting fines for sexual offences . . . are written in a way that implies that the *dolos* or *woikeus* paid the fine himself. . . . Scholars generally assume that these fines would be paid by the slave's master, but the Greek suggests otherwise." Davies ("Gortyn Laws," 316) holds a similar view based on **72** IV 13–14, in which a fine is prescribed for a slave woman who exposes her child: "In any case the possibility of being fined (e.g. **72** IV 13–14) and the admissibility of action if a divorced or widowed *woikea* takes away more than her own property (**72** III 40–44) clearly imply that 'serfs' could own at least moveable property"; cf. John K. Davies, "Gortyn within the Economy of Archaic and Classical Crete," in *La grande inscrizione di Gortyna*, ed. Emanuele Greco and Mario Lombardo (Athens: Scuola Archeologica Italiana di Atene, 2005), 153–74, at 161. On **72** IV 13–14, see the appendix to the present chapter.

6. Finley, *Economy and Society*, 137.

7. David M. Lewis, "Slave Marriages in the Laws of Gortyn: A Matter of Rights?," *Historia* 62, no. 4 (2013): 390–416. Finley believed that Gortynian slaves enjoyed some rights not found in, e.g., Athens, particularly a right to marry (see his *Economy and Society*, 135–39). As I have pointed out, the rules at **72** IV 18–23 show that the slave marriage arrangement was not entirely informal, since its existence affected the rights of slave owners regarding the ownership of the children of their slaves (Lewis, "Slave Marriages," 403–4). This legal or quasi-legal character, however, did not provide the slaves with any rights vis-à-vis their owners.

8. Gagarin and Perlman, *Laws*, 83.

9. For references on the debate between the two scholars, see Michael Gagarin, "Women's Property at Gortyn," *Dike* 15 (2012): 73–92.

10. Alain Bresson, "Women and Inheritance in Ancient Sparta: The Gortynian Connection," *Studi Ellenistici* 30 (2016): 9–68.

11. Athenian women found creative ways to exercise agency within this restrictive institutional framework: see Edward M. Harris, *Democracy and the Rule of Law in Clas-*

sical Athens (Cambridge: Cambridge University Press, 2006), 333–46; cf. Harris, "Wife, Household and Marketplace: The Role of Women in the Economy of Classical Athens," in *Donne che contano nella storia greca*, ed. Umberto Bultrighini and Elisabetta Dimauro (Lanciano: Casa Editrice Rocco Carabba, 2015), 185–207.

12. As J. K. Davies has perceptively noted ("Gortyn Laws," 322), "it looks as if lawmakers are trying to minimize the leaching of property via women away from the direct chain of male-to-male inheritance."

13. Gagarin, "Women's Property," 74.

14. Alberto Maffi, "Lo statuto di 'beni materni' nella Grecia classica," *Index* 40 (2012): 91–111, at 100–101. Cf. Maffi, *Il diritto*, 124, where Maffi follows Link, *Kreta*, 34–35, as do I (Lewis, "Slave Marriages," 404–5).

15. Gagarin, "Women's Property," 82.

16. Gagarin and Perlman, *Laws*, 359.

17. Cf. Angelos Chaniotis, "The Great Inscription, Its Political and Social Institutions, and the Common Institutions of the Cretans," in Greco and Lombardo, *La grande inscrizione di Gortyna*, 175–94, at 178: "The Law Code does not define any of the social, economic, legal and political institutions, for which norms are introduced, modified, or just written down; it *presupposes* the understanding of all these institutions, and this is why the interpretation of terms and clauses is still a matter of controversy."

18. For suggestions, see Aikaterini Mandalaki, "Ο κλᾶρος στὴ μεγάλη δωδεκάδελτο ἐπιγραφὴ τῆς Γόρτυνος," *Tekmeria* 5 (2000): 71–86. Cf. Chaniotis, "Great Inscription," 183; Davies, "Gortyn Laws," 320.

19. Debt bondage in ancient Greece has been treated in two excellent recent essays. Edward M. Harris's "Did Solon Abolish Debt Bondage?" (*Classical Quarterly* 52 [2002]: 415–30 = Harris, *Democracy and the Rule of Law*, 249–69) looks at the Solonian reforms but also provides a general overview of the phenomenon. Kristensen's "Debt Bondage" provides a lucid and convincing analysis of the Gortynian situation, though I do not agree with her description of debt bondage as "temporary enslavement" (77–78). As Harris shows in his essay, debt bondage and enslavement for debt are two substantively different phenomena.

20. Kristensen, "Debt Bondage," 74.

21. Thus *arkaios pastas* should not be translated "old master" or "former master." When a slave was sold, liability for his misdeeds transferred to the new owner, who had a sixty-day warranty period within which he could return the slave (**72** VII 10–15, quoted on p. 80). The phrase means "original owner." That wording mirrors the language of credit in Greek, where the principal of a loan is called, among other things, τὸ ἀρχαῖον, the "original amount" (e.g., Ar. *Nub.* 1156; Dem. 1.15, 34.26). See also LSJ[9] s.v. ἀρχαῖος II.2, for comparable examples when the term means "original" rather than "former." Kristensen ("Debt Bondage") translates the term correctly and provides a clear overview of the legal positions of the respective parties.

22. Link, *Kreta*, 37 (citing Reinhard Koerner, *Inschriftliche Gesetzestexte der frühen*

griechischen Polis [Cologne: Böhlau Verlag, 1993], no. 138 [= **47**]): "Nur vor dem Hintergrund, daß selbstverständlich die Herren für Vergehen ihrer Sklaven hafteten, ist auch zu verstehen, daß nach dem Wortlaut eines anderen Gesetzes für die Missetaten eines verpfändeten Sklaven sein alter Eigentümer zu haften hatte—es sei denn, der Pfandgläubiger habe dem Sklaven das Verbrechen befohlen und damit die Verantwortung übernommen. Die Möglichkeit, daß auch der Sklave selbst haften könnte, kam dem Gesetzgeber offenbar gar nicht in den Sinn." Cf. Domingo Avilés, "Slaves, Noncitizens and Written Law in Ancient Greece," *Ancient History Bulletin* 25 (2011): 1–8, at 5.

23. Detlef Lotze, ΜΕΤΑΞΥ ΕΛΕΥΘΕΡΩΝ ΚΑΙ ΔΟΥΛΩΝ: *Studien zur Rechtsstellung unfreier Landbevölkerungen in Griechenland bis zum 4. Jahrhundert v. Chr.* (Berlin: Akademie Verlag, 1959), 15–16: "Darauf könnte besonders die Bestimmung in der etwa gleichaltrigen Inschrift 47, 10ff. führen, daß die Strafsumme für Verletzung eines verpfändeten Sklaven durch einen Dritten zwischen Verpfänder und Pfandgläubiger geteilt werden soll. Zeigt sich darin nicht doch die Vermögensunfähigkeit des Sklaven? Zunächst nur das Fehlen der aktiven Gerichtsfähigkeit. Der Sklave kann nicht selbst Klage erheben, sondern nur sein Herr, und daher kann auch nur dieser die Strafsumme zugesprochen erhalten. Während jedoch dem halbfreien Pfandling die Hälfte davon garantiert ist, ist beim Sklaven nicht davon die Rede. Der Vergleich beider Inschriften lehrt vielmehr, daß der Sklave nichts bekommt; denn in seinem Falle macht das Gesetz keinen Unterschied zwischen εἰσπράττειν und ἔχειν des Geldes, sondern spricht nur vom ἔχειν, und zwar seitens des Herrn. Folglich hatte der Sklave keinen Rechtsanspruch darauf."

24. Lilian Jeffrey, *The Local Scripts of Archaic Greece*, 2nd ed., with a supplement by A. W. Johnston (Oxford: Oxford University Press, 1990), 315.

25. Davies, "Deconstructing Gortyn," 40.

26. Edward Harris points out to me that the second canon in the canons of statutory interpretation used by US courts presumes that even modern US laws might not always have a "plain and unambiguous meaning" and that one has to look at the whole statutory scheme rather than an isolated part of it to understand its meaning: "Our first step in interpreting a statute is to determine whether the language at issue has a plain and unambiguous meaning with regard to the particular dispute in the case. Our inquiry must cease if the statutory language is unambiguous and 'the statutory scheme is coherent and consistent'" (Robinson v. Shell Oil Co., 519 US 337, 340 [1997]).

27. A case in point is the scale and ratio of fines for sexual offenses set out in **72** II. At a glance, one must agree with Davies' view that this section of the code is "rather a mess." But Gagarin ("Serfs and Slaves," 17) has usefully compiled these data into tables, converting all fines into drachmas. Only when this is done can one properly grasp the intelligence and consistency that lies behind this ostensibly rather scrappy part of the code: in the circumstances where slaves commit an offense, the penalty is consistently twice that exacted in an otherwise identical scenario where the perpetrator is a free man. Conversely, in the circumstances where a slave is the victim of an offense, the penalty is

consistently one-fortieth of that exacted if the victim were a free person. (Here, as before [see n. 3 above], I take *dolos* and *woikeus* to indicate the same slave status.) For further discussion, see David M. Lewis, *Greek Slave Systems in Their Eastern Mediterranean Context, c. 800–146 BC* (Oxford: Oxford University Press, 2018), 147–65, especially 152. For the coherence of Gortynian law, see also Edmond Lévy, "La cohérence du Code de Gortyne," in *La codification des lois dans l'Antiquité*, ed. Edmond Lévy (Paris: De Boccard, 2000), 185–214.

28. Lewis, "Slave Marriages," 411–15.

29. On coinage in Crete during this period, see Georges Le Rider, *Monnaies crétoises du Ve au Ier siècle av. J.-C.* (Paris: Librairie orientaliste P. Geuthner, 1966); Manolis Stefanakis, "The Introduction of Coinage in Crete and the Beginning of Local Minting," in *From Minoan Farmers to Roman Traders: Sidelights on the Economy of Ancient Crete*, ed. Angelos Chaniotis (Stuttgart: Franz Steiner Verlag, 1999), 247–68.

30. On the difficult passage **72** IV 31–43, see Lewis, "Slave Marriages," 406–8. Cf. Philomen Probert, *Early Greek Relative Clauses* (Oxford: Oxford University Press, 2015), 374–77. Probert adopts a similar explanation to mine and provides a useful dissection of the grammar of the passage. Her view is unpacked in greater detail in Eleanor Dickey and Philomen Probert, "Houses in Which a Serf Living in the Country Does Not Reside: A Reconsideration of Gortyn Laws Column 4 Lines 31–37," in *Sprachgeschichte und Epigraphik: Festgaben für Rudolf Wachter zum 60. Geburtstag*, ed. Andreas Willi (Innsbruck: Universität Innsbruck, 2017), 57–81.

31. Cf. David M. Lewis, "The Market for Slaves in the Fifth and Fourth Century Aegean: Achaemenid Anatolia as a Case Study," in *The Ancient Greek Economy: Markets, Households and City-States*, ed. Edward M. Harris, David M. Lewis, and Mark Woolmer (Cambridge: Cambridge University Press, 2016), 316–36, at 325–30.

32. Cf. Link, *Kreta*, 37n130: "Ob der Herr die Strafsumme, die er für das Vergehen eines seiner Klaroten hatte zahlen müssen, von dem Täter wieder eintrieb und sich so an ihm schadlos hielt, war rechtlich unerheblich und dürfte von Fall zu Fall geschwankt haben, je nachdem, wieviel dem Herrn daran lag, und je nachdem, ob der Täter über ein ausreichendes *peculium* verfügte oder nicht." Edward Harris pointed out to me a parallel in the sacred law of Andania (*LSCG* 65, lines 75–78): a slave found guilty of theft is to be beaten and pay double the amount of the stolen item; if he is unable to pay, the owner gives him over in debt bondage to repay the fine. There is a similar sense here that the slave may have the wherewithal to pay but that his owner is ultimately liable. Harris also points me to Ira Berlin, *Many Thousands Gone* (Cambridge, MA: Harvard University Press, 1998), 33: "In Virginia, the justices of one county allowed a miscreant slave the choice of the lash or a fine which he could pay 'out of that hee calls his owne estate.'"

33. Michael Gagarin, *Writing Greek Law* (Cambridge: Cambridge University Press, 2007), 67–92.

34. This has been most dramatically illustrated by Merle Langdon's discovery of over twelve hundred rupestral verbal graffiti, some quite elaborate, written by herders in the

vicinity of Vari and Voula in Attica and dating to the sixth century BC. Most remain unpublished, but for a selection of eleven examples, see Merle K. Langdon, "Herders' Graffiti," in *Axon: Studies in Honor of Ronald S. Stroud*, ed. Angelos Matthiou and Nikolaos Papazarkadas (Athens: Elleniki Epigrafiki Etaireia, 2015), 49–58.

35. For a cogent defense of the historical value of such literary sources, see Gunnar Seelentag, *Das archaische Kreta: Institutionalisierung im frühen Griechenland* (Berlin: De Gruyter, 2015), 93–117.

36. Gagarin is surely right to note (Gagarin and Perlman, *Laws*, 360) that *guna* in lines 8–9 is a general term that can apply to free and slave women, though others have doubted that interpretation.

37. Gagarin and Perlman, *Laws*, 359.

CHAPTER 4

Free in Fact?

Legal Status and State in the Suits for Freedom

Nicole Giannella

"It can be difficult to distinguish a freeman from a slave" (*difficile dinosci potest liber homo a servo*).[1] So acknowledges the Severan jurist Paul when explaining how a freeman may be accidentally purchased as a slave. But despite the occasional mix-up, legal status—that is, whether people were free Roman citizens, freed men or women, slaves, or foreigners—was relatively straightforward for the majority of the population of the Roman world. As a result, scholars of antiquity tend to think about legal status as an objective and knowable fact: someone is either slave or free. That fact, in turn, conjures up a particular existence: because of his status, a slave has an owner, while a citizen has particular rights and responsibilities on account of his status. Put in more legalistic language, a slave is in a state of slavery, and a freeman is in a state of liberty. But Paul's dictum indicates that perhaps status and state did not always match up and that it was sometimes impossible to know whether a man in a state of slavery was really a slave.

While the jurists discussing suits for freedom (*causae liberales*,[2] suits that sought to settle disputed legal status) wanted status to be dispositive of state, there were not always documentary records available to allow suits to be settled with such certainty. In such cases, the jurists did not always aim to uncover what we might think of as the latent truth of a person's status (i.e., an originary status that can be unearthed), nor did the jurists treat the legal ruling as a revelation of an objective and knowable fact.[3] In this chapter, I examine the mechanisms the jurists employ when considering this fundamental aspect of human life, namely, the determination of whether someone is a free person or a slave. The reasoning of the jurists is governed by three at times seemingly competing ethical norms: (1) the protection of the rights of a buyer acting in good faith (*bona fides*); (2) the principle of favoring liberty (*favor libertatis*); and, ultimately and perhaps most consequentially, (3) the conviction that a person behaving as a slave ought to be legally rendered a slave—or, put differently, the cultural fiction that some essential marker distinguished free and slave and was made known through the convincing performance of either free or slave status.[4]

To understand which of these ethical norms the jurists privilege while creating the legal fact of a person's status under Roman law, I focus on two extraordinary scenarios in which jurists either correct or explicitly change a person's legal status. The first is a case of the second-century jurist Julian, in which two men claim to own half of one man each and, accordingly, pursue two suits for enslavement, which end with contradictory results (*Dig.* 40.12.30). The second is a case of the Severan jurist Ulpian, in which a freeman sells himself fraudulently to two buyers—one unsuspecting, the other not (*Dig.* 40.12.7). These cases show that the jurists are not always seeking to adjust or reaffirm status so that it matches truth (e.g., so that following a suit, a slave is in a state of slavery or a freeman is in a state of liberty). Rather, the jurists make legal rulings, in the first case, in the place of truth, and, in the second, creating truth. As these cases are extreme situations, they allow us to see the manner in which jurists resolve a case when the evidence as reported is insufficient to establish a ruling that necessarily lines up with the person's original status.

Suits for Freedom and Cultural Fictions

A suit for freedom is a trial that takes place when someone challenges his or her own status or that of another person. Suits could arise, as will be discussed in further detail below, from honest errors (e.g., unknown parentage suddenly revealed) or from duplicitous action (e.g., if a slave runs away and pretends to be a freeman or if a freeman fraudulently sells himself as a slave). The first step in such a suit was determining the type of proceeding that was to occur, whether from liberty to slavery (*ex libertate in servitutem*) or from slavery to liberty (*ex servitute in libertatem*). The person whose status was in question had to be represented by another person (an *adsertor libertatis*), as a slave lacked standing to bring suit.[5] The burden of proof was always on the plaintiff and, as such, depended on the type of proceeding. In a trial from liberty to slavery, the burden of proof rested on the would-be owner who claimed that the defendant was his slave; in a trial from slavery to liberty, the burden rested on the person asserting the slave's freedom.[6] To determine what type of trial was to proceed, the jurists considered whether the person in question was "in a state of liberty" (*in libertate fuisse*) and if he or she was in that state "without fraud" (*sine dolo malo*).

Before turning to the two cases that are the focus of this chapter, it is worth looking at these preliminary proceedings, as represented in the juristic commentary on suits for freedom, in some detail. While these trials arise from an uncertainty about the legal status of a person (free, slave) and state (in liberty, in slavery), the jurists acknowledge that there is uncertainty in their method of determination as well. A lengthy text from the Severan jurist Ulpian shows the method of deliberation about who is in a state of liberty and whether that liberty is nonfraudulent.

> *Quod autem diximus "in libertate fuisse" sic est accipiendum non ut se liberum doceat is, qui liberale iudicium patitur, sed in possessione libertatis sine dolo malo fuisse. Quid sit autem "sine dolo malo fuisse," videamus. Nam Iulianus ait omnes, qui se liberos putant, sine dolo malo in libertate fuisse, si modo se pro liberis gerant, quamvis servi sint. Varus autem scribit eum, qui se liberum sciat, dum in fuga sit, non videri sine dolo malo in libertate esse: sed simul atque desierit quasi fugitivus se celare et pro libero agere, tunc incipere sine dolo malo in libertate esse: etenim ait eum, qui scit se liberum, deinde pro fugitivo agit, hoc ipso, quod in fuga sit, pro servo agere. Igitur sciendum est et liberum posse dolo malo in libertate esse et servum posse sine dolo malo in libertate esse.*

Our expression "in a state of liberty" should be taken to mean not that the man subject to a trial for freedom is to show that he is a freeman, but that he was in a state of liberty without fraud. But let us consider what "without fraud" means: for Julian says that all who think themselves freemen have been in a state of liberty without fraud, provided that they behave as freemen, although they could be slaves. But Varus writes that a man who knows himself to be a freeman, while he is in flight, is not regarded to be in a state of liberty without fraud. But once he has ceased to hide as if a fugitive and to behave like a freeman, he begins from that moment to be in a state of liberty without fraud. In fact, he says that the man who knows himself to be a freeman but behaves as a fugitive is behaving as a slave because he is in flight. It should then be known that a freeman can be in a state of liberty fraudulently and a slave can be in a state of liberty without fraud.[7]

The jurists distinguish between legal status (slave, freeman) and being in a state (in liberty, in slavery).[8] The basis of determining whether someone was in a state of liberty was fraudulent behavior, not the objective or even the believed, though mistaken, legal status. As Ulpian explains, a slave can be in a state of liberty without fraud: among other reasons, this can happen if a will manumitting a slave is rendered invalid without the slave's knowledge or if it is revealed that a man raised as a freeman, with everyone thinking he was freeborn, was actually born a slave.[9] Wills and birth are the main factors for determining status in cases not involving fraud,[10] but things become more complicated when discussing the state someone is in. In the passage quoted above, Ulpian cites two earlier jurists, Alfenus Varus and Julian, both of whom hold, in slight variation, that the key to showing that one is in a state of liberty is to behave as if a free person and to do so without fraud (*sine dolo malo*).

Though Alfenus Varus, a jurist of the first century BCE, speaks about a man certain (*scire*) of his status, Varus emphasizes behavior over a person's actual status: a freeman in flight (*in fuga*) is in a state of liberty fraudulently until he ceases to behave like a runaway (*pro fugitivo agere*) or slave (*pro servo agere*). Irrespective of the man in question knowing he is actually a freeman, his behavior determines whether he is in a state of liberty fraudulently.[11] For Julian, writing in the second century CE, a man is in a state of liberty without fraud if he thinks (*putare*, in contrast to Varus' *scire*) himself to be a freeman and conducts himself as such (*se pro libero gerere*), regardless of the fact that he is actually a slave.[12] Certainty is not necessary in the mind of the man who is acting, as long as he acts honestly and to the best of his understanding. The jurist Gaius, a contemporary of Julian, notes, in a chapter on suits for freedom in his commentary on the praetorian edict, that while a freeman could behave as a freeman even in flight, such a freeman is still in a state of liberty fraudulently.[13]

Through these juridical twists between self-knowledge, honesty, and action, we see the acknowledged difficulty of accessing truth. While Varus and Julian present a shared understanding of what *sine dolo malo* means (the deceitful intention of a person not behaving according to his or her known status), Varus' version more plainly reveals the limitations of this understanding. We might view Varus' account also as a caution: all that can be seen is behavior, which can either reveal or mislead. The shift in nuance from Varus' *scire* to Julian's *putare* further demonstrates the allowance extended by the later jurist: such a situation might arise through confusion or error rather than duplicity. Gaius, also writing in the second century CE, seemingly elaborates on the scenario of Varus, making the situation more forgiving in expression, but he presents a view equally as strict in practice: a freeman in flight is in a state of liberty fraudulently. This strict view allows the jurists to bolster the divide between free and slave without regard for actual status.

The jurists weigh whether a person behaved like a slave or a free person and whether the performance was genuine or duplicitous; to be in flight serves as a sign of bad intention and extralegal behavior for both a slave and a freeman. Varus' passage also gives us an understanding of servile behavior: running away, hiding from one's status, and neglecting duties and responsibilities is the behavior not of freemen but of slaves—specifically, bad slaves. Varus' language suggests that a freeman may not engage in the performance of slavehood. The freeman, regardless of his concern for his status, may not hide from a situation, and he is only in a state of liberty when he ceases to hide and flee.

The jurists' discussion of the runaway slave, which Varus mentions explicitly and which Gaius evokes, provides a good example of how the juridical space between status and state allows a subversion of legal boundaries and can cause uncertainty. Gaius' assertion that a freeman can behave as a freeman in flight is mirrored in the first-century CE jurist Caelius' claim that a slave can behave as a freeman in flight. Ulpian provides the passage of Caelius in his commentary on the edict of the aediles, which covers the regulations on the slave market: *Idem recte ait libertatis cuiusdam speciem esse fugisse, hoc est potestate dominica in praesenti liberatum esse* (Rightly [Caelius] says flight is an appearance of a kind of liberty, since the slave is freed from the power of his master in that present moment).[14] There is a very pragmatic financial concern with slaves running away, but there are other underlying concerns about slaves engaging in free behavior. The fugitive slave disrupts the convenient cultural fiction that slaves and freemen necessarily and essentially behave differently and therefore are different. This fiction is perhaps further driven home by the jurists' understanding that a slave who runs away has a mental defect (*vitium animi*)[15]—that is, he or she does not have the correct mentality for a slave. Fugitive slaves trouble Roman status boundaries, because for runaway slaves not to be caught, they must convincingly behave and portray themselves as a free people (not as fugitive slaves) while in flight. We might think the reason runaways so consume the Roman literary and juridical imagination is not solely a preoccupation with economic loss but, rather, that they embody the Roman investment in the cultural fiction about status difference and blur the ethical boundaries of free and slave.[16]

As well as representing the uncertain nature of legal status, the runaway fails, on all fronts, to behave in good faith (*bona fides*). The runaway is not behaving as a slave without fraud, because if he were, he would not be running away. Nor is he in a state of slavery, either with or without fraud, because he left his servile duties behind when he became a runaway. Since he is a slave, he is clearly not behaving as a freeman without fraud or in a state of liberty without fraud. The question of a freeman's state of liberty lies in this mental realm: his behavior is taken to show his belief in his status as a freeman. This is contrasted with a person, such as the fugitive, who knows he is a slave but may be behaving like a free person, in bad faith.

The language of these passages, particularly *se gerere* or *agere*, highlights both the use of behavior or conduct as a means to understand if someone is in a state of slavery or liberty and, at the same time, the imperfect nature of this understanding. Its formulation with *pro libero*, *pro servo*, or *pro fugitivo* indicates the jurists' awareness that while this state may indeed all be a performance, it is sometimes a legally acceptable one. As Clifford Ando has recently noted in an article on facts and fictions, the preposition *pro* plus a noun representing the status assigned to a person or thing for the purposes of the case at hand (not their actual status) is one of the formulations jurists use when proceeding with a legal fiction.[17] This formulation, found already in the late republic in what appears to be a reference to statute law, is used in numerous imperial rescripts discussing people uncertain or mistaken about their status.[18] This passage on determining the state of a person provides an understanding of the way in which uncertainty not only could come into, but was an acknowledged element of these proceedings. It simultaneously underscores the difficulties of having accurate self-knowledge and of reading and trusting the presentation of such knowledge through the deportment of others. But it is possible that while such a situation was ripe with uncertainty, the judges got it right in the end. In any case, right or wrong (i.e., whether or not in accord with the person's true status), the ruling is now the person's legal status. In the case I turn to next, the focus is not on how to get a legal ruling from dubious evidence (social facts) but, rather, on the uncertainty that arises from legal rulings themselves (legal facts).

The Problem of the Half-Slave and Half-Free Man

A case from the second century CE jurist Julian's commentary on the work of jurist Minicius (*Ex Minicio*) discusses two suits involving one man. The suits resulted in conflicting verdicts, rendering him half-slave and half-free. Here, rather than an evidentiary uncertainty, we have disputed certainties: two legal rulings that do not agree. In the different solutions posited, the jurists emphasize the importance of upholding a sale in good faith and of favoring liberty, but the legal rule ultimately presents a compromise of these principles that stresses the sharp ethical divide between free and slave.

> *(A) Duobus petentibus hominem in servitutem pro parte dimidia separatim, si uno iudicio liber, altero servus iudicatus est, (B) commodissimum est eo usque cogi iudices, donec consentiant: (C) si id non continget, Sabinum refertur existimasse duci servum debere ab eo qui vicisset: cuius sententiae Cassius quoque est et ego sum. (D) Et sane ridiculum est arbitrari eum pro parte dimidia duci, pro parte libertatem eius tueri. (E) Commodius autem est favore libertatis liberum quidem eum esse, compelli autem pretii sui partem viri boni arbitratu victori suo praestare.*

> (A) If two persons in separate suits claim a man [who purports to be free] as a slave, each as to a half-share, and he is adjudged free in one trial and a slave in the other, (B) it is most suitable that pressure should be brought on the judges until they agree; (C) if this does not happen, Sabinus is reported to have thought that the successful claimant should lead him away as a slave; Cassius too and I are of the same opinion. (D) And it is perfectly absurd to suppose that he is half a slave and half free. (E) However, it is more suitable under the principle of favoring liberty that he should be free and yet be compelled to pay half his value to the successful claimant, as assessed by a good man.[19]

This passage exemplifies different stages of the uncertainty of the man's legal status: first, (A) how it may arise (in two trials with two alleged owners); second, methods for resolving this uncertainty, such as (B) pressure on the judges, (C) disregarding the suit in which the slave won his freedom, or (E) favoring liberty, but with a price. The passage additionally provides a justification for this ruling: (D) a man cannot be half-slave and half-free.

As often, there are no details given about this man's particular circumstance, but for whatever reason, one owner was successful in his case, while the other was not. We might imagine that the would-be freeman was more successful in defending his nonfraudulent liberty in one trial than in the other. Or perhaps one alleged owner was around the supposed slave more and could more convincingly prove his case. The complicated nature of this case allows us to follow the reasoning of the jurist more closely than in a simpler case where such explanations would not be needed.

Possible Solutions

The greater part of the text quoted just above discusses possible solutions for the seemingly paradoxical half-slave, half-free man and provides justifications for why each solution may be reasonable. The first, most suitable (*commodissimus*) proposal is (B) that "pressure [*cogi*] should be brought on the judges [of the separate cases] until they agree." As the judges would compare notes on their respective trials in order to convince one another, it is possible that one judge would reveal a bit of evidence that would make it clear whether the man should be judged a slave or a freeman. It is then possible that truth would prevail. But even this first attempt at resolution is not framed as a means of accessing the truth; rather, it has merely the virtue of collective agreement. The failure of the method of agreement underscores the difficulty in communally reading performances of liberty or slavery with enough certainty to establish the new legal fact that the man is wholly a slave or a freeman. This difficulty is also clear in the subsequent solutions, which are concerned not with truth but with who has the better claim: the person who has proved the man to be a slave or the person who has defended his freedom.

Sabinus and Cassius, both jurists of the first century CE, and Minicius (or possibly Julian)[20] think that (C) the owner who won his case should lead the man off as a slave. This solution protects the rights as owner of the successful master, who presumably bought half of the slave in good faith. The importance of the ethical notion of *bona fides* in the Roman law of sale is seen in these three jurists' thinking that this is the next best solution. However, it gives too much to the owner—he only paid for and owns half of the slave. In the previous solution (B), one trial influences the other; here, one trial is ignored. This approach is a form of fictional workaround, but unlike other legal workarounds that are generally procedural in nature, this one provides a solution. This solution introduces several problems: first, it is a bad precedent to simply ignore legal rulings if they are meant to establish facts; second, instead of resolving a discrepancy, it creates one between the man's reaffirmed status as a slave and the reality that this master only owns half of him; lastly, the result could run the risk of keeping a freeman incorrectly in slavery. As a result of this solution, a man is in a state of slavery, but in terms of status, he is still only half a slave. No legal principle is given as to why the trial that found for one of the owners should be given priority, only that these three first-century jurists judge this to be the best solution.[21] From the discussion above about the preliminary proceedings of a suit for freedom, we see that the jurists want to have someone's status be in agreement with his behavior, but this solution asks for one set of behaviors to be ignored.

The rejection of the second solution (C), which has the consensus of the three jurists, is explained in the third (E): "It is more suitable under the principle of favoring liberty that he should be free and yet be compelled to pay half his value to the successful claimant, as assessed by a good man." While the owner who won his case is compelled to accept money for his share of the slave (compulsion that may be viewed as an infringement on an owner's rights), the half-free and half-slave man here still has to perform his slavehood: he must purchase his freedom from his master. Though it is acknowledged that legal status does not allow for someone to be part free and part slave, he is, in that moment, exactly half a slave.[22] As he has bought half of himself and won the other half at trial, both rulings are upheld. Yet the reason why this is the more convenient solution is not the acknowledgment of the man's mixed status but the idea of favoring liberty. While the first-century jurists Sabinus, Cassius, and Minicius make explicit their conviction that the man should just be wholly enslaved, the second-century jurist Julian settles on the principle of favoring liberty as the more suitable solution.

In general, *favor libertatis* was used either when a situation involving a person's freedom was unclear or to carry out the intention of an owner wanting to free a slave, when the manumission was held up due to procedural impediments.[23] Following Julian's codification of the edict in the reign of Hadrian, the principle of favoring liberty, grounded in natural law, came into prominent use by jurists and emperors alike in the second century CE.[24] Favoring liberty only goes so far, however. In other situations where the jurists employ the language or spirit of favoring liberty, they do so to settle one case rather than to bring two rulings together. Julian's use of *favor libertatis* does not change the ruling of the case in which the man was judged a slave; it merely keeps the jurist from ignoring the trial in which the defendant was ruled a freeman. Rather than settling the whole matter in favor of a person who was possibly truly free, Julian's reasoning that the man must pay for half his freedom forefronts the performative aspect of slavery: the man ruled a slave must purchase his freedom. It is nowhere suggested that the man go free without purchasing half his freedom, in the same way that the other jurists think he ought to be led off as a slave regardless of his half freedom (C). The appeal to *favor libertatis*, while able to compromise the successful master's rights as owner, is not enough here to push a man ruled both free and slave over the boundary line of status.[25]

Uncertainty in suits for freedom is treated differently from uncertainty in other cases. The difference can be seen in a passage of the jurist Paul, who cites a constitution of Hadrian's successor, the emperor Antoninus Pius. Discussing split votes, Paul says, *Inter pares numero iudices si dissonae sententiae proferantur, in liberalibus quidem causis, secundum quod a divo Pio constitutum est, pro libertate statutum optinet, in aliis autem causis pro reo. Quod et in iudiciis publicis optinere oportet.* (When the number of judges is equal, and different opinions are given in a case involving freedom, judgment shall be rendered in favor of liberty in accordance with the Constitution of the Divine Pius, but, in all other cases, judgment shall be rendered in favor of the defendant. This rule must also be observed in criminal cases.)[26] In other matters, if the judges cannot come up with a majority, the defendant is favored. The preferential treatment is not surprising, as suits for freedom affect the most basic level of the law of persons. In the texts collected under the title of the *Digest* pertaining to these suits (40.12), there are a number of instances where the jurists express their understanding or even empathy that a person would want to free a family member or relation that was in slavery by mistake.[27] In our case from Julian, which is different because it discusses two trials that come to a certain ruling, both liberty and the defendant are favored, but only to the point of turning Julian away from the his fellow jurists' opinion that the man should be wholly enslaved (C). The principles that Paul outlines allow us to see another reason why it would be problematic for the winning owner to lead the slave off: it disrupts the basic idea that the verdict goes to the defendant in an undecided trial.

Because of the fundamental nature of the suits for freedom, the principle of favoring liberty causes the burden of proof for the would-be owner to be higher regardless of whether he is the plaintiff or the defendant. Nevertheless, it seems likely that proving liberty enough to cause uncertainty would often be an insurmountable challenge.[28] Citing the second-century jurist Pomponius, Paul also explains that if one judge in a suit for freedom is unable to reach a decision though the rest agree, the undecided judge can elect to remain silent; in any case, if he did object, it would not matter, as the majority would rule.[29] The first and best option proposed to solve the case of Julian (B) is a variant of that approach: the two judges should try to come to a consensus. However, if the evidence does not provide sufficient certainty that the judges could rule unanimously, the jurists do not seek to uncover the truth of an underlying status. Instead, they use the principle of favoring liberty to create a legal fact, the status of the man, in the face of an uncertain reality where there is no expressly convincing proof to lead to this conclusion.[30]

Self-Sale and the Problem of Fraud

Unsurprisingly, the compiled suits for freedom in the *Digest* are replete with cases of fraud;[31] the jurists' discussions of people's statuses in these fraud cases reveal the motivations and mechanisms for the creation of legal fact in a much more explicit way. Here, the jurists are not interested in upholding the underlying truth about someone's status, since the penalty if a man sold himself to defraud his purchaser was enslavement.[32] While some freemen sold themselves into slavery to become accountants for an estate, the issue of fraud arose when a freeman got another man to sell him to an unsuspecting buyer. After the buyer paid, a third man (who could be yet another accomplice or just someone who recognized the sold man from his previous, free life) asserted that the sold man was actually a freeman. The penalty was mediated by age, as freemen under twenty who sold themselves into slavery in order to share in the price were not barred from proclaiming their freedom. If they were over twenty, they could proclaim their freedom only if they had not shared in the price—that is, if they had not sold themselves fraudulently but for some other purpose.[33] A text of Ulpian discusses the penalties if these adults had sold themselves to defraud their purchaser.

> *2. Si quis sciens liberum emerit, non denegatur vendito in libertatem proclamatio adversus eum qui eum comparavit, cuiusque sit aetatis qui emptus est, idcirco quia non est venia dignus qui emit, etiamsi scientem prudentemque se liberum emerit. Sed enim si postea alius eum emerit ob hoc, qui scivit, ignorans, deneganda est ei libertas. 3. Si duo simul emerint partes, alter sciens, alter ignorans, videndum erit, numquid is qui scit non debeat nocere ignoranti: quod quidem*

magis est. Sed enim illa erit quaestio, partem solam habebit is qui ignoravit an totum? Et quid dicemus de alia parte? An ad eum qui scit pertineat? Sed ille indignus est quid habere, quia sciens emerit. rursum qui ignoravit, non potest maiorem partem dominii habere quam emit: evenit igitur, ut ei prosit qui eum comparavit sciens, quod alius ignoravit.

2. If anyone has bought a freeman in knowledge of his freedom, a proclamation of freedom against the purchaser is not denied to the man sold, whatever his age, on the ground that the purchaser deserves no favor, even if the man he bought knew the position and was of sound mind. However, if subsequently another person, in ignorance of his status, bought him from the purchaser, freedom should be denied to him. 3. If two persons have bought shares [in the man], one in knowledge of the position, the other without, we shall have to see whether it can really be that the former by his knowledge ought not to prejudice the latter; indeed, this is the view to be preferred. But then the question will arise whether the purchaser without knowledge is to have only a share in the whole. And what shall we say of the other share? Would it belong to the purchaser who knew the facts? Yet, he does not deserve to have anything, since he made the purchase in knowledge. On the other hand, the purchaser without knowledge cannot have a larger share in the property than he bought. So, it comes about that the ignorance of the one is beneficial to the other who bought the man in knowledge of his status.[34]

These cases are punitive rather than corrective. In the first scenario (2), the action of the purchaser—buying a man he knows to be a freeman—is deemed more harmful than the action of the freeman who sold himself despite his age, knowledge of his true status, and soundness of mind. As a result, the man who sold himself can proclaim his freedom and thereby uphold his true status; the freedom of his newly bought freeman serves as punishment for the purchaser with knowledge. While the freeman is in a state of slavery fraudulently, the buyer who acts without *bona fides* has committed the worse action. The outcome changes if the purchaser with knowledge sells the man off to an unsuspecting third party: he can make back his money, and the penalty shifts to the sold freeman. At this point, the freeman who sold himself is no longer able to claim his freedom, which effectively changes his legal status to slave. This is not a case of disputed status (there is no uncertainty on the part of the original buyer or the man being sold), but the desire to uphold the truth of the man's free status is no longer given prime importance. The result swaps the liberty of the sold freeman not only for the rights of the buyer in good faith but also for the sold freeman's behavior: the man that is sold is acting like a slave.

In the subsequent scenario (3), Ulpian considers a case parallel to Julian's half-slave, half-free scenario: the outcome if the man was purchased by two men, one knowing the true status of the man, the other ignorant. To the benefit of the purchaser with knowledge of the man's true status, the right of the ignorant purchaser is upheld. Protecting the right of the purchaser in good faith trumps both the fraud and any appeal to the man's liberty. In this case, unlike with the owner who lost his suit for his share of the slave, the successful claim of the ignorant buyer creates a situation in which both owners win.[35] The jurist's desire to protect the interests of the ignorant purchaser rewards the purchaser with knowledge at the expense of the sold man, and as a by-product, the previous idea that the purchaser with knowledge has erred more than the sold man is reversed. The sold man is not able to proclaim half of his freedom, but because two-thirds of the people involved in the transactions know the sold man to be a freeman, no kind of majority of knowledge rules. In this scenario, then, *res iudicata* does not smooth over the potentially rough edges of truth but, rather, replaces it and creates a new version: the man is now a slave.

The situation here is different than the case of the man found to be free in one trial and a slave in the other. In that case, one trial affects the other, but here, the knowledge of one buyer is not meant to affect the ignorance of the other. The end results are different as well: while the man in question in the two suits for freedom must, like a slave, purchase his freedom from the master that won his suit, there is not necessarily a change in his true status. He may very well be a freeman incorrectly being transferred into a state of slavery. But in the case of self-sale with two purchasers, there is a change in a known status, as the man was, in reality, a freeman. For trying to profit from a temporary self-slavery, he is denied his liberty (*deneganda est ei libertas*). We see the importance of performative status enunciated much more explicitly in this case, which expressly punishes the man who sold himself, while still protecting the rights of the purchaser.

Ulpian's language while discussing self-sale is careful and moralizing: he writes that the praetor is "absolutely right" (*rectissime*) to stop the wiliness (*calliditas*) of freemen who sell themselves. The subsequent passage in Ulpian's commentary on the edict, which explains when self-sale should count as fraud (i.e., when it is *dolus*), notes that this pertains precisely to the man who fashions himself as a slave (*qui finxit se servum*) with the express purpose of deceiving his buyer (*decipiendi emptoris causa*).[36] This deception must originate from the mind and plan of the would-be slave, as Ulpian adds that the man would be innocent of fraud if he was sold under the compulsion of force or fear (*si tamen vi metuque compulsus fuit his qui distractus est, dicemus eum dolo carere*).[37] A particular characteristic, his wiliness (*calliditas*), is being punished; he is unable to proclaim his freeborn status before the law and, instead, is made into a slave, a *servus callidus*.[38] The ethical varnish the jurist applies to the matter is perhaps tied to the number of references to fraudulent self-sale in the texts on suits for freedom; these were not men who were genuinely confused or coerced, nor were they making some calculation to the effect that it would not be in their interest to proclaim their own freedom. Instead, these were men who behaved as slaves and used the courts as a money-making scheme.

The change in status derives, then, from the intention of the man who orchestrated his own sale instead of from luck, presentation of evidence, or the judge's understanding of the situation in the suit for freedom. Taken as punishment, the ruling can disregard a known legal fact—that the man is actually free—and create a new truth: he is now a slave in fact. This new reality has severe consequences; when discussing the liability that a freeman who has been sold as a slave with knowledge has to his purchaser, the third-century jurist Modestinus notes that the sold freeman will be liable even if the vendor or any other third party is as well, because, as he says, "this action is penal."[39] The second-century jurist Pomponius tells us that a free woman who has sold herself as a slave will bear slave children with no right to proclaim freedom while she is a slave.[40] And the later jurist Hermogenian notes that a man over twenty who has put himself up for sale with an agreement to share in the price cannot, even after manumission, proclaim his free birth.[41] Despite the fact that he very well may have been born free, his new status as a slave precludes that proclamation. Given that exposed children subsequently sold as slaves remain untainted by slavery and could proclaim their freeborn status, the punitive nature of this situation is clear. The exposure cases are explained as an error of fact; the exposed child was never truly a slave.[42] None of these penalties should be surprising, as the man who sold himself is a slave in legal fact, and what we see here is the jurists' correction: following the ruling, status does indeed drive state. The person that is a slave is in a state of slavery, legally speaking; the man is no longer freeborn, and the children of the woman are born slaves.

The aim of this chapter is not to suggest that a great number of people were going about their lives with an unknown and unknowable legal status. This was not the case for several reasons. First, most people were born slaves or free persons and remained in that status. Second, in most suits for freedom, there likely was clear evidence that would lead to a sound and correct verdict. Third, at least some of the people proclaiming their freedom or claiming someone as a slave were probably lying. The thin line between duplicity and honest error can be seen in the language shared between passages discussing whether the proceedings were to be from liberty to slavery or the opposite (*se libero sciat . . . pro servo agere, Dig.* 40.12.10) and passages on cases of fraudulent sale (*se liberos scirent . . . se pro servis venum dari, Dig.* 40.12.14). Additionally, the attention to flight and the runaway in the discussion of uncertain status and state suggests that jurists presumed some amount of duplicity in claiming a different status. The idea of lying is explicit in the cases of fraud, as those are cases of known status, and the jurists change the status of the person as a punishment. The true status of a person plays a crucial role: in order to defraud a purchaser, the man selling himself must know he really is a freeman. Thinking about the two cases together, one in which the status of the man is truly uncertain and one in which the man is perpetrating a fraud, we see that the issue is resolved in each situation in such a way that the criterion for reaffirming or rendering legal status is not upholding the true status of the man. The elaborate nature of these cases reveals the ethical considerations the jurists weigh when reaching particular rulings. While the significance of favoring liberty or upholding the notion of *bona fides* in the Roman law of sale are stressed by the jurists, the performative nature of status drives the legal rulings, as it cements the cultural fiction of tangible difference between free and slave.

Notes

1. Paul, *Sabinus*, book 5, fr. 1705 Lenel = *Dig.* 18.1.5. Lenel = Otto Lenel, *Palingenesia iuris civilis*, 2 vols. (Leipzig: Tauchnitz, 1889). *Dig.* = Alan Watson, ed., *The Digest of Justinian*, 4 vols. (Philadelphia: University of Pennsylvania Press, 1985).

2. On the *causa liberalis* generally, see W. W. Buckland, *The Roman Law of Slavery: The Condition of the Slave in Private Law from Augustus to Justinian* (Cambridge: Cambridge University Press, 1908), 652–75; Mathieu Nicolau, *Causa liberalis: Étude historique et comparative du procès de liberté dans les législations anciennes* (Paris: Recueil Sirey, 1933); Gennaro Franciosi, *Il processo di libertà in diritto romano* (Naples: E. Jovene, 1961); Elisabeth Herrmann-Otto, "*Causae liberales*," *Index* 27 (1999): 141–59; Salvatore Sciortino, *Studi sulle liti di libertà nel diritto romano* (Turin: Giappichelli, 2010).

3. On the phenomenon of constructing legal truths that do not correspond to objective truths, see, generally, Charles Nesson, "The Evidence or the Event? On Judicial Proof and the Acceptability of Verdicts," *Harvard Law Review* 98 (1985): 1357–92. In the legal history of slavery specifically, see Rebecca J. Scott, "Social Facts, Legal Fictions, and the Attribution of Slave Status: The Puzzle of Prescription," *Law and History Review* 35 (2017): 9–30. I thank Will Sullivan for bringing these sources to my attention and for his many insightful comments on the present chapter.

4. On the performance of status in the courts, see Ariela J. Gross, *What Blood Won't Tell: A History of Race on Trial in America* (Cambridge, MA: Harvard University Press, 2010), especially 1–72.

5. Buckland, *Roman Law of Slavery*, 655.

6. Cf. Ulpian, *Edict*, book 54, frr. 1291, 1296 Lenel = *Dig.* 40.12.7.5, 40.12.12.3–4; Ulpian, *Duties of Consul*, book 2, fr. 2060 Lenel = *Dig.* 22.3.14. See, further, Buckland, *Roman Law of Slavery*, 660.

7. Ulpian, *Edict*, book 55, fr. 1296 Lenel = *Dig.* 40.12.10, 12, trans. P. A. Brunt. Acknowledged translations of the jurists, with or without modifications, are taken from the Watson edition of the *Digest of Justinian*. This fragment is interrupted by the *Digest* compilers with a text from the second-century jurist Gaius. While the passage of Ulpian is considered genuine (see Sciortino, *Liti di libertà*, 217n550; more generally on this passage, see 217–22), the phrase *in possessione libertatis* is most likely a later gloss (see Claudia Moatti, "Les erreurs de statut et la définition de la liberté dans l'espace judiciaire romain jusqu'au IIIe siècle de notre ère," in *Recht haben und Recht bekommen im Imperium Romanum: Das Gerichtswesen der Römischen Kaiserzeit und seine dokumentarische Evidenz*, ed. Rudolf Haensch [Warsaw: Faculty of Law and Administration of the University of Warsaw, Institute of Archaeology of the University of Warsaw, and Fundacja im. Rafała Taubenschlaga, 2016], 543, 543n83).

8. This distinction can be seen in literary exempla. E.g., Dio Chrysostom's second discourse on freedom uses language that evokes the legal understanding of the difference between status and state (*Or.* 15.13): "Τί δέ;" εἶπε, "δοκοῦσί σοι πάντες οἱ δουλεύοντες δοῦλοι εἶναι;" ("What, do you think that all those who are in a state of slavery are slaves?").

9. Ulpian makes mention of these possibilities in the same passage (*Edict*, book 55, fr. 1296 Lenel = *Dig.* 40.12.12.2, trans. P. A. Brunt): *Potest et servus sine dolo malo in libertate morari, ut puta testamento accepit libertatem, quod nullius momenti esse ignorat, vel vindicta ei imposita est ab eo, quem dominum esse putavit, cum non esset, vel educatus est quasi liber, cum servus esset* ("It is also possible for a slave to live in a state of liberty without fraud; for example, he has accepted liberty under a will without knowing that it has no validity, or he has been freed by 'vindicta' by someone whom he mistakenly supposed to be his owner, or he has been brought up as a freeman, although a slave.").

10. For the opposite scenario, see Hermogenian, *Epitome of Law*, book 1, fr. 5 Lenel = *Dig.* 5.1.53 (the suppression of a will that gave freedom); Paul, *Edict*, book 44, fr. 603

Lenel = *Dig.* 22.6.1.2 (the exposure of freeborn children that are then enslaved), discussed below.

11. This chapter is much indebted to the work done on these passages by Moatti ("Les erreurs de statut," especially 532, 546–47). She shows how cases of status determination explicitly tie intention (*voluntas*) to the action of the person, and she underscores the importance of performativity as a method of reading status (see especially 549, 558).

12. This same language is used in the discussion of whether a slave can be *infamatus*. The Augustan jurist Mela argues that the target of the *infamia* is not the master if the slave was behaving like a freeman (Ulpian, *Edict*, book 77, fr. 1359 Lenel = *Dig.* 47.10.15.45 [placed in Lenel's *Palingenesia* in book 57 of Ulpian's commentary on the edict], trans. J. A. C. Thomas): *Interdum iniuria servo facta ad dominum redundat, interdum non: nam si pro libero se gerentem aut cum eum alterius potius quam meum existimat quis, non caesurus eum, si meum scisset, non posse eum, quasi mihi iniuriam fecerit, sic conveniri Mela scribit* ("An affront to a slave sometimes affects the master also, sometimes not; for if the slave is posing as a freeman or if the person who beats him thinks that he belongs to someone else and would not have done it if he knew the slave was mine, Mela writes that the striker cannot be sued as having affronted me.").

13. Gaius, *Urban Praetor's Edict, Chapter on Suits for Freedom*, fr. 42 Lenel = *Dig.* 40.12.11: *Licet fugae tempore pro libero se gesserit: dicemus enim eum in eadem causa esse* ("Although in the time of flight he behaved as a freeman, certainly we will say he is in the same situation."). The Justinianic compilers place this passage in the midst of Ulpian's text.

14. Ulpian, *Curule Aediles' Edict*, book 1, 1761 Lenel = *Dig.* 21.1.17.10.

15. Ulpian, *Curule Aediles' Edict*, book 1, 1760 Lenel = *Dig.* 21.1.4.3 (citing Pomponius), trans. J. A. C. Thomas: *Et ideo nominatim de errone et fugitivo excipitur: hoc enim animi vitium est, non corporis* ("Hence, the express reservation of the wandering or runaway slave; for their defects are of the mind, not the body.").

16. An example taken (again) from Dio's second discourse on liberty offers what this form of fraudulent liberty might look like (*Or.* 15.15–16, trans. J. W. Cohoon, with modifications): ὁπότε καὶ ὁ Καλλίου υἱὸς ἔδοξε δουλεῦσαι πολὺν χρόνον ἐπὶ Θρᾴκης μετὰ τὴν μάχην, ἣν Ἀθηναῖοι περὶ Ἄκανθον ἡττήθησαν· ὥστε καὶ ὕστερον διαφυγὼν καὶ ἀφικόμενος ἠμφισβήτει τοῦ κλήρου τοῦ Καλλίου καὶ πολλὰ πράγματα παρεῖχε τοῖς ξυγγενέσιν, ἐκεῖνος μὲν οἶμαι ψευδόμενος· ἦν γὰρ οὐχ υἱός, ἀλλ' ἱπποκόμος Καλλίου, τὴν δὲ ὄψιν ὅμοιος τῷ τοῦ Καλλίου μειρακίῳ, ὃ ἔτυχεν ἐν τῇ μάχῃ τελευτῆσαν· ἔτι δὲ ἡλλήνιζεν ἀκριβῶς καὶ γράμματα ἠπίστατο, ἀλλὰ ἕτεροί γε μυρίοι τοῦτο πεπόνθασιν ("The son of Callias was thought to have been enslaved for a long time in Thrace after the battle in which the Athenians suffered a defeat at Acanthus. When he escaped afterwards and reached home, he laid claim to the estate left by Callias and caused a great deal of trouble for Callias' kinsmen, on the one hand, because I think that man was lying: he was not the son, but the groom of Callias. But, on the other hand, he was similar in appearance to Callias' son, who did die in the battle, and also he spoke Greek accu-

rately and could read and write. —But there have been innumerable others who have suffered this fate."). The groom fraudulently impersonates a free person. His skills are certainly not exclusive to the free population, but in this particular performance they are suggestive markers of liberty.

17. Clifford Ando, "Fact, Fiction, and Social Reality in Roman Law," in *Legal Fictions in Theory and Practice*, ed. Maksymilian Del Mar and William Twining (Cham: Springer, 2015), 295: "the preposition *pro*, one among several lexemes employed to effect substitutions and assert equivalence across taxonomic boundaries." In addition, Ando (309; see also 310–11) gives the example of *pro consule*, which he argues means "as if" rather than "in place of" in Livy 8.23.10–12.

18. For further information on the use of this language for those mistaken about their legal status and the history of the formulation, see Clifford Ando, *Roman Social Imaginaries: Language and Thought in Contexts of Empire* (Toronto: University of Toronto Press, 2015), 92, 92n10.

19. Julian, *From Minicius*, book 5, fr. 875 Lenel = *Dig.* 40.12.30, trans. P. A. Brunt. While there is some debate about the origin of the legal rule found in the final sentence (E), most scholars agree that it is genuinely Julian's rather than the work of Tribonian or some other later hand. For a summary of the argument and reasons why the passage should be viewed as Julian's, see Sciortino, *Liti di libertà*, 244–54, 245n639, 259.

20. The question of whether the *ego* in section C refers to Julian or Minicius is partly what leads some to believe that the ruling in section E is interpolated. I follow Capone's reading of Minicius in section C and of Julian giving his ruling in section E. See Piera Capone, "Una quaestio di Minicio e una nota di Giuliano: Rileggendo D. 40.12.30," in *Fides, humanitas, ius: Studi in onore di Luigi Labruna*, ed. Cosimo Cascione and Carla Masi Doria (Naples: Editoriale Scientifica, 2007), 2:695–722; contra Pia Starace, "Un confronto testuale in tema di causa liberalis," in *Diritto e giustizia nel processo: Prospettive storiche costituzionali e comparatistiche*, ed. Cosimo Cascione and Carla Masi Doria (Naples: Editoriale Scientifica, 2002), 51–92.

21. The very little we know about Minicius comes from Julian. Frier suggests Minicius may, like Cassius, have been a student of Sabinus; see Bruce Frier, "Early Classical Private Law," in *The Cambridge Ancient History*, ed. Alan K. Bowman et al., 2nd ed. (Cambridge: Cambridge University Press, 1996), 10:972n65.

22. The view that a man cannot be half-slave and half-free is also seen in Gaius, *Urban Praetor's Edict, Chapter on Suits for Freedom*, fr. 38 Lenel = *Dig.* 40.12.9.2: *minime autem praetor pati debeat, ut pro parte quis servus sit* (the praetor could not possibly allow anyone to be partly a slave).

23. See, e.g., Pomponius, *Sabinus*, book 7, fr. 520 Lenel = *Dig.* 50.17.20; Ulpian, *Edict*, book 60, fr. 1395 = *Dig.* 40.5.2.

24. On this shift toward equity and the principle of *favor libertatis*, see Hans Ankum, "L'expression *favor libertatis* dans les travaux des juristes classiques romains," in *Extravagantes: Scritti sparsi sul diritto romano* (Naples: Jovene, 2007), 45–78; P. A. Brunt, "Mar-

cus Aurelius and Slavery," *Bulletin of the Institute of Classical Studies* 71 (1998): 144–48; Carlo Castello, "In tema di *favor libertatis*," *Studia et documenta historiae et iuris* 22 (1956): 348–61; A. M. Honoré, "The Nature of Slavery," in *The Legal Understanding of Slavery: From the Historical to the Contemporary*, ed. Jean Allain (Oxford: Oxford University Press, 2012), 9–16. On the effects that Julian's codification of the edict of the praetor had on jurisprudence, see Richard A. Bauman, *Lawyers and Politics in the Early Roman Empire: A Study of Relations between the Roman Jurists and the Emperors from Augustus to Hadrian* (Munich: C. H. Beck, 1989), 236; H. F. Jolowicz and Barry Nicholas, *Historical Introduction to the Study of Roman Law*, 3rd ed. (Cambridge: Cambridge University Press, 1972), 356–59; Barry Nicholas, *An Introduction to Roman Law*, rev. ed., ed. Ernest Metzger (Oxford: Oxford University Press, 2008), 21–22.

25. In Louisiana slave law, there was sometimes an argument for "freedom by prescription," which held that someone who lived as a free person in good faith for a number of years may be entitled to legal freedom. But that prescription appealed not to natural law (in the way *favor libertatis* is viewed) but to practice or performance; see Scott, "Social Facts, Legal Fictions," 9–30. The use of *favor libertatis* in the antebellum South was rather rare and fell out of use as slavery was further under threat from abolitionists: see William M. Wiecek, "Emancipation and Civic Status: The American Experience, 1865–1915," in *The Promises of Liberty: The History and Contemporary Relevance of the Thirteenth Amendment*, ed. Alexander Tsesis (New York: Columbia University Press, 2010), 80–81; Judith Kelleher Schafer, "Roman Roots of the Louisiana Law of Slavery: Emancipation in American Louisiana, 1803–1857," *Louisiana Law Review* 56, no. 2 (1996): 412; Judith Kelleher Schafer, *Slavery, the Civil Law, and the Supreme Court of Louisiana* (Baton Rouge: Louisiana State University Press, 1994), 225–26, 269–71.

26. Paul, *Edict*, book 17, fr. 267 Lenel = *Dig.* 42.1.38, trans. J. A. C. Thomas.

27. E.g. Gaius, *Urban Praetor's Edict, Chapter on Suits for Freedom*, fr. 35 Lenel = *Dig.* 40.12.2.

28. The challenge would especially be insurmountable, e.g., if the claim was due to exposure as an infant rather than testamentary issues. On exposure, see Paul, *Edict*, book 44, fr. 603 Lenel = *Dig.* 22.6.1.2.

29. Paul, *Edict*, book 17, fr. 266 Lenel = *Dig.* 42.1.36.

30. Ando ("Fact, Fiction, and Social Reality," 312) examines a passage of Ulpian that he has shown pertains to his discussion on how to proceed after it is discovered that a suit for freedom was resolved erroneously (*Lex Julia et Papia*, book 1, fr. 1978 Lenel = *Dig.* 50.17.207 [also *Dig.* 1.5.25 pr.], trans. Ando): *res iudicata pro veritate accipitur* ("a legal judgment is accepted in the place of truth").

31. E.g., *Dig.* 40.12.4, 7, 9, 14.

32. This penalty would not apply to being forced to sell yourself through fear or violence (Ulpian, *Edict*, book 55, fr. 1300 Lenel = *Dig.* 40.12.16.1) or to someone taking away another person's evidence of free status and then claiming them as a slave (Paul, *Edict*, book 11, fr. 199 Lenel = *Dig.* 4.2.8.1). There is some evidence that there were cases

outside of fraud that did not let a person recover his status; see Buckland, *Roman Law of Slavery*, 427–36. Indicating the difficulty of understanding these scenarios, J. A. Crook (*Law and Life of Rome* [Ithaca: Cornell University Press, 1967], 61n114) notes that "Buckland discusses the problem, with less than his magisterial confidence."

33. Ulpian, *Edict*, book 54, fr. 1290 Lenel = *Dig.* 40.12.7 pr.–2. There is some discussion about the age being twenty-five rather than twenty; see Alan Watson, *Roman Slave Law* (Baltimore: Johns Hopkins University Press, 1987), 9.

34. Ulpian, *Edict*, book 54, fr. 1290 Lenel = *Dig.* 40.12.7.2–3, trans. P. A. Brunt. On self-sale, see Buckland, *Roman Law of Slavery*, 427–36; Watson, *Roman Slave Law*, 8–10 (the passage is cited at 9n9); Alfred Söllner, ed., *Irrtümlich als Sklaven gehaltene freie Menschen und Sklaven in unsicheren Eigentumsverhältnissen—Homines liberi et servi alieni bona fide servientes* (Stuttgart: F. Steiner, 2000), 27–28, 86 (on this passage); Hans Wieling, *Die Begründung des Sklavenstatus nach ius gentium und ius civile* (Stuttgart: F. Steiner, 1999), 26, 62–68 (which contains discussion of this passage).

35. A similar sentiment is expressed by Paul, but he holds that the purchaser with knowledge will not get ownership at all (*Senatus Consultum Claudianum*, sole book, fr. 1898 Lenel = *Dig.* 40.13.5, trans. P. A. Brunt): *Si duo liberum hominem maiorem annis viginti emerimus, unus sciens eius condicionem, alter ignorans, non propter eum qui scit ad libertatem ei proclamare permittitur, sed propter eum qui ignorat servus efficietur, sed non etiam eius qui scit, sed tantum alterius* ("If two of us have bought a freeman over twenty, one in knowledge of his status, the other without, the knowledge of the one does not entitle him to proclaim his freedom; the ignorance of the other will make him his slave; the purchaser who knows the facts will not have a share.").

36. Ulpian, *Edict*, book 55, fr. 1299 Lenel = *Dig.* 40.12.14: *rectissime praetor calliditati eorum, qui, cum se liberos scirent, dolo malo passi sunt se pro servis venum dari, occurrit* ("The praetor is absolutely right to check the craft of those who, knowing themselves to be free, have fraudulently permitted themselves to be sold as slaves.").

37. Ulpian, *Edict*, book 55, fr. 1300 Lenel = *Dig.* 40.12.16.1.

38. It may be that Ulpian is thinking specifically of the trickster slave; a scene in Terence's *Self-Tormenter* (5.1.14–16) uses similar language to describe the *calliditas* of the slave Syrus, who is able to shape (*fingo*) the appearance of people.

> CHREMES: *Servi venere in mentem Syri / Calliditates.* (The wily tricks of my slave, Syrus, just came to mind.)
>
> MENEDEMUS: *Itane?* (Yeah?)
>
> CHREMES: *Vultus quoque hominum fingit scelus.* (The scoundrel can even mold the countenances of people.)

39. Modestinus, *Penalties*, book 1, fr. 152 = Dig. 40.12.21, trans. P. A. Brunt: *Secundum quae id, quod alter eorum solverit, nihil ad exonerandum alterum pertinebit, quia placuit hanc actionem poenalem esse* ("Accordingly, what one of them has paid will not

contribute to relieving the other of liability, since it has been decided that this action is penal.").

40. Pomponius, *Letters and Readings*, book 11, fr. 201 = *Dig.* 40.13.3, trans. P. A. Brunt: *Dubitari non potest, quin ei quoque, quae maior annis viginti venire se passa est, ad libertatem proclamandi licentia fuerit deneganda. his quoque danda non est, qui ex ea nati tempore servitutis eius erunt* ("It cannot be doubted that the right to proclaim freedom should also be denied to a woman over twenty who has let herself be sold; it is also not to be given to her children born while she is in slavery").

41. Hermogenian, *Epitome of Law*, book 5, fr. 77 Lenel = *Dig.* 40.12.40, trans. P. A. Brunt: *Cum pacto partitionis pretii maior viginti annis venalem se praebuit, nec post manumissionem ad libertatem proclamare potest* ("A man over twenty who has put himself up for sale with an agreement to share the price cannot even after manumission proclaim his free birth.").

42. Paul, *Edict*, book 44, fr. 603 Lenel = *Dig.* 22.6.1.2, trans. A. M. Honoré: *Ignorantia vel facti vel iuris est. . . . Si quis nesciat se cognatum esse, interdum in iure, interdum in facto errat. nam si et liberum se esse et ex quibus natus sit sciat, iura autem cognationis habere se nesciat, in iure errat: at si quis (forte expositus) quorum parentium esset ignoret, fortasse et serviat alicui putans se servum esse, in facto magis quam in iure errat* ("Ignorance is of fact or law. . . . 2. Someone who does not know he is a cognate may be mistaken as to fact or law. If he knows he is free and who his parents are, but not that he has rights as a cognate, his error is of law. But if someone, perhaps exposed at birth, does not know his parents and acts like someone's slave, believing he is one, his error is of fact rather than law.").

CHAPTER 5

Gossip, Slander, Hearsay, Truth

Oral Evidence in Athenian Courts

Esther Eidinow

Introduction

Gossip and Truth

In modern parlance, "gossip" is "idle" talk, usually about a person, evaluative in nature, and in some way "superfluous (in the sense of being unnecessary or excessive)."[1] Modern scholarship on the fourth-century Athenian lawcourt speeches has long identified this kind of "informal information" in litigants' speeches and has argued persuasively that it worked to enforce social norms.[2] This chapter builds on these arguments to examine, in more detail, the role of gossip as evidence in the forensic speeches of the fourth century.[3] While acknowledging the key relationship between gossip and social control, it suggests that gossip played a more complex role in the Athenian law courts, interacting with epistemological, ethical, and legislative frameworks to become a key rhetorical resource for a speaker in the construction of his case.

In the first half ("Informal Discourse in the Courts"), this chapter explores the ways in which gossip was employed and to what end, analyzing how its epistemic value was established. It examines the different processes that were available for constraining the delivery of various kinds of informal information, including the rules of hearsay and their application. It suggests that an examination of that aspect not only gives further insight into the epistemological framework of this context, but also illuminates the ethical and legislative assumptions that shaped the nature and use of evidence. This reveals the crucial role, not of the content or context of the information presented but, instead, of the level of presence—and therefore liability—of those whose knowledge was being invoked, with implications for the role of gossip and its attendant framing.[4]

The second part of this chapter ("Telling Stories") then turns to this aspect in more detail, examining how individual speakers employed gossip as evidence. It argues that the strategic deployment of particular kinds of information helped individual litigants to generate and communicate the specific constructions of their cases. To make this argument, the chapter draws on the socio-cognitive linguistic theory of Teun van Dijk and the idea that "it is not the social situation that influences (or is influenced by) discourse, but the way the participants *define* such a situation."[5] The chapter draws on a number of examples but focuses particularly on one case of gossip, in which the orator Demosthenes was repeatedly, and over a twenty-year period, described as being responsible for a horrible murder; this story is described in the next section.[6]

The Stories and Their Significance

The legal case of Nicodemus appears to have been notorious in Athens in the second half of the fourth century. It occurs in a number of legal speeches, most of which were written for cases targeting Demosthenes (indirectly, if not explicitly) over a period of roughly twenty years. As far as we know, the basic facts are as follows: some time after 348 BCE, a man called Nicodemus, from the deme of Aphidna in Athens, was murdered and horribly mutilated; his eyes were gouged out, and his tongue was cut off. The various sources reveal that Nicodemus was a supporter of Meidias and Eubulus, enemies of Demosthenes, and was part of a group, formally led by Euctemon, who had tried to convict Demosthenes of deserting from the campaign by Athens against Euboea in 348 BCE.[7] The orator Aeschines provides us with one version of the events that led to this killing.

> Demosthenes, after he had spent his patrimony, went up and down the city, hunting rich young fellows whose fathers were dead, and whose mothers were administering their property. I will omit many instances, and will mention only one of those who were outrageously treated. He discovered a household that was rich and ill-managed, the head of which was a woman, proud and of poor

> judgment. A fatherless young man, half crazy, was managing the estate, Aristarchus, son of Moschus. Demosthenes, pretending to be a lover of his, invited the young man to this intimacy, filling him up with empty hopes, assuring him that without any delay whatever he should become the foremost man in public life, and he showed him a list of names. So, he became prompter and teacher of the young man in conduct that has made Aristarchus an exile from his fatherland; while Demosthenes, getting hold of the money that was to support him in his banishment, has cheated him out of three talents! In addition, at the hands of Aristarchus, Nicodemus of Aphidna has met a violent death. The poor man had both eyes knocked out, and that tongue cut off, the tongue with which he used to speak out freely, trusting in the laws and in you.[8]

This was not the only time that Aeschines mentioned these events. He brought Nicodemus up again, not so long after, in *On the Embassy* (343 BCE). This time he did not bother to support his statement with any kind of testimony or reference to general knowledge but left it as a bald accusation.

> It is my good fortune, too, that all the members of my mother's family are freeborn citizens; and today I see her here before my eyes in anxiety and fear for my safety. And yet, Demosthenes, this mother of mine went out to Corinth an exile, with her husband, and shared the disasters of the democracy; but you, who claim to be a man—that you really are a man I should not venture to say—you were once indicted for desertion, and you saved yourself by buying off the man who indicted you, Nicodemus of Aphidna, whom afterward you helped Aristarchus to destroy; wherefore you are polluted, and have no right to be invading the market-place.[9]

A similarly brief reference occurs in a forensic speech made twenty years later, wielded by Dinarchus during the trials of those accused of taking bribes from Harpalus.[10] Rather than providing any evidence for the main charge, the case against Demosthenes turned on a thorough presentation of his character as corrupt, venal, and deceitful. The mention of this murder was brief but powerful, delivered in a punchy series of rhetorical questions.

> Could any one of you, or of the bystanders, say what public or private affairs he has not ruined by his contact with them? After gaining access to the home of Aristarchus and planning with him the death of Nicodemus, which

> they contrived, an affair of which you all know the details, did he not banish Aristarchus on the most shameful charges? And did not Aristarchus find in Demosthenes such a friend as to make him think that this was some evil spirit which had visited him and the originator of all his misfortunes? Is it not true that once this man began to advise the city, and would he had never done so—I shall pass over his private affairs, for time does not permit me to speak at length—absolutely no good has befallen it; indeed not only the city but the whole of Greece has been involved in dangers, misfortunes, and dishonour?[11]

Finally, in summarizing Demosthenes' character flaws, Dinarchus touched on the case once more: "He has been proved to have taken bribes against Athens, has cheated the people and the council in defiance of the curse, professing views he does not hold, and in private has recommended to Aristarchus a course both cruel and unlawful."[12]

The information about these events is, obviously, presented in these passages by enemies of Demosthenes. But, remarkably, the case for the opposition has also survived. Even before Aeschines first raises the case in *Against Timarchus*, we are given a very different version of the relevant events by Demosthenes himself in his speech *Against Meidias* (347/6).[13] Demosthenes relates how his opponent, Meidias, "went round the Marketplace and ventured to spread impious and atrocious statements about me to the effect that I was the author of the deed."[14] Meidias apparently also tried to persuade the relatives of the dead man (who were prosecuting Aristarchus) to accuse Demosthenes of the crime.[15] Finally, according to Demosthenes, Meidias changed his approach and aimed his attack ostensibly at Aristarchus. Demosthenes emphasizes how Meidias had socialized with Aristarchus—he pictures Meidias in Aristarchus' house, putting his hand in his, treating him as a friend—just the day before he denounced him in the Council Chamber.[16] Demosthenes also brings forward witnesses who testify to the whereabouts of Meidias.[17]

Demosthenes' aim is clearly to defend himself against allegations that have recently been leveled against him: the ways in which he chooses to do this, and the language he employs, are examined in more detail below. The role that the story of Nicodemus' death plays for other speakers who mention it in court is less obvious.[18] In each case, the story has no direct connection to the case being heard: it could be (indeed has been) described as irrelevant detail. But it is far more significant than that; it is gossip.[19]

Informal Discourse in the Courts

Facts and Framings

It has been argued that in Athens, procedural law held "a chronological and a logical priority" over substantive law,[20] while the courts were "more concerned with dispute-settlement than with the enactment of justice in our objective sense."[21] But this argument must be nuanced: while it seems highly likely that at least some of the litigants and *dikastai* in Athenian courts viewed the courts as an arena for the continued pursuit of "long-term competitive and feuding relations," this did not exclude a sophisticated approach to the laws and their aims.[22] As David Mirhady has recently argued, the Athenian *dikastai* tried "to abide by their oath to vote 'according to the laws,'" but they did so "with a comprehensive understanding of the multiplicity of laws and the legal principles implicit in them."[23]

To that argument, we can, in turn, add—or make more explicit—the *dikastai*'s appreciation of how these legal principles reflected, or were reflected by, the sociopolitical context, in a judicial system that, in practice, explicitly conflated "justice" with a particular characterization of the interests of the city qua demos.[24] This aspect is manifest in forensic rhetoric, which indicates that the dikasts decided cases, at least partly, on their assessments of not only the actions but also the character of the litigants. While the primary aim of the court was to establish whether the crime itself was committed, there appears to have been just as much interest in establishing the nature of the person on trial. In the Athenian courts, this information was not only a part of the interpretative context of the case that each speaker presented, it was also an element in what we would now call the "fact pattern" presented by each speaker. Information about a person's character was intended to suggest the likelihood of his (or, more rarely, her) having committed the crime. Appealing to the shared values of the community, speakers would describe, evaluate, and/or criticize the activities and personalities of those on trial—holding up to criticism those who had erred; lauding those whose actions were admirable—even (perhaps especially) when they were talking about themselves.[25]

In this context, it seems, any and all information was welcomed—including gossip, which brought the private into the public sphere, as Aeschines points out in *Against Timarchus*, a speech that is riddled with reports of Timarchus' youthful indiscretions.[26] It also seems likely that as well as drawing in this kind of informal intelligence, the courts helped to spread it: we can imagine how information voiced in a litigant's speech before potentially hundreds of dikasts must have quickly entered the gossip networks of a community—and perhaps traveled even beyond these. As the evidence shows us, by its nature, this kind of information was about more than just the specific events of the trial; it encompassed the character and long-term past actions of the litigants. Adriaan Laani has observed how such a broadcasting of a person's possible nature and actions would be likely to reach not only a litigant's residential community, but also individuals outside his community with whom he interacted.[27]

To what extent, however, this kind of information may have been understood to influence day-to-day interactions—or actually did—is unclear.[28] Lanni notes the apparent rarity of informal social sanctions, while acknowledging that fear of talk and loss of reputation may have been important in exerting some control over some behavior.[29] In considering more formalized responses to gossip, Wallace provides an important nuance, emphasizing how "every infringement of individual liberty responded to substantive, material dangers to other citizens or the community."[30] He gives the case of Timarchus as an example: Aeschines' repeated appeals to the dikasts' own knowledge of the gossip about Timarchus presented in this case suggest that it had not been an important consideration before that point. Wallace argues that this illustrates the general Athenian attitude toward their politicians: "such gossip was typically disregarded by a majority of the demos, who went on supporting them," but this attitude changed when the case had significant political consequences.[31]

This argument is hard to evaluate, since it is, in the end, circular. But the case study examined in this chapter may help to break that apparent deadlock. The stories that appear to have been circulating about Demosthenes' role in a murder did not bring him to court. Nevertheless, what the evidence reveals of Demosthenes' own reaction to them does imply that he was concerned that these rumors *could* have had some adverse effect. And, as the forensic speeches demonstrate, he was not alone in manifesting anxiety about gossip. This suggests that while our evidence may indicate a general tolerance for social indiscretions in Athenian society, litigants did not take it for granted. Their approach may indicate a concern with individual honor (as others have argued);[32] but litigants may also have feared that, if presented in a particular way by a skillful speaker, their personal conduct could be portrayed as a threat to the city.[33]

There were certainly rhetorical conventions for the delivery of this kind of information: in the forensic speeches, gossip was often framed with particular verbal formulas—that made it more or less clear what kind of information this was. Many of the formulas drew on characteristics of what we recognize as informal conversation, in which information is left, as Niko Besnier has described it, "unsaid, understated, or waiting to be filled in by the audience."[34] As we see in the examples above and in many other passages across the forensic corpus, speakers could refer to or hint at what was generally known or could explicitly ask the jurors to recall what they knew. For example, in *Against Timarchus*, by apparently drawing the example of Aristarchus out of a selection of many, Aeschines is implying that there is a pool of unstated but widely held knowledge: "I will omit many instances, and will mention only one of those who were outrageously treated."[35] Again, in talking about the death of Nicodemus, Dinarchus says to the assembled jurors that this is "an affair of which you all know the details."[36]

Such formulas mark this information as gossip, but modern commentators need to exercise caution in their treatment of it. While to modern audiences, gossip is unverifiable, heard via others, and, thus, inherently untrustworthy, in their Athenian audience, these formulaic phrases may have prompted a very different response. For example, they may have recalled the way that this kind of informal talk occurs between people in daily life, thus suggesting reliable firsthand knowledge. In an arena that revolved around the judgment of the demos, in which speakers claimed authority by asserting their own knowledge, rhetorical appeals to the personal knowledge of their fellow citizens, including the dikasts themselves, could, therefore, have strengthened a legal case, not undermined it.

These observations about the presentation of informal information in the law courts resonate with evidence from other contexts for the underlying structure of contemporary epistemological frameworks in which what was seen firsthand was regarded as more reliable than what was heard from others.[37] It explains why speakers who wanted to present themselves as authorities in a case needed to give the impression that they either themselves had, or had access to sources with, relational or physical proximity to those involved. In Demosthenes' account of Meidias' behavior, we see this approach in operation, as Demosthenes brings in witnesses to support his account. Demosthenes may not have been in the marketplace when Meidias was there trying to find citizens willing to take him to court, but he can bring in witnesses who were; similarly, Demosthenes was not present when Meidias visited Aristarchus, but he can introduce others who were there into the courtroom.[38]

This situation brings us back to the importance of character. The corroborative role of witnesses is significant: while we can describe it as a "ritualized, socio-political act of support," it extended beyond any simple verbal affirmation, introducing the complexity of community relations into the courtroom.[39] Sally Humphreys, examining the role of witnesses, analyzed the social function of this "face-to-face" knowledge, noting how this approach was an attempt "to retain some of the qualities of village dispute-settlement procedures in an urban setting."[40] She observed how more than one witness could be used to testify repeatedly to the same story: such a technique was not about providing factual testimony; rather, it demonstrated that the litigant on whose behalf the witnesses spoke was "surrounded by a substantial group of respectable and law-abiding kin, friends, and associates."[41]

Their social significance was not the only contribution of witnesses: they also provided crucial epistemological support. Since they were likely to have had close personal experience of the litigant, their proximity could corroborate his testimony. Aeschines makes use of both these modes of verification, albeit in a slightly indirect way, when he lists his family members in *On the Embassy*. He intersperses his descriptions of them with observations about Demosthenes' crimes—among them, the murder of Aristarchus.[42] The contrast that he develops between his family's experiences and that of Demosthenes redounds to the benefit of his own character; but it also reinforces his claims about Demosthenes' dreadful deeds, enfolding his accounts of those events alongside descriptions of family events about which he is, of course, more likely to have insight. What we might describe as gossip is, in this context, transformed into an insight about personal experience, apparently delivered by someone in a position to know. It reinforces the fact pattern, as well as (or even by) providing information about character—not only that of the man accused of a crime, but also that of the speaker making the accusation.

Limits and Regulations

The importance of, and emphasis on, this personal aspect of reported knowledge was, in turn, reinforced by the different processes available for constraining the delivery of certain kinds of informal information. The ways in which these were structured (and differed from each other) is significant for developing our understanding of the epistemic, ethical, and legislative principles that seem to have underpinned the Athenian legal system. First of all, to challenge statements made about his own character and/or actions, a litigant could protest against what had been said against him, by claiming that these words were slander (*diabole*), or abuse, or, even worse, that they had been delivered for personal reasons. For example, in protesting against Meidias' reported accusations of murder, Demosthenes intensifies his protestation of innocence by describing Meidias as committing acts of impiety and hubris. He argues that Meidias' accusations could have resulted in Demosthenes being taken to court on a charge of homicide and condemned to death.[43] In effect, this was fighting fire with fire: it was an attempt to blacken the character of the opposition, in order to weaken their attempts at character assassination.

Moving beyond this level, litigants could also invoke particular legal procedures. For example, a litigant could attack an opponent with a *dike kakegorias*, the penalty for which was five hundred drachmas. This procedure could be invoked against speech made in certain contexts; it was apparently designated by Solon, who, the sources report, made it illegal to speak ill of the living in temples, legal trials, public offices, or festival contests, and of the dead in any situation.[44] An example is found in Lysias 9, where Polyainos defends his nonpayment of a fine for insulting the generals, not on the grounds that what he said was true, but by arguing that the fine should not have been imposed.[45] He notes that the case was brought on the basis of a report from someone who had not included the information that he was "at Philius' bank," and so he was not in a place in which his remarks made him liable.[46] He then produces witnesses who testify that he was not in the magistrates' hall at the time of his speech.[47]

Our sources indicate not only that it mattered where the reported statement had been made, but it could also be crucially important which words had been used. The arguments made by speakers in relevant cases indicate that certain terms were specified in the statutes as *aporrheta*, that is, "not to be spoken"; the accusation that they had been used could become the basis of a court case. In Lysias 10 (*Against Theomnestos*), the speaker, who had been called a parricide by Theomnestos in an earlier trial, has brought a *dike kakegorias* against him. In the speech, the speaker attacks the defense put forward by Theomnestos—that he did not use the *aporrheta* words specified (he said that the defendant had killed his father, but he did not call him a murderer).[48] The focus of most commentary on this passage has been on the role of the argument in support of synonyms for the term *aporrheta*.[49] But the speech also provides some useful insight into what might make the speaker's argument plausible.

Considering in more detail how these speakers frame their arguments can illuminate the role of informal information in the law courts. In the first case, Lysias 9, Polyainos' language emphasizes the importance of firsthand knowledge. In his summary, his repetition of cognates of *phaino* stresses the role of sight and seeing in the provision of evidence for his alleged crime—and his defense against it: "For if I manifestly [*phaneros*] did not go into the court, and the law enjoins that the fine is to be due from those who misbehave inside it, I can be seen [*phainomai*] not to have acted against the law."[50] This is also the case in Lysias 10: the speaker not only frames his argument with formulas that emphasize his own experience (obvious for his own case), but also appeals to the memories of those among the dikasts themselves who, he claims, were present at the previous case in which the use of the key words took place.[51]

But while we can observe the similarities in terms of the epistemic emphasis on personal knowledge, there is also a crucial difference between these two cases: that is, the level of presence, and therefore liability, of those whose knowledge is invoked. For example, in the first case, Polyainos contrasts the anonymity of the person who is the source of the accusation with the witnesses that he calls to support his own defense: the latter, as we know, are liable for their testimony, but the former cannot be held liable since he is unknown. In the second case, no witnesses are called on this matter (although witnesses are called for other facets of the case); instead, the speaker relies on a claim that some of those who were present may remember what had happened.

The importance of the presence and therefore potential liability on the part of witnesses is supported further by two other regulatory procedures. The first and most obvious is the *dike pseudomarturion*, or case for false witness, which could be used to challenge witnesses for the information that they had brought to court.[52] Being found guilty of this charge three times would mean the loss of one's citizenship.[53] As Stephen Todd persuasively argues, this would mean that an act of witnessing was associated with risk. It was also surely a key reason why women and slaves were unable to act as witnesses, since they could not be taken to court on this charge.[54] In contrast to our own idea of false witness—and in line with the previous examples—such a case was concerned with challenging not only information that was untrue but also information that was disallowed, specifically what we might call "hearsay."[55] In Greek, such information is described as *akoe*, a term that can refer to both the act of "hearing" or the "sound heard."[56] A passage from Demosthenes 57 provides us with an overview of the problems with such evidence, introducing again the contrast between what has been heard but not seen by a witness.

> I should have thought, men of the jury, that it was fitting for Eubulides, and for all those who are now making accusations in cases of disfranchisement, to state only things of which they have accurate knowledge and to bring forward no hearsay evidence [μηδεμίαν προσάγειν ἀκοὴν] in a trial of this sort. Such a procedure has from time immemorial been recognized as so clearly unjust that the laws do not admit the production of hearsay testimony [οὐδὲ μαρτυρεῖν ἀκοὴν] even in the case of the most trifling charges and with good reason; for when persons who claim to have sure knowledge have ere now been convicted of falsehood, how can it be right to give credence in matters regarding which even the speaker himself has no knowledge? And when it is not permitted a man, even when he makes himself responsible, to harm another by evidence which he declares he has heard [δι' ὧν ἂν ἀκοῦσαι τις φῇ], how can it be right for you to give credence to one who speaks without responsibility?[57]

Further insights into the Athenian regulation of such information and its admission into court are provided by Pseudo-Demosthenes 46 (*Against Stephanus* ii), where Apollodoros argues that the testimony of Stephanus in support of Phormio is either false or hearsay.

> And surely, if he says that he believed this to be true because Phormio said it was, it would be like the same man to believe him when he said this, and to testify to it at his bidding. The laws, however, do not say this, but ordain that a man may testify to what he knows, or to matters at the doing of which he was present, and that his testimony must be committed to writing in order that it may not be possible to subtract anything from what is written, or to add anything to it. Hearsay evidence they do not admit from a living person, but only from one who is dead [ἀκοὴν δ' οὐκ ἐῶσι ζῶντος μαρτυρεῖν, ἀλλὰ τεθνεῶτος]; but in the case of those who are sick or absent from the country they allow evidence to be introduced, provided it be in written form, and the absent witness and the one submitting his testimony shall alike be liable to action under the same impeachment, in order that, if the absent witness acknowledges his evidence, he may be liable to action for giving false testimony, and if he does not acknowledge it, the one who submitted his testimony may be liable.[58]

As this passage suggests, there were situations in which hearsay could be admitted. For example, if the witness was ill or absent, an "extrajudicial deposition" was allowed (*ekmarturia*), where the information was put into a deposition in the presence of a witness or witnesses who then appeared in court to authenticate it.[59] In these cases, both the absent witness and the one deposing the evidence could be liable for a *dike pseudomarturion*.[60] If the original witness acknowledged the evidence, an impeachment (*episkepsis*) might be brought against him; if he denied it, then it would be brought against those who had confirmed it.[61]

Going back to the passage from Pseudo-Demosthenes 46, it appears that hearsay evidence was also allowed if the original witness was dead. Stephen Todd has argued that such evidence was admissible, not, as others have argued, because those who were about to die were perceived to be speaking the truth, but because "where possible the original author should run his own risk"—the risk in question being that of *dike pseudomarturion*.[62] But although said person would have run this risk while alive, by the time the evidence was given that person would have been deceased, and so was no longer vulnerable; this makes Todd's explanation seem unlikely. Instead, in such a situation, the risk came to rest with the person who introduced the evidence.[63] And, in fact, this interpretation also seems to align better with Todd's larger point about the risks attending the act of witnessing, that the evidence was admissible because the person who actually brought the information to court was potentially liable for such a charge.[64]

Indeed, this aspect marks a subtle but important difference between ancient and modern regulation of hearsay.[65] The rules differ between the United Kingdom and the United States, but research suggests that the overriding concern in both instances is that the jury will not be able to evaluate the credibility of the speaker, especially by means of the cross-examination of the opposing party.[66] In contrast, in the ancient Greek context, it was not the potential for cross-examination that mattered, but the potential to be sued for false witness. This is illustrated by examples where these laws appear to have been transgressed. For example, the law against hearsay seems to be broken in Demosthenes 41, when the plaintiff notes that the defendant's wife had acknowledged that the seals on a will were genuine. Harrison suggested that the gender of the evidence-giver may be relevant here, but did not elaborate on this idea.[67] If we pursue Todd's suggestion that it is liability to prosecution that is significant in a case of hearsay, then gender is clearly an, if not the, important factor. A woman could not give evidence herself, so the information must be brought into court through the testimony of another party. Moreover, another consideration may have been the way in which the woman gave her evidence: if the speaker is alluding to an oath taken by the woman, then, as Todd has argued, this form of evidence also could not be challenged by a *dike pseudomarturion*.[68] Thus, it is possible that although this would appear to be a situation of hearsay to modern eyes, a Greek audience may simply not have perceived that information as "hearsay" in a technical sense.

A further and more complex example occurs in Demosthenes' *Against Phormion*, where the speaker introduces witnesses who testify to what Lampis, the agent of Phormion, had said to the speaker before the case was brought: Lampis had not received the money owed from Phormion—which was (the plaintiff argues) the reason why he brought the case. Once the case came to arbitration (and the plaintiff had received his payoff from Phormion), Lampis changed his position, claiming that he had in fact received the money—and had been out of his mind when he made his previous statement.[69] The plaintiff tells this story himself, and then introduces witnesses to support it: to modern eyes, this is hearsay evidence. Harrison, suggesting that this case "may be an exception proving the rule," argues that the introduction of this evidence may have been allowed because Lampis was "almost a party to the suit."[70] This argument seems compelling, insofar as the speaker refers to Lampis as "an accomplice in the crime."[71] But other, more technical reasons may also be significant: first, it is possible that Lampis was in fact a slave, which would mean that his evidence could not be produced in court other than by a third party.[72] More tentatively, it is also possible that the justification for submission of third-party evidence lay in the claim made by Lampis (and repeated during the case) that he had been out of his mind when he made his first statement about the money.[73] To begin with, evidence suggests that madmen were not deemed to be criminally responsible.[74] But that aside, the implication would have been that Lampis' previous insane self could not be called to give evidence, since he was no longer in that state. This was then, in effect, the provision of evidence about a dead or absent party.[75]

These different procedures provided some regulation of the introduction of reported information into the courtroom; they reveal awareness of the potential for abuse of a system that relied on information that had been heard by third parties. So too, perhaps, does the introduction of written depositions for evidence (ca. 380 BCE). This may have reinforced the reliability of evidence, insofar as it turned what was heard into what was read—and therefore seen. Michael Gagarin has argued that "the process for presenting these documents in court underlies the fundamental division Aristotle establishes for forensic rhetoric": that is, these written documents conform to Aristotle's non-artistic proofs as opposed to artistic ones.[76] But there may still have been some ambiguity: after all, the witnesses were still required to be present in court.[77] Moreover, written evidence was no indication of objectivity: Todd suggests that, during the fourth century, "Athenians juries . . . remained consistently and deeply suspicious of unattested written documents."[78] Some of our sources suggest that suspicion may also have been extended to those witnesses' statements that were often written by the litigant himself.[79]

In sum, in a legal system that relied on assessments of the lives and characters of the litigants, the role of "evaluative social talk"—what we would call "gossip"—often played a crucial role.[80] This section has discussed some of the ways in which the legal context structured the presentation of that kind of information. The emphasis on personal testimony reflected the epistemological frameworks of this culture, in which firsthand knowledge was highly valued. But the focus on the liability of those who volunteered such information suggests that there was a concomitant emphasis on the importance of individuals taking responsibility for their reports.

As well as giving insight into the difference between ancient and modern definitions of hearsay, this analysis also provides better understanding of the role and framing of "gossip" in the courts. The kinds of statements examined in the preceding section ("Facts and Framings"), which attributed knowledge to everyone, carried epistemological power, since they appealed to an apparent wealth of firsthand knowledge. But because no named individual delivered the information, no one was legally liable for its presence in the courtroom—other than the speaker, of course. I stress here the sense of *legal* liability, since, by appealing to the general knowledge of all those who were present, the speaker's formulation could be said to be implicating everyone present. This strategy of suggesting the collective guilt of the *dikastai* was used explicitly in lawcourt speeches, strongly suggesting that it was a rhetorical feint that exerted some leverage.[81]

Building on this argument, the next section of this chapter turns to a closer examination of the speeches in the case study, exploring how each speaker frames and deploys the story of the murder of Nicodemus. Drawing on the socio-cognitive linguistic theory of Teun van Dijk, it argues that the strategic deployment of particular kinds of information offered one possible and important technique by which individual litigants could define the specific constructions of their cases.

Telling Stories

Corruption and Betrayal

The first three examples of the use of this story occur in speeches made by Demosthenes' enemies. In each case, the emphasis of the account is on a different aspect of the story. The variations demonstrate how one event can be employed to help shape the discourse of a court case and thus to establish the parameters of the case itself.

Aeschines' first extant mention of the murder of Nicodemus, in the speech *Against Timarchus*, is something of a sleight of hand. It is intended to draw attention away from accusations he states Demosthenes will make, involving Aeschines' behavior toward Alexander of Macedon during the embassy to Philip, a smaller part, presumably, of the larger charge of treason. Demosthenes' accusations will, apparently, suggest a sexual aspect, through the use of certain terms. Aeschines' response is to establish his opponent as a far worse offender in this respect, by telling the court the story of Nicodemus' murder and by placing his emphasis not on the killing but on Demosthenes' relationship with Aristarchus. Aeschines stresses how Aristarchus was one of a number of fatherless young men whose relationship with Demosthenes fitted a particular pattern; nowadays, we might describe it as "grooming."[82]

The story is framed as informal discourse. The phrase with which it begins—"I will omit many instances, and will mention only one of those who were outrageously treated"—is similar to those introductions to gossip that are found elsewhere (as noted above). This pointed anecdote is, as in other instances of gossip, intended to provide us with information about a person's character; it makes clear (as if it were needed) that Aeschines' case against Timarchus is aimed also at Demosthenes. The story of Aristarchus offers a report on the character of Aeschines' primary enemy and, as a story of corruption, it not only reinforces the case against Timarchus, but is itself strengthened by appearing in this context.

Aeschines enfolds this information in a rhetorical appeal to the jurors, which not only stresses the horror of the crime but also underlines the potential dangers of inaction by the dikasts. He compares Demosthenes to Socrates: "Did you put to death Socrates the sophist, fellow citizens, because he was shown to have been the teacher of Critias, one of the Thirty who put down the democracy, and after that, shall Demosthenes succeed in snatching companions of his own out of your hands, Demosthenes, who takes such vengeance on private citizens and friends of the people for their freedom of speech?"[83] The comparison makes an explicit plea to the dikasts to recognize that they should punish Demosthenes just as they punished Socrates, but its terms reinforce, and are reinforced by, the story of Nicodemus' murder and the particular emphasis that Aeschines has put on it. Without referring explicitly here to Aristarchus, the analogy with Socrates draws attention to the dangers of the teacher-pupil relationship. Moreover, the reference to free speech is a reminder of the mutilation of Nicodemus, whose tongue, as Aeschines has just told us, was ripped out: thus, here, Aeschines also implicitly accuses Demosthenes of murder. The informal information about the murder, coupled with the comparison of the case of Socrates, vividly depicts Demosthenes as a corruptor of individuals, a murderer, a threat to the city and its democracy. But in addition, as noted above, the introduction of this informal information also implicates the *dikastai* in the fate of their community, underlining their responsibility to protect the young—and their likely guilt if they do not.

Aeschines' second employment of these events, in *On the Embassy*, shows a marked change of both emphasis and tone. The accusations against Demosthenes are stated more baldly: Aristarchus is mentioned, but here the main point of the story is the murder itself. Although Aeschines is careful not to deny that Aristarchus was the main protagonist, he nevertheless implies that Demosthenes was closely involved, by stating that Demosthenes should not enter the marketplace because he has been polluted—presumably through association with the murderer. Aeschines does not support this statement with any kind of testimony or reference to general knowledge, but leaves it as a bald accusation.

The story's use here seems, at first sight, tenuous: Aeschines seems to be assembling any material he can that might indicate that Demosthenes lacks the qualities of a citizen, in terms of either his character or his current status. The accusation receives almost no special emphasis, but appears as just one of a number of observations about the nature of Demosthenes' character. In the framing of this information, however, Aeschines develops a very specific sense of the situation. He creates for the dikasts a vivid picture of the network of citizens and family that surrounds him. His accusations against Demosthenes involve a roll call of individuals who are present in the courtroom. Thus, again, the Aristarchus anecdote is enfolded in the larger story of the city and citizenry who have suffered at Demosthenes' hands and, thus, draws attention to the need for the *dikastai* to protect their own. This approach comes to a climax when Aeschines calls a witness, Aristophanes of Olynthus, to testify to Demosthenes' attempts to persuade him to blacken Aeschines' character (155–56).[84]

And finally, we come to Dinarchus' use of the story (323 BCE). Again, the account is told with a particular emphasis that helps to define Dinarchus' charge against Demosthenes. Here, the speaker underlines neither the murder nor the corruption of a youth but the betrayal of a friend. Dinarchus seeks to show that Demosthenes simply cannot be trusted—indeed, is a liability as a politician acting for Athens. Whether deliberately or not, Dinarchus appears to echo the language used by Aeschines of Demosthenes in *Against Ctesiphon* (330 BCE), which evokes the idea that Demosthenes has or is an evil *daimon* for the city.[85] The result, again, is that the introduction of gossip generates a familiar discourse in which the *dikastai* are called upon to protect their city. The reference to this well-known, but unsubstantiated and unattributed, accusation against Demosthenes creates a context of collusion in the courtroom, in which those who hear this story are called upon to protect their community.

Murderer . . . or Victim?

One of the many problems for historians confronted by this material is the question of its historical value. Aeschines' account of the murder in *Against Timarchus* does suggest that there were such stories circulating. This suspicion is reinforced by the attention that Demosthenes pays to this charge in *Against Meidias*, and is further strengthened by the nature of Demosthenes' approach. The basis for his account is remarkably thin: it is clear from what he says that, in an official civic setting, Meidias was seen and heard to accuse Aristarchus. As noted above, Demosthenes must introduce reports (of reports) of gossip and bribery to support his argument that Meidias accused him. This may be why Demosthenes implicitly repositions himself in this section of the speech so that, in a number of ways, he appears to be in the role of a defendant. This repositioning is achieved, in part, through the adoption of certain rhetorical strategies: for example, as Demosthenes describes how Meidias tried to persuade Nicodemus' family to prosecute him for the murder, he is, in effect, providing a typical defendant's counternarrative, offering a different version of events from that which Meidias (now cast in the role of prosecutor) was apparently promulgating.[86]

Crucially, there is in fact no original prosecution narrative; the dikasts have only Demosthenes' versions of both accusation and defense. It is perhaps no surprise to find Demosthenes marking Meidias' reported accusations as gossip of a kind that is to be despised. Demosthenes effects this categorization through the use of a phrase found elsewhere to evoke the activities of those who gossip: "going around [in this case the marketplace] spreading stories."[87] But although he uses this dismissive language, he does not stop there: he simultaneously suggests that Meidias' accusations in this respect were somehow impious (*asebema*).

The introduction of impiety reinforces a larger argument, made across the speech, that establishes Meidias as a threat not just to Demosthenes but also to the *dikastai*, the wider city, and indeed, the city's relationship with the gods.[88] At the end of the speech, Demosthenes challenges the jurors to defend their city from the likes of Meidias. Here, we see him foreshadowing this argument when, at the end of this passage, he asks the jurors, "What compassion shall he deserve at your hands?"[89] This plea marks another characteristic of such defensive counternarratives: the idea that Demosthenes is a murderer has been transformed into an accusation of murder against Meidias.[90] Here, it also eases the audience back into the main narrative, since it is subsumed into, and reinforces, a broader charge against Meidias, of hubris, a charge that pervades Demosthenes' case against Meidias of "wrongdoing concerning a festival."[91] Finally, as we have seen, this introduction of impiety is a way of turning his accuser's use of gossip back against him: through the unattributed report of this informal information, Demosthenes has been depicted as a threat to the community, and his response is to accuse his enemy of the same charge.

Conclusion

As this last example demonstrates, "gossip" or informal, evaluative talk, used skillfully, could acquire a crucial weight in the context of the courtroom. Scholars have noted its role in reflecting social values, but this chapter's analysis has suggested that gossip's role was more complex and significant than that. To begin with, the examination of the various ways in which informal information was framed and regulated gives insight into the epistemological framework of this culture. Above all, the deployment of this kind of information in speeches draws particular attention to the importance allocated to firsthand experience, which resonates with evidence from other, nonforensic sources. This insight in turn, highlights the ethical dimension of this epistemology. An examination of the regulation of this kind of information reveals that witnesses and rapporteurs of various kinds had to be prepared to take responsibility for the information they provided. Again, as the case study illustrates, gossip was a powerful strategy for introducing information for which, for one reason or another, no one could or would take responsibility: what if that information was simply too dangerous to attribute to anyone?

Finally, while the legal context, with its conventions, rules, and procedures, shaped the ways in which this kind of information was used in forensic discourse (influencing what could be considered relevant evidence, why, and how it should be framed), examination of the diverse ways in which individual speakers strategically deployed such information as evidence reveals how gossip was a key rhetorical resource for a speaker in constructing and defining a case. In particular, it was used to draw attention to specific people and to portray their character and actions as risks that potentially threatened the city and its citizens.[92] As the case study shows, litigants might introduce this kind of information into a case not only to reflect on character (their own or, more usually, that of their opponent) or to evoke social mores (with some attempt to elicit social disapproval), but also with more specific epistemological considerations: for example, to redirect the attention of the dikasts, to underline an implicit theme of the speech, or to refine perceptions of the initial charge. In sum, in the fourth-century Athenian law courts, gossip was not so much "idle talk" but, rather, a powerful form of "social action."[93]

Notes

1. Ralph Rosnow, "Rumor and Gossip in Interpersonal Interaction and Beyond: A Social Exchange Perspective," in *Behaving Badly: Aversive Behaviors in Interpersonal Relationships*, ed. Robin M. Kowalski (Washington, DC: American Psychological Association, 2001), 201–11. I have discussed definitions of gossip at some length, so I keep my remarks here to a minimum. See Esther Eidinow, *Envy, Poison, and Death: Women on Trial in Classical Athens* (Oxford: Oxford University Press, 2016), especially 171–79.

2. See especially Virginia Hunter, *Policing Athens: Social Control in the Attic Lawsuits, 420–320 B.C.* (Princeton: Princeton University Press, 1994); Adriaan Lanni, "Social Sanctions in Classical Athens," in *Symposion 2011: Études d'histoire du droit grec et hellenistique (Paris, 7–10 septembre 2011)*, ed. B. Legras and G. Thür, Akten der Gesellschaft für griechische und hellenistische Rechtsgeschichte 23 (Vienna: Austrian Academy of Sciences Press, 2012), 99–110; Lanni, *Law and Order in Ancient Athens* (Cambridge: Cambridge University Press, 2016), 17–46.

3. In making such an analysis, I return to a theme raised by Sally Humphreys in "Social Relations on Stage: Witnesses in Classical Athens," *History and Anthropology* 1, no. 2 (1985): 313–72. Her examination of the identity and role of witnesses is structured by the question of "the bases of authority and the social factors influencing perception" (314). She argues that "the selection and presentation of witnesses was designed to recreate in court the social context from which the litigant had been detached" (316).

4. See Hunter, *Policing Athens: Social Control in the Attic Lawsuits.*

5. Teun A. van Dijk, *Discourse and Context: A Sociocognitive Approach* (Cambridge: Cambridge University Press, 2008), ix.

6. I alluded to this story in Eidinow, *Envy, Poison, and Death*, 257–60; the present chapter gives me the opportunity to examine it in in greater detail.

7. Dem. 21.103–4; Aeschin. 2.148. Demosthenes argues (103) that Meidias was behind this prosecution, that Meidias planned it after attacking Demosthenes in the theater in 348/7; Demosthenes returned to serve as *choregos* (responsible for funding a dramatic or lyric chorus) at the Great Dionysia.

8. Aeschin. 1.170–73 (trans. here and below, Charles Darwin Adams, trans., *The Speeches of Aeschines* [Cambridge, MA: Harvard University Press, 1919]; here slightly revised).

9. Aeschin. 2.148–49 (trans. Adams 1919).

10. For a full account of these events and the trials that ensued, see Ian Worthington, *Demosthenes of Athens and the Fall of Classical Greece* (Oxford: Oxford University Press, 2015), especially chap. 14.

11. Din. 1.30–31 (trans. here and below, J. O. Burtt, trans., *Minor Attic Orators*, vol. 2: *Lycurgus, Dinarchus, Demades, Hyperides* [Cambridge, MA: Harvard University Press, 1954]).

12. Din. 1.47.

13. Dem. 21.104–22 (trans. here and below, J. H. Vince, trans., *Demosthenes, Orations*, vol. 3: *Orations 21–26* [Cambridge, MA: Harvard University Press, 1935]).

14. Dem. 21.104 (trans. Vince). See Douglas MacDowell, ed. and trans., *Demosthenes, "Against Meidias" (Oration 21)* (Oxford: Clarendon, 1990).

15. Dem. 21.104–5.

16. Dem. 21.116–19.

17. Demosthenes tells the story at 21.104, attributing statements to Meidias; at 21.107, the kinsmen of Aristarchus testify to what Meidias had said to them in the process of trying to bribe them.

18. Any of the speakers may have intended that their account lead to a homicide charge, but if so, they were unsuccessful. Although Demosthenes' enemies apparently persisted in introducing this story into both the formal setting of the courtroom and the informal arena of the agora, there is no certain evidence that Demosthenes was ever prosecuted on a charge of murder. While discussing Demosthenes' use of relative terms, Aristotle (*Rhet.* 2.23.3) refers to a trial in which Demosthenes and those who killed

"Nicanor" were concerned. Dionysius of Halicarnassus (*Ep. ad Am.* 1.12) notes that this is the speech made by Demosthenes on behalf of Ctesiphon (*On the Crown*), but that speech makes no mention of this murder, so there seems to be some confusion in the sources.

19. Chris Carey calls this material introduced into Aeschines 1 "an irrelevant character assassination," in *Aeschines* (Austin: University of Texas Press, 2000), 22.

20. See Stephen Todd and Paul Millett, "Law, Society and Athens," in *Nomos: Essays in Athenian Law, Politics and Society*, ed. Paul Cartledge, Stephen Todd, and Paul Millett (Cambridge: Cambridge University Press, 1990), 1–18, at 5.

21. See Todd and Millett, "Law, Society and Athens," 14; Robin Osborne, "Law in Action in Classical Athens," *Journal of Hellenic Studies* 105 (1985): 40–58.

22. David Cohen, *Law, Violence, and Community in Classical Athens* (Cambridge: Cambridge University Press, 1995), 183.

23. David Mirhady, "Knowing the Law and Deciding Justice: Lay Expertise in the Democratic Athenian Courts," *Comparative Legal History* 3, no. 2 (2015): 231–44, at 233.

24. Mirhady seems to suggest this aspect in his discussion of the activities of arbitrators: "Emphasis here was clearly put on the experience that came from age and lengthy active participation in order to achieve an ideal of justice rather than a strict reading of law or the blunt winner-take-all demands of one side or the other" ("Knowing the Law," 243). To what extent these values and attitudes were shared is a question raised by Todd and Millett ("Law, Society and Athens," 13). See also Kenneth J. Dover, *Greek Popular Morality in the Time of Plato and Aristotle* (Berkeley: University of California Press, 1974).

25. Hunter, *Policing Athens*, 96. Lanni's "Social Sanctions in Classical Athens" (the basis for Lanni, *Law and Order in Ancient Athens*, 20–33, where the argument is developed) argues for a modified version of this approach (in which the courts play a crucial role in enforcing social sanctions and internalized norms), but rejects what Lanni reads as Hunter's picture of a highly coercive environment (citing Hunter, *Policing Athens*; Cohen, *Law, Violence, and Community in Classical Athens*, 88–94).

26. On the role of gossip bringing the private into the public realm, see Aeschin. 1.127.

27. Lanni, "Social Sanctions in Classical Athens," 108.

28. See Lanni, "Social Sanctions in Classical Athens"; Lanni, *Law and Order in Ancient Athens.*

29. Lanni, "Social Sanctions in Classical Athens," 104; and Lanni, *Law and Order in Ancient Athens*, 27. Lanni stresses that the idea "implicit in the scholarship that emphasizes informal social control" that violation of community norms would lead not just to talk but also to material loss and social sanction may be exaggerated.

30. Robert Wallace, "The Legal Regulation of Private Conduct at Athens: Two Controversies on Freedom," *Etica e Politica* 9, no. 1 (2007): 155–71, at 171.

31. Wallace, "Legal Regulation of Private Conduct," 170.

32. See Paul Cartledge, "Fowl Play: A Curious Lawsuit in Classical Athens," in Cartledge, Todd, and Millett, *Nomos* (Cambridge: Cambridge University Press, 1990), 41–61. Cartledge notes how the *agon* of litigation revealed the "relative *time* of the opposing litigants" (55).

33. As Demosthenes portrays Meidias and his actions; on the development of this theme in *Against Meidias*, see Esther Eidinow, "Ancient Greek Religion: Embedded . . . and Embodied," in *Communities and Networks in the Ancient Greek World*, ed. Claire Taylor and Kostas Vlassopoulos (Oxford: Oxford University Press, 2015), 54–79.

34. Niko Besnier, *Gossip and the Everyday Production of Politics* (Honolulu: University of Hawaii Press, 2009), 124.

35. Aeschin. 1.170.

36. Isae. 5.39 (Edward Seymour Forster, trans., *Isaeus* [Cambridge, MA: Harvard University Press, 1927]): "Everyone saw [Dicaeogenes'] mother seated in the shrine of Eileithyia and charging him with acts which I am ashamed to mention but which he was not ashamed to commit"; Dem. 57.61 (A. T. Murray, trans., *Demosthenes, Orations*, vol. VI: *Orations 50–59* [Cambridge, MA: Harvard University Press, 1939]): "These facts all the older ones know"; Dem. 18.129 (C. A. Vince and J. H. Vince, trans., *Demosthenes, Orations*, vol. 2: *Orations 18–19* [Cambridge, MA: Harvard University Press, 1926]): "everybody knows that without being told by me"; Andoc. 1.139 (K. J. Maidment, trans., *Minor Attic Orators I* [Cambridge: Harvard University Press, 1941]): "whom every one of you sitting in this court knows too well to trust with anything belonging to him." See also Dem. 39.16, 54.34; [Dem.] 45.63–65, 70; [Dem.] 58.28; Din. 1.30; Din. 2.8, 11; Lys. 6.32; Isoc. 17.33–34.

37. This ambiguity is nicely summarized in the comments of the Athenian envoys (Thuc. 1.73.2; C. Forster Smith, trans., *Thucydides*, vol. 1 [Cambridge, MA: Harvard University Press, 1919]): "[2] But what need we now to speak of matters long past, confirmed more by hearsay than by the eyes of those that are to hear us relate them?" (καὶ τὰ μὲν πάνυ παλαιὰ τί δεῖ λέγειν, ὧν ἀκοαὶ μᾶλλον λόγων μάρτυρες ἢ ὄψις τῶν ἀκουσομένων;) Other examples where sight is stressed over hearsay as a source of knowledge include Hdt. 2.147.1, 2.148.6; Diod. 13.32; Paus. 5.12, 9.39; Dem. 4.47, 38.7; Aesch. *PV* 338–39; Soph. *Trach.* 744–47; Phil. 676; Eur. *IT* 900; Eur. *Hel.* 117–18.

38. Dem. 21.104–7, 119.

39. Stephen Todd, "The Purpose of Evidence in Athenian Courts," in Cartledge, Todd, and Millett, *Nomos*, 27, citing Sally Humphreys, "Introduction: Law, Anthropology and History; Law as Discourse," *History and Anthropology* 1, no. 2 (1985): 241–64. From Todd's analysis of the term *martus* in other literary contexts, it is clear that it was not understood to indicate a neutral source of information. See Dem. 43.9–10, 30. Cf. Apollodorus, *Against Stephanus* 2.46.4 (trans. Murray): "Otherwise you would not know whether what they severally say is true or false, if they did not bring forward the witnesses also. But when they do bring in witnesses, you rely upon these as being respon-

sible, and so from the statements and the testimony offered you cast your votes for what seems to you to be a just verdict."

40. Humphreys, "Social Relations on Stage," 350.

41. Humphreys, "Social Relations on Stage," 324. Humphreys gives the examples of [Dem.] 43 and Dem. 57.

42. Aeschin. 2.148–49.

43. Dem. 21.104–5.

44. An example of *dike kakagorias* occurs when the speaker in Lysias' *Against Theomnestos* brings a case for a slander uttered against him in an earlier hearing (when Theomnestos characterized the speaker as a parricide); see Stephen Todd, *The Shape of Athenian Law* (Oxford: Oxford University Press, 1993), 259 (it may be that Lys. 10.12 offers another example, if the emendation of Lysitheos for Theon is accepted, Lysitheos having been the plaintiff of the original trial against Theomnestos).

45. Lys. 9.6–12; Todd, *Shape of Athenian Law*, 260.

46. Lys. 9.6.

47. Lys. 9.9.

48. In *The Law in Classical Athens* (Ithaca: Cornell University Press, 1978), 128, Douglas MacDowell argues that, as the speaker argues, the law probably did include synonyms, and that it was sufficient defense to be able to argue that what had been said was true, but Todd (*Shape of Athenian Law*, 260–61) disagrees. There were likely to have been other forbidden insults, further to those mentioned in this speech (see MacDowell, *Law in Classical Athens*, 128), such as abuse of citizens for working in the marketplace (Dem. 57.30), along with laws concerning the abuse of magistrates.

49. E.g., Todd, *Shape of Athenian Law*, 260–61; MacDowell, *Law in Classical Athens*, 127–28.

50. Lys. 9.10 (adapted).

51. Lys. 10.1–3.

52. In the mid-fifth century, it appears to have been possible for someone other than the victim to bring this case, but Dem. 48.45 suggests that this rule changed in the fourth century. See MacDowell, *Law in Classical Athens*, 244.

53. See MacDowell, *Law in Classical Athens*, 245.

54. Todd, "Purpose of Evidence," 28.

55. In his discussion of the main methods of proof, Todd ("Purpose of Evidence," 22) raises the subject of hearsay and opinion but does not pursue it in detail. Cf. Hunter (*Policing Athens*, 108) who elides "innuendo, rumor, hearsay, and gossip."

56. LSJ s.v. ἀκοή, ἡ.

57. Dem. 57.4–5 (trans. Murray).

58. [Dem.] 46.6–8 (trans. Murray).

59. A. R. W. Harrison, *The Law of Athens* (Oxford: Oxford University Press, 1971), 2:146. See Isae. 3.20; Dem. 46.2.7; Aeschin. 2.19; Dein. fr. 60. Dem. 35.20, 33 for the depositions of several witnesses (it is contested as to whether they are genuine or forgeries).

60. See Robert J. Bonner and Gertrude Smith, *The Administration of Justice from Homer to Aristotle* (Chicago: University of Chicago Press, 1938), 2:134, on the confusion between extrajudicial evidence and hearsay in the lexicographers and some speeches (e.g., Is. 3.77).

61. Harrison (*Law of Athens*, 146–47) suggests that the one who had evidence falsely attributed to him would have had a *dike blabes* against those who confirmed the deposition and against the litigant who introduced it into the case; similarly, there was probably a procedure against the witness who falsely repudiated evidence.

62. Todd, "Purpose of Evidence," 29. For other examples, see Robert Bonner, *Evidence in Athenian Courts* (Chicago: University of Chicago Press, 1905), 20–23.

63. As Harrison has observed (*Law of Athens*, 145), bringing such a charge would only test whether the living witness had heard the dead/absent witness testify; it did not test whether that person had said it or not.

64. Harrison, *Law of Athens*, 145.

65. For studies primarily concerned with North American approaches, see R. A. Clark, "The Changing Face of the Rule against Hearsay in English Law," *Akron Law Review* 21, no. 1 (1988): art. 4; Roger C. Park, Peter Miene, and Eugene Borgida, "Juror Decision Making and the Evaluation of Hearsay Evidence," *Minnesota Law Review* 76 (1992): 683–701; Roger C. Park, Margaret Bull Kovera, and Steven D. Penrod, "Jurors' Perceptions of Eyewitness and Hearsay Evidence," *Minnesota Law Review* 76 (1992): 703–22; Andrew Paglia and Regina Schuller, "Jurors' Use of Hearsay Evidence: The Effects of Type and Timing of Instructions," *Law and Human Behavior* 22, no. 5 (1998): 501–18; Paul Roberts and Adrian Zuckerman, *Criminal Evidence*, 2nd ed. (Oxford: Oxford University Press, 2010), especially chap. 9, on the CPS "Hearsay" and UK Criminal Justice Act (2003).

66. Stephan Landsman and Richard F. Rakos, "Research Essay: A Preliminary Empirical Enquiry concerning the Prohibition of Hearsay Evidence in American Courts," *Law & Psychology Review* 65 (1991): 66–85. See Park, Kovera, and Penrod, "Jurors' Perceptions"; Park, Miene and Borgida, "Juror Decision Making," 684–85; Roberts and Zuckerman, "Criminal Evidence," especially 401–2.

67. Harrison, *Law of Athens*, 145: "whether the sex of the witness was relevant here we cannot say."

68. See Todd, "Purpose of Evidence," 28. The speaker refers to the wife "agreeing" or "acknowledging" (forms of ὁμολογέω) that the seals were genuine.

69. Dem. 34.20

70. Harrison, *Law of Athens*, 146n1.

71. Dem. 34.46.

72. See Dem. 34.5, 10. Todd (*Shape of Athenian Law*, 192–93) includes Lampis in his discussion of the rights and duties of typical slaves: as Todd notes, the speech does not make clear the current status of Lampis or that a distinction between present and former slave status would not have mattered to the court.

73. Dem. 34.20, 35, 49: the Greek is literally "being within."

74. On the criminal liability of the insane, see Agnes Carr Vaughn, *Madness in Greek Thought and Custom* (Madison: University of Wisconsin Press, 1919), 59–69.

75. In *On the Embassy* (2.55), Aeschines calls Aristophanes (an Olynthian) to give evidence that Demosthenes had asked him to substantiate a discreditable story about Aeschines, then he calls men who were present when Aristophanes told Aeschines about what Demosthenes had done. Harrison (*Law of Athens*, 146) argues that this testimony is barely hearsay, since Aristophanes himself had already given evidence, which is true; more straightforwardly, it may have escaped criticism as hearsay because the witnesses were only testifying to the fact that they had heard a particular story from Aristophanes, even though including their testimony reinforces the evidence about Demosthenes' wrongdoing.

76. Michael Gagarin, *Writing Greek Law* (Cambridge: Cambridge University Press, 2008), 189–91. According to Aristotle, *pisteis entechnoi* are produced by the art of the orator (Aristot. *Rhet.* 1355b35), as opposed to proofs that do not require such art, *pisteis atechnoi*, which include laws, witnesses, agreements, tortures, and oaths (1375a24–25).

77. Bonner and Smith, *Administration of Justice*, 357. As noted there, the witnesses may have been required to face the judges (see Andoc. 1.18); thus, it is perhaps unsurprising that this approach may also have been boosted by an accumulation of witnesses (see Isae. 3.21).

78. Todd, "Purpose of Evidence," 29n15.

79. Dem. 43.38–47, 54.26

80. Cohen, *Law, Violence, and Community in Classical Athens*, 188: "the speakers invite the judges to compare their lives, they open themselves to a formal and ritualized form of the kind of public scrutiny and evaluation which operates in informal ways through the politics of reputation in so many societies."

81. E.g., see Dem. 59.110–11, when the speaker imagines the responses of the *dikastai*'s female relatives on hearing that Neaera has been acquitted.

82. Aeschin. 1.171.

83. Aeschin. 1.173.

84. On the use of this witness in this context, see n. 77.

85. See Esther Eidinow, *Luck, Fate and Fortune: Antiquity and Its Legacy* (London: Tauris, 2011), 143–50.

86. On the different kinds of counternarrative used in defense speeches, see Steven Johnstone, *Disputes and Democracy: The Consequences of Litigation in Ancient Athens* (Austin: University of Texas Press, 1999), 56–57.

87. Dem. 21.104 (cf. Din. 1.32; Dem. 4.48–49, 6.14, 18.127, 21.198).

88. See Eidinow, "Ancient Greek Religion."

89. See especially Dem. 21.213–22, foreshadowed at 21.105.

90. See Lys. 3, *Against Simon*. For this and further examples, see Johnstone, *Disputes and Democracy*, 56–57.

91. On the *probole* charge in this instance, see MacDowell, *Demosthenes, "Against Meidias,"* especially 16–17.

92. In this sense, it perhaps has more in common with modern definitions of "rumor": see, e.g., Nicholas DiFonzo and Prashant Bordia, *Rumor Psychology: Social and Organizational Approaches* (Washington, DC: American Psychological Association, 2007), where the authors argue that rumors comprise "unverified statements, arising in contexts of ambiguity, used to make sense of puzzles that seem to contain an element of danger or risk." In the case of Nicodemus, for example, Demosthenes' opponents try to elevate gossip to the level of rumor, using it across a variety of contexts to highlight the risk that Demosthenes presents; on theories of gossip with reference to a different set of trials, see Eidinow, *Envy, Poison, and Death*.

93. See Eidinow, *Envy, Poison, and Death*, 8.

CHAPTER 6

Truth and Athenian Court Verdicts

Adriaan Lanni

The primary role of the trial in the Western tradition has been to make determinations of fact. As Blackstone wrote in the eighteenth century, "experience will abundantly show, that above a hundred of our lawsuits arise from disputed facts, for one where the law is doubted of."[1] Much of the development of the law of evidence and procedure in medieval and early modern Europe and England can be traced to anxiety about how to handle "hard cases" where definitive proof of the facts is unavailable, particularly where conviction would result in capital punishment. The ordeal handed over to divine judgment only those criminal cases in which the truth could not be determined from witness or documentary evidence or where the case could not be resolved by compurgation (that is, the use of oath helpers to support a defendant's oath of innocence).[2] When the ordeal was abandoned on the Continent, anxiety over the fallibility of human judgment engendered a strict system of proof aimed at factual accuracy. In serious cases, conviction required two eyewitnesses or a confession; torture could be used to obtain a confession only in the presence of half proof (typically one eyewitness or significant circumstantial evidence) and could be carried out only according to complicated rules designed to elicit a reliable confession.[3] In England, the ordeal was replaced primarily by lay juries. Scholars have pointed out the counterintuitive similarities between the ordeal and trial by jury: just as in the case of the ordeal, the inscrutability of the jury verdict obscured any factual doubts or deficiencies in proof.[4]

While medieval and early modern trial procedures[5] were designed largely to generate factual accuracy or at least a decision whose factual accuracy could not be easily challenged,[6] an Athenian popular court verdict generally did not represent a simple determination of fact. In many popular court cases, the resolution of factual disputes was intertwined with and subsumed within broader normative judgments. The analysis in this chapter shows that the broader role of the Athenian popular court jury had important implications for the Athenian court procedure and the meaning of verdicts. The procedures of the special homicide courts, by contrast, *do* seem to have been designed to focus litigants, witnesses, and jurors narrowly on the circumstances of the death that were the basis of the charge. However, the focus on narrow fact-finding in the homicide courts seems to have grown out of a practical need to encourage compliance with verdicts and limit vendetta, rather than from a commitment to getting at the truth as an independent goal of the trial.

The Meaning of Athenian Popular Court Verdicts

In the popular courts, the Athenians favored a discretionary rather than formal or numerical approach to proof that empowered jurors to make normative judgments about the broad context of the dispute rather than focus narrowly on disputed questions of fact relating to the charge. This approach had important implications for evidence law and procedure and particularly for the meaning of popular court verdicts and their role in the ability of courts to adapt to changing norms and circumstances.

A Discretionary Approach to Proof

One of the distinctive aspects of the Athenian legal system is the exclusive reliance on discretionary rather than formal modes of proof and on human rather than divine legitimation of legal decisions. Formal modes of proof are known from at least the time of Hammurabi's code, which provides for ordeals and the use of decisive oaths. The Gortyn code uses a mixture of formal and discretionary forms of proof. Judges in Gortyn have two distinct functions: in some cases, a judge is to give judgment (*dikadden*) according to nondiscretionary rules of proof, such as a specified number of witnesses or an oath; in other cases, the judge takes an oath and judges according to his discretion. It appears that the Athenians rarely, if ever, used formal modes of proof in court. The number of witnesses supporting each litigant had no predefined significance in an Athenian court.[7] Although oaths were used in various contexts, yet in most cases, the resulting evidence was persuasive but not decisive (as, for example, when a litigant swears an oath or imposes one on a reluctant witness).[8] There is, however, some evidence that accepting an opponent's challenge to swear an oath was decisive, though in practice it seems that such challenges were generally worded in such a way as to guarantee that they would not be accepted.[9]

Athenian popular court verdicts were not only discretionary judgments. They also represented the product of human reason, without any pretense to divine intervention or justification. Aside from the oaths sworn by litigants and jurors,[10] there is little evidence of the divine in the procedures of the popular courts, the largest jurisdiction in the Athenian system. (The homicide courts, discussed below, may be a partial exception.) While the use of a lottery in the popular courts might be conceived of as the introduction of randomness to permit divine participation, in Athens the lot was the standard mechanism for choosing magistrates and jurors, and seems to have been introduced not for religious reasons but primarily to prevent the accumulation of power by individual magistrates. It is true that the random selection procedure used to assign members of the jury pool to individual courtrooms was unusually elaborate and filled with fanfare.[11] Yet this complex procedure need not suggest divine participation in juror selection. It seems more likely that this juror selection ritual was intended to prevent bribery of jurors and to instill in the jurors, who were formally unaccountable for their verdicts, a sense of the seriousness of their task.[12]

What of divine intervention in the verdict itself? Ancient voting systems often included some provision for the gods to affect the outcome. The voting procedure at the Athenian dramatic festival the Dionysia, for example, seems to have included the possibility of divine intervention. Although a representative of each of the ten tribes cast a ballot, only five ballots were counted initially. If one of the three competitors had a majority of the five votes selected, they were declared the winner, even though it was possible that the "winner" actually had not received the highest number of the ten ballots cast.[13] This procedure is commonly interpreted in theological terms: Dionysus is "the ultimate theatrical arbiter."[14] The use of the lot in the election procedure in Roman tribal assemblies similarly has been interpreted as a mechanism to permit Jupiter to influence the outcome.[15] By contrast, there is no suggestion in our sources that the gods influence Athenian jury verdicts. Interestingly, when prospective litigants created "curse-tablets" against their opponents, they commonly asked that the gods interfere with the opposing litigant's presentation, by, for example, making him tongue-tied in court, but they do not request that the gods insure a favorable verdict. Finally, it is worth noting that notions of informal juror accountability tend to take the form of informal social sanctions by fellow citizens rather than divine punishment. Litigants in the popular courts warn jurors that an unfair verdict will tarnish their worldly reputations and ask jurors to contemplate how they will defend their verdict when questioned by the spectators as they leave the courtroom, but do not threaten divine sanctions for an incorrect verdict.[16]

The Subordination of Facts to Normative Judgments

So far, I have argued that popular court verdicts reflect the discretionary judgment of lay jurors. But what were Athenian jurors expected to decide? I have argued at length elsewhere that Athenian juries did not simply determine whether the factual elements of the charge were met, but rather aimed at reaching a just resolution that incorporated the broader context of the dispute, general notions of fairness, and sentencing considerations.[17] According to this view, Athenian litigants could present jurors with a wide variety of legal and extralegal arguments, and it was up to the jury to decide (and the litigants to make a case for) which types of information were most important in reaching a just outcome to the particular case.[18] I won't repeat the case for that interpretation of the jurors' role here. Instead I want to focus more narrowly on the comparative point that while the purpose of many trials in the Western tradition, including modern trials, is to resolve disputed questions of fact, Athenian popular court verdicts rarely turned on a simple question of fact. The broader conception of the jury's role had important implications for the Athenian approach to evidence and procedure.

To be sure, there are many questions of disputed fact in our surviving Athenian cases, and litigants attempt to prove through argument and evidence that their version of the facts is correct. But it is striking that even where the charge would suggest that the case should turn on a straightforward factual question, litigants go to great lengths to argue that justice, in a broad sense, is on their side. Demosthenes' *Against Nicostratus* provides an example. The suit is an *apographe*, a procedure through which any Athenian citizen could proclaim property belonging to a state debtor subject to seizure and public sale. The issue in the case is quite simple: Apollodorus is challenging the defendants' claim of ownership over two slaves, arguing that they actually belong to the defendants' brother Arethusius, a state debtor, and should therefore be confiscated. Apollodorus offers witness testimony of Arethusius' debt and ownership of the slaves, arguing that the defendants, Nicostratus and Deinon, are asserting that they own the slaves to protect their brothers' property from confiscation.[19] From a modern perspective, one might expect the speech to begin and end with this apparently quite damning evidence. Apollodorus does not, however, discuss the slaves until the last quarter of his speech, but instead devotes the bulk of his time to a detailed narrative of how the defendants had betrayed his friendship and why Arethusias' status as state debtor was deserved. Of course, we don't know how the individual jurors went about evaluating the case. The factual question of who owned the slaves may well have played an important role, but given the nature of the arguments in the speech, it seems unlikely that the litigants, jurors, or audience viewed the verdict as merely a determination on this narrow factual issue.

Other examples of speakers going beyond the narrow factual question raised in the charge abound. Speeches in suits charging false testimony generally include an attempt to re-argue the previous case as well as evidence that the statement made by one of the opponent's witnesses was false. For instance, in one false testimony suit the plaintiff states, "I now present to you a just request, that you both determine whether the testimony is false or true, and at the same time, examine the entire matter from the beginning."[20] Similarly, in *paragraphe* cases in which the speaker is seeking to quash a lawsuit on the ground, for example, that a discharge or release for a debt had been executed, speakers do not limit themselves to the question raised in the counter-suit.[21]

The notion that a popular court jury might reach a verdict contrary to the facts by acquitting defendants who are factually guilty is explicit in the *apophasis* procedure. *Apophasis* was a procedure introduced in the 340s most commonly used in charges of corruption, official misconduct, and treason. Much of our information about this procedure comes from the surviving speeches in the Harpalus affair of 323 BCE, in which a number of prominent Athenians were prosecuted for accepting bribes from the Macedonian Harpalus. Under this procedure, the Areopagus Council conducted an investigation and published a non-binding report. It seems from the surviving speeches connected to the Harpalus affair that the report did not include the evidence against the accused, but simply provided a list of those guilty of corruption and the amount of money each had taken as a bribe.[22] The case was then passed to a popular court for final decision. The surviving prosecution speeches in the Harpalus affair are remarkable in that they do not discuss the evidence at all; the speakers repeatedly insist that the jury should simply accept the report of the Areopagus.[23] Thus in the Harpalus affair the jurors were expected to render a verdict upholding or overturning the Areopagus' report even though they were not presented with any evidence regarding the facts of the case. A passage in the first speech of Dinarchus explains this paradox by suggesting that the popular court jury's task may have included more than reaching a decision on the factual question of guilt. He notes that the Areopagus' inquiry is limited to establishing the facts:

> Unlike you [popular court jurors] who (now don't get angry at me for saying this) sometimes are accustomed when rendering a verdict to privilege mercy over justice, the [Areopagus] council simply seeks to report anyone who is liable to the charge and has committed crimes contrary to your ancestral ways.[24]

Dinarchus goes on to list cases in which the popular court jury acquitted men found guilty by the Areopagus in *apophasis*, adding this (doubtless at least partially self-serving) explanation:

> Judging the case, you [the popular court jurors] acquitted them. It was not that you were charging the Areopagus Council with being incorrect, but that you placed mercy rather than justice first, believing the penalty to be too harsh given the crime committed by the defendant. . . . The report of the Areopagus Council was not shown to be false. Rather, even though the report was true, it seemed best to the jurors to acquit. . . . For the Areopagus Council was assigned to seek out the truth; but the court, I say, judged him worthy of pardon.[25]

The surviving prosecution speeches in the Harpalus affair support this account of the jury's role: the prosecutors devote most of their time to broad attacks on the character of the defendants and to other arguments suggesting that full punishment is merited and pity inappropriate.[26] Thus, the two-staged *apophasis* procedure highlights what was likely one of the elements of popular court decision-making in ordinary cases as well: the determination of whether the allegations, even if true, merit punishment in light of the particular circumstances of the case and the defendant.

So far, we have been discussing situations in which the charge might seem to call for a straightforward determination of fact, but the popular court jury's verdict seems to have incorporated broader notions of a fair and just result to the dispute. Of course, there were also many cases in which evaluating the merits of the charge itself involved normative as well as factual determinations. Athenian statutes were notoriously vague and offered little guidance regarding potential exceptions, defenses, and aggravating and mitigating factors. The presence of these types of arguments in our surviving speeches suggests that Athenian jurors sometimes considered them in reaching their verdicts,[27] and there is some evidence suggesting that jurors in particular cases were swayed by these arguments.[28] But there were no clear rules, written or unwritten, about when particular defenses or mitigating factors might trump the straightforward determination of whether the factual allegations in the charge had been met. As a result, Athenian jurors were regularly called on to make normative judgments as well as finding facts.

Hyperides' *Against Athenogenes* may offer an example. The prosecutor in this case, Epicrates, fell in love with a slave boy and offered to buy the freedom of the boy as well as that of his brother and father from their owner, the defendant Athenogenes. When they met to conclude the deal, Athenogenes proposed that Epicrates buy the slaves instead, along with the perfume shop they managed. This would make Epicrates liable for any debts they owed, but Athenogenes assured him that the stock in the shop was worth far more than any debts. Epicrates admits that Athenogenes read out the contract, but he claimed that he was too distracted and eager to get access to the boy to listen carefully. Soon after concluding the deal, he learned that the boy's father had considerable debts and that the contract included a provision that Epicrates would assume responsibility for any debts owed by the slave to anyone else. The applicable law stated simply that any voluntary agreement made between two parties was binding, but Epicrates argues that an unjust contract such as this one should be voided.[29] This case likely turned not on fact-finding but on the jurors' interpretation of the vague contract statute; that is, the jury had to make a normative judgment about whether to punish the unscrupulous seller even though the contract was in order, or to take the position that the careless and gullible buyer got what he deserved. In sum, although questions of fact were often raised in Athenian court cases, in many suits fact-finding was subsumed within a normative judgment concerning the just resolution to the dispute.

Implications for Evidence and Procedure

The fact that popular court juries were as focused on normative judgments as on factual determinations was reflected in several aspects of Athenian court procedure and the treatment of evidence. There is no parallel in Athenian law to the Roman praetor's *formula* which narrowed and spelled out the issues to be decided at trial.[30] In Athens a magistrate who had been selected by lot for a one-year term held a pre-trial preliminary hearing, but the magistrates do not seem to have dismissed suits on legal grounds or set out particular issues to be decided at trial.[31] Moreover, while most modern trials aimed at fact-finding focus on the introduction of testimony and other forms of evidence, often in a highly fragmented form, Athenian litigants provided a largely uninterrupted narrative of their case, punctuated with the reading of evidence to support the speaker's statements. Thus in an Athenian court the evidence did not make the case but rather reinforced claims and rhetorical and normative arguments presented in the litigant's speech.

In a modern trial focused on factual disputes, a great deal of effort is put into bolstering the credibility of one's witnesses and attacking the credibility of the opponent's witnesses. But as Stephen Todd has pointed out, our surviving speeches include very few discussions of witness credibility.[32] Witnesses support the story presented by the litigant, but where a fact is disputed, we don't see the kind of careful parsing of testimony in an attempt to reveal bias or inconsistencies and to get at the truth that dominates modern trials. Some scholars have suggested that the role of an Athenian witness was as much to indicate that the litigant was supported by kin and respectable members of the community as to testify to questions of fact.[33] There may well be something to this, but I also think that Athenian witness testimony may have been given less scrutiny than witness testimony in modern courts in part because Athenian cases so rarely turned on discrete factual questions.

Finally, the Athenians employed a comparatively broad approach to relevance and admissibility to provide jurors with the information necessary to reach normative judgments that reached beyond the narrow confines of the charge. For example, Athenian litigants routinely introduce evidence that moderns would consider relevant, if at all, only to sentencing, such as prior crimes and other character evidence and even information about the effect that a penalty would have on a defendant and his family.[34] The subordination of fact-finding also had implications for the meaning of verdicts. Because multiple factual disputes and normative questions might be in play in any given case, it could be difficult to know which argument had swayed the jury or even whether there was a consensus among the jurors who had voted for the same verdict. Like medieval English jury verdicts, Athenian popular court verdicts were inscrutable. But while early English verdicts may have obscured factual uncertainty, the inscrutability of Athenian verdicts may have served a different role. The lack of clarity in Athenian court verdicts may have made the legal system more flexible and able to adapt to changing norms and circumstances.

As is well known, the Athenians were very conservative when it came to their laws.[35] Court cases provided an opportunity to challenge the normative underpinnings of a law as applied in a particular situation without challenging the law itself.[36] The incremental nature of court cases made it easier for litigants and jurors to critically examine norms that might be in flux, and to slowly change the law case by case without actually overturning any statute. In the modern context, scholars have shown that "norm entrepreneurs"—that is, actors seeking to shift society's thinking about a particular norm—are more successful when they proceed slowly, using "gentle nudges" in the desired direction rather than risking a backlash by getting too far ahead of popular sentiment.[37] Athenians may have been more receptive to attempts to change norms, if, for example, they came in the form of an argument that a particular litigant had crossed the line in using self-help in a specific situation, rather than an argument that the Athenians should adopt a new rule limiting the use of self-help more generally. Moreover, norms could be questioned and tentatively challenged in the context of a court case, beginning a public debate on an issue without eliciting a direct vote on the question. In this way, even arguments raised by a losing litigant might begin to shift public opinion, while fledgling changes raised in the Assembly might be squelched by the clear statement of public disapproval generated by a negative vote.[38]

Homicide Court Verdicts

In contrast to the many potential meanings of a popular court verdict, the special homicide court procedures appear to be aimed at enhancing factual accuracy on the ultimate question of guilt. Although the reasons for the different approaches in the homicide and popular courts are ultimately speculative, I believe the explanation lies not in an Athenian view that truth was a particularly important value in homicide cases but in the practical need to generate legitimacy for the verdict and limit vendetta in the early period when the homicide courts were established. In the classical period, five special courts shared jurisdiction over most cases involving homicide. The Areopagus Council, which tried cases of intentional killing and wounding, arson, and poison, was the most celebrated of these courts. Other types of homicide—for example, unintentional homicide or alleged justifiable homicide—were tried in specialized courts and judged, it seems, by a subset of members of the Areopagus. Several aspects of the homicide procedures encouraged litigants, witnesses, and jurors to focus on the narrow factual question of guilt.

One major difference concerned the treatment of oaths. Prior to trial, each litigant swore that the defendant had or had not committed the homicide,[39] and after trial the victorious litigant swore that the verdict was true.[40] While witnesses in popular court cases did not routinely swear an oath, witnesses in the homicide courts were required to swear not just to the truth of their testimony, but to whether the accused had or had not committed the homicide.[41] This requirement certainly helped to focus the case on the ultimate question of fact, though it is not clear that in practice it would always have helped the truth come to light. No doubt it cut down on witness testimony on extraneous matters, but it may also have prevented relevant testimony from witnesses who did not have enough information to swear to the ultimate question of guilt. For example, a doctor might have information about the nature of a wound or cause of death that would be highly relevant, but he might not have any idea whether the defendant was guilty or not. The lack of witness testimony in Antiphon 1, which involved an allegation of poisoning, is often noted; and Antiphon 6, a case involving accidental poisoning of a chorus boy, includes no testimony about the nature of the drug that was given, but only that the speaker was not involved in the decision to give him the potion. It seems at least possible that more evidence was available in these cases from witnesses who felt unable to testify given the strictures of the oath. Moreover, the requirement that witnesses swear to the ultimate factual question may have made it more likely that witnesses who knew the defendant well and were confident of his guilt or innocence, and thus were biased, were the most likely to provide evidence in the homicide courts.

Another distinctive aspect of the homicide courts was the oath taken by litigants to speak only to issues relevant to the homicide charge. One speaker describes the oath: "You had to swear the greatest and most powerful oath, . . . in very truth that you would accuse me only concerning the homicide itself (*auton ton phonon*), [arguing] that I killed, with the result that, had I done many bad acts, I would not be convicted for any reason other than the charge itself, and, had I done many good deeds, I would not be saved because of this good conduct."[42] The Athenian definition of material "outside the issue" (*exo tou pragmatos*) for purposes of the homicide courts appears to have centered on character evidence. Although our surviving speeches indicate that homicide court speakers fell far short of complete compliance with the relevancy rule, these speeches generally remain focused on the factual circumstances of the death and do not invite the jury to make equitable and normative judgments based on the broader context of the dispute or the character of the parties.[43]

Perhaps most important, the Athenians themselves perceived the homicide courts as focused on the factual allegations in the charge in a way that popular courts were not. Antiphon states, "the laws, the oaths, the sacrifices, the public announcements, and all the other things that happen in a homicide suit, are very different from other procedures because the facts themselves, concerning which the stakes are the greatest, must be known correctly."[44] Several passages attest to a widespread belief that the homicide court verdicts, unlike popular court verdicts, represented a straightforward determination regarding the homicide charge.[45] Moreover, while popular court speakers tend to speak in terms of *dike* (justice), *aletheia* (truth) (or, at times truth and justice together[46]) plays a prominent role in the surviving homicide court speeches.[47]

Why did the Athenians judge cases in the homicide courts differently? Factors such as the seriousness of the offense and penalty and concern over pollution may have played a role.[48] But our evidence suggests that these characteristics of homicide may have been less important in the classical period than one might expect. In the medieval and early modern period, concern about the potential for incorrectly sentencing an innocent man to death drove much of the focus on insuring accurate fact-finding at trial. But in Athens, intentional homicide was only one of many crimes that could result in the death penalty, alongside treason, impiety, theft, robbery, and corruption, among others. There was no sense that a heightened attention to fact-finding applied to these other potentially capital offenses. Moreover, recent scholarship has suggested that the relative importance of pollution in the treatment of homicide has been exaggerated, and that by the fourth century, concern over pollution in relation to homicide was in steep decline.[49] Perhaps most important, near the end of the fifth century, a new procedure, *apagoge*, was introduced for dealing with at least some forms of homicide through the popular court system.[50] If the crime of homicide and any resulting pollution required a special focus on fact-finding in the fourth century, we would not expect the Athenians to permit some homicide cases to proceed through the popular court system without any of the special homicide court procedures.

If concerns over wrongly imposing the death penalty and pollution cannot completely explain the focus on fact-finding in the homicide courts, then what might be the explanation? My own, necessarily speculative, view is that the homicide courts' more narrow focus on the homicide charge grew out of an urgent need to foster obedience of and respect for verdicts in a fledgling legal system that was just beginning to assert control over the private use of violence. The homicide court procedures were likely quite old, predating the popular courts by about a century and remaining largely unchanged throughout the classical period. The traditional response to homicide in pre-Draconian Athens was retaliatory murder carried out by the victim's family unless they agreed to accept a blood price. Draco's law set limits on the family's power over a homicide: unintentional killers were to be permitted to flee the city unharmed; at least one type of justifiable homicide was proclaimed to be without penalty; and although the family retained the final decision on whether to accept compensation from unintentional homicides, a finding that a killing was unintentional likely put pressure on the family to do so. The process of convincing relatives of a man who had been killed to relinquish their traditional right of immediate retaliation and to abide by the findings of the homicide courts must have been a slow and difficult one. Procedures like the relevancy rule and special litigant and witness oaths that focused the case on the homicide itself may have assisted this process in a few different ways. First, by limiting the judges' discretion and discouraging evidence about the parties' character and social background, these procedures may have fostered a belief in the impartiality of the judges and thereby encouraged families to appeal to and abide by the results of the official homicide procedures. Second, by forcing families to cast their arguments in terms of the narrow question of the homicide, the homicide procedures promoted the view that the homicide was an isolated event to be resolved rather than simply one part of an ongoing and escalating cycle of violence that reached beyond the individual killer and victim to encompass their families as well.

If the interpretation I've sketched is broadly correct, the focus on fact-finding in the homicide courts may have been unrelated to a sense that discovering the truth was an independent value in legal decision-making. A focus on truth and narrow fact-finding in the homicide courts may have helped generate compliance with verdicts, but the Athenians consciously rejected this potential model when they created the popular court system. Perhaps most interesting, the Athenian approach to verdicts belies an evolutionary account of the development of the law of evidence and proof. The greater focus on the narrow legal charge in the homicide courts actually *predated* the open-ended, ad hoc approach of the popular courts.

Let's return to the question we started with—what was distinctive about the Athenian approach to fact-finding? What is most striking is how untroubled Athenians were about resolving important questions of fact: there were no safeguards to prevent factual errors in most cases, none of the evidentiary and procedural rules that are ubiquitous in continental European legal history from the medieval period forward. It could be that the Athenians, blissfully pre-Christian, simply did not care as much about errors, even errors of life and death. But another way to look at it is that disputes over key facts seem somehow to have been less common in Athenian litigation, and that this was partially the result of the way the Athenian system was designed. The familiar modern focus on accurate fact-finding is partially an artifact of a system where litigants cannot dispute what the applicable legal rules should be. This limit has channeled litigation into disputes over facts and neuroses about what constitutes admissible and adequate proof. Athens was different: the openness of the popular courts to arguments of any kind subtly encouraged all litigants to tell a full and persuasive story about what happened, and why the defendant's conduct should or should not merit punishment. Instead of shoehorning events into legal categories and formulas, as lawyers do for their clients to this day, the stories in Athenian litigation came out to the jury more or less as the parties always understood them. Paradoxically, this more naïve version of storytelling and of justice probably let the Athenian jury come closer to the truth of what really happened in most cases than occurs in modern courts today, where evidentiary and procedural rules, though aimed at a strict pursuit of truth, far more often hide basic realities. We have sacrificed justice for truth, but have really obtained neither.

Notes

1. William Blackstone, *Commentaries on the Laws of England*, Book III: *Of Private Wrongs* (Oxford: Oxford University Press, 2016), 218.

2. Robert Bartlett, *Trial by Fire and Water* (Oxford: Oxford University Press, 1986), 1–38.

3. John Langbein, *Torture and the Law of Proof: Europe and England in the Ancien Régime* (Chicago: University of Chicago Press, 2006), 3–26.

4. Bartlett, *Trial by Fire and Water*, 139.

5. In setting up a dichotomy between medieval and later courts' focus on truth and

classical Athens' preference for normative judgments over fact-finding, I have not included classical Roman procedure, because it appears to have elements of both.

6. In practice, English jurors seem to have committed "pious perjury" and acquitted contrary to the evidence with some regularity. See Thomas A. Green, *Verdict According to Conscience: Perspectives on the English Criminal Trial Jury, 1200–1800* (Chicago: University of Chicago Press, 1985).

7. See David C. Mirhady, "Athens' Democratic Witnesses," *Phoenix* 56 (2002): 255–74.

8. See Stephen C. Todd, "The Purpose of Evidence in Athenian Courts," in *Nomos: Essays in Athenian Law, Politics and Society*, ed. Paul A. Cartledge, Paul Millett, and Stephen C. Todd (Cambridge: Cambridge University Press, 1990), 35. Testimony obtained from a slave under torture was not decisive. See Todd, "Purpose of Evidence," 34–35; cf. David C. Mirhady, "Torture and Rhetoric in Athens," *Journal of Hellenic Studies* 116 (1996): 119–31.

9. There are only a couple examples of accepted challenges. See Todd, "Purpose of Evidence," 35 and n. 29. *Diamartyria*, a procedure used exclusively in inheritance cases in the classical period, may be another example of formal proof in Athens.

10. E.g., Aesch. 2.87 (litigants' oath); Dem. 24.149–51 (jurors' oath sworn to Zeus, Poseidon, and Demeter).

11. For a description of this procedure, see [Ar.] *Ath. Pol.* 59.

12. See Victor Bers, "Just Rituals: Why the Rigamarole in Fourth-Century Athenian Lawcourts?," in *Polis and Politics: Studies in Ancient Greek History*, ed. Pernille Flensted-Jensen, Thomas Heine Nielsen, and Lene Rubinstein (Copenhagen: Museum Tusculanum Press, 2000), 553–62.

13. For a discussion of the voting procedure, see C. W. Marshall and Stephanie van Willigenburg, "Judging Athenian Dramatic Competitions," *Journal of Hellenic Studies* 124 (2004): 90–107.

14. Marshall and Willigenburg, "Judging Athenian Dramatic Competitions," 91. As Marshall and Willigenburg note (91n10), in the New Testament, the successor to Judas is selected by lot from a short list (Acts 1:21–26).

15. See Lilly Ross Taylor, *Roman Voting Assemblies* (Ann Arbor: University of Michigan Press, 1990), 80–83; Roberta L. Stewart, "Publicity and the Lot: The Politics of Sortition," in *The Shapes of City Life in Rome and Pompeii*, ed. Mary T. Boatwright and Harry B. Evans (New Rochelle, NY: Aristide D. Caratzas, 1998), 9–26; Roberta Stewart, *Public Office in Early Rome* (Ann Arbor: University of Michigan Press, 1998), 12–51.

16. E.g., Din. 2.19; Dem. 20.165, 25.98; Aesch. 3.247. See Adriaan Lanni, "Publicity and the Courts of Classical Athens," *Yale Journal of Law and the Humanities* 24 (2012): 127–30.

17. Adriaan Lanni, *Law and Justice in the Courts of Classical Athens* (Cambridge: Cambridge University Press, 2006), 41–74.

18. For more detailed discussion of how the jury evaluated extralegal and legal argumentation, including discussion of the juror's oath, see Lanni, *Law and Justice*, 70–74.

19. Dem. 53.18–25.

20. Dem. 47.46. See also Dem. 29.9, 27; Dem. 45.1–2; Is. 2.27–37.

21. See A. R. W. Harrison, *The Law of Athens* (Indianapolis: Hackett, 1998), 2:10–119.

22. Hyp. 5.6.

23. Din. 1.84, 2.6. See also Edwin Carawan, "*Apophasis* and *Eisangelia*: The Role of the Areopagus in Athenian Political Trials," *Greek, Roman, and Byzantine Studies* 26 (1985): 134.

24. Din. 1.55.

25. Din. 1.57–59.

26. Din. 1.47, 71ff., 82, 94ff., 110–11; 2.1–2, 11ff.; 3.11, 15, 18, 20. See also Hyp. 5.26, 40.

27. In *Performing Interpersonal Violence: Court, Curse, and Comedy in Fourth-Century B.C.E. Athens* (Chapel Hill: University of North Carolina Press, 2012), 22–101, Werner Riess sketches various aggravating and mitigating factors regarding violence that seem to have affected jurors, including public versus hidden violence, inebriation versus sobriety, old age versus youth, and escalation versus de-escalation.

28. Din. 1.55–57; Dem. 21.71–76.

29. Hyp. 3.13. Cf. Dem. 42.12, 47.77, 56.2. Epicrates suggests that the law provides that the agreement must be just, but since this provision is not cited in other cases discussing the law, it is unclear whether the provision was part of the law itself or an interpretive gloss provided by Epicrates. For a convincing argument that the general contract law did not include limitations, see David Phillips, "Hypereides 3 and the Athenian Law of Contracts," *Transactions of the American Philological Association* 139 (2009): 89–122.

30. Some scholars have recently argued that Athenian litigants were less focused on interpreting and applying the applicable statute than on proving or disproving the specific allegations in the written indictment (called a *graphe* in public suits, an *enklema* in private cases), which sometimes included a detailed list of alleged wrongs in addition to and sometimes instead of the statutory charge. See Gerhard Thür, "The Principle of Fairness in Athenian Legal Procedure," *Dike* 11 (2008): 51–73; Michael Gagarin, "Law, Politics, and the Question of Relevance in the Case on the Crown," *Classical Antiquity* 31, no. 2 (2012): 293–314; Edward Harris, *The Rule of Law in Action in Democratic Athens* (Oxford: Oxford University Press, 2013), 114–36. That argument may well be right, but the plaint was a far cry from the Roman formula. For one thing, it was created unilaterally by the plaintiff; there was no official determination of how to narrow the issues at trial, and there was not even agreement by both parties as to how to characterize the issue. Moreover, that our surviving evidence shows routine use of extralegal arguments, such as character evidence and appeals to pity, suggests that litigants and jurors did not restrict themselves to arguments related to the indictment.

31. Possible exceptions include Lys. 13.86 and Is. 10.2. See Adriaan Lanni, "Precedent and Legal Reasoning in Ancient Athenian Courts: A Noble Lie?," *American Journal of Legal History* 43 (1999): 27, 33–34.

32. Todd, "Purpose of Evidence," 24.

33. Sally Humphreys, "Social Relations on Stage: Witnesses in Classical Athens," *History and Anthropology* 1 (1985): 313–69; Todd, "Purpose of Evidence." Cf. Mirhady, "Athens' Democratic Witnesses"; Lene Rubinstein, "Main Litigants and Witnesses in the Athenian Courts: Procedural Variations," in *Symposion 2001: Vorträge zur griechischen und hellenistischen Rechtsgeschichte*, ed. Michael Gagarin and Robert Wallace (Vienna: OAW, 2005), 99–120.

34. For extensive discussion of "extralegal" argumentation in Athenian popular courts, see Lanni, *Law and Justice*, 42–64.

35. See, e.g., Alan L. Boegehold, "Resistance to Change in the Law at Athens," in *Demokratia: A Conversation on Democracies, Ancient and Modern*, ed. Josiah Ober and Charles Hedrick (Princeton: Princeton University Press, 1996), 203–14; Rosalind Thomas, "Written in Stone? Liberty, Equality, Orality, and the Codification of Law," in *Greek Law in Its Political Setting: Justifications Not Justice*, ed. Lin Foxhall and A. D. E. Lewis (Oxford: Oxford University Press, 1996), 9–31.

36. In fact, litigants do not directly argue that the law is wrong or that the jurors should ignore the law in favor of justice; rather, they tend to argue that both the law and justice/equity are on their side. See, e.g. Christopher Carey, "*Nomos* in Attic Rhetoric and Oratory," *Journal of Hellenic Studies* 116 (1996): 41, 33–46.

37. See, e.g., Dan Kahan, "Gentle Nudges vs. Hard Shoves: Solving the Sticky Norms Problem," *University of Chicago Law Review* 67 (2000): 607–45.

38. On the tendency that one decision maker's disapproval of a proposed norm change could result in "self-reinforcing resistance" to the change, see Kahan, "Gentle Nudges vs. Hard Shoves," 608.

39. Ant. 6.16; Lys. 10.11; Dem. 23.67–69.

40. Aesch. 2.87.

41. Ant. 1.28, 5.12; Isoc. 18.56.

42. Ant. 5.11. See also Lyc. 1.11–13. For discussion, see Lanni, *Law and Justice*, 75–114. The report at *Ath. Pol.* 67.1 that litigants in private cases before the popular courts took a similar oath to speak to the issue has no corresponding trace in our surviving speeches, and the sources make it clear that the Athenians viewed the homicide courts as enforcing a stricter standard of relevance than the popular courts (Lyc. 1.11–13; Dem. 23.65–66; Xen. *Mem.* 3.5.20; Ant. 5.8–14, 6.6). See Adriaan Lanni, "The Role of the Complaint (*graphe/enklema*) in the Athenian Legal System," in *Symposion 2017: Vorträge zur griechischen und hellenistischen Rechtsgeschichte*, ed. Uri Yitach (Vienna: OAW, forthcoming).

43. See Lanni, *Law and Justice*, 96–105.

44. Ant. 6.6.

45. Lyc. 1.11–13; Dem. 23.65–66; Xen. *Mem.* 3.5.20; Ant. 5.8–14, 6.6.

46. This formulation of truth and justice is particularly prominent in Ant. 6 (see 24, 26, 32).

47. E.g., Ant. 1.6, 10, 13; Ant. 5.14, 18, 24, 26, 29, 32, 41; Lys. 1.5.

48. For example, in Ant. 6.6 (quoted above), the speaker states that the wrongful conviction of an innocent man would be a sin against the gods as well as the laws. Several aspects of the homicide procedures, such as the requirement that trials be held in the open air, seem to suggest concern about pollution.

49. E.g., Robert Parker, *Athenian Religion: A History* (Oxford: Oxford University Press, 1996), 104–43; Ilias Arnaoutoglou, "Pollution in the Athenian Homicide Law," *Revue Internationale des Droits de l'Antiquité* 40 (1993): 109–37; Edwin Carawan, *Rhetoric and the Law of Draco* (Oxford: Oxford University Press, 1998), 17–19.

50. See, e.g., Eleni Volonaki, "*Apagoge* in Homicide Cases," *Dike* 3 (2000): 147–76.

CHAPTER 7

The Certainty of Documents

Records of Proceedings as Guarantors of Memory in Political and Legal Argument

Clifford Ando

Legal institutions often present themselves as adjudicating issues of fact. Their operations also produce facts, by affirming some statements and evidence entered in pursuit of judgment as true (or more likely to be so), and also insofar as legal judgments amount to new facts in the world in which those institutions intervene.[1] They are sometimes self-aware about their capacity to assess the gap between the social and epistemic status of the things they affirm as facts: the instructions delivered by Roman magistrates to lay judges, for example, urged them to proceed to judgment not on the grounds that some condition were in fact true, but merely if it seemed to them to be so.[2] Likewise, through rules of evidence, practices of ceremonial and procedure, and claims to forensic expertise, legal institutions promote particular cultures of knowledge.[3] They seek, one might say, to bring into being a recognition of their own operations as rational and disinterested, the better to claim legitimacy for the effects they produce. This was also true of the forms of publicity and genres of publication that they cultivated.

In this chapter, I focus on a practice of institutions of Roman public law with astonishing effects in the broader cultures of knowledge and memory in the ancient Mediterranean: their tendency, in issuing judgments, to cite the representations made by the party or parties to the issue at hand, whether singly or adversarially. One aspect of my topic concerns the tendency of institutions of Roman public law to cite the factual basis of their actions as part of the issuance of a decision. (Indeed, as we shall see, they often employ the same lexical means to cite both the factual and normative bases for their actions.) In employing this language, I am not saying either that the Romans claimed that the representations made by parties before Roman tribunals were true or that the Romans were proceeding on the basis of facts that they had been able to verify. Rather, what Roman tribunals did, was to provide a formal account of both the claims about the world, and the arguments about those claims, that were made before them; and these are proffered as the basis for Roman action. This is true already in the earliest surviving evidence for the publication of decisions of the Roman Senate.

Though the subsequent development of stenography in the Roman world and its widespread use to record the proceedings of courts and councils are, at some level, well known, they deserve more thorough study than they have heretofore received, and the evidence has never been fully collated. My interest here, however, is not so much in the practice of recording proceedings as in the influence achieved by the documentary form of the Roman record of proceedings, via what appears to be massive subscription to its efficacy as a means of memorialization. This came about, I suggest, precisely because of long experience with the practice on the part of Roman officials of citing proceedings by way of authorizing their actions. Records of proceedings necessarily advanced simultaneous claims about knowledge and about the appropriate means to acquire it. The citation and imitation of records of proceedings in nonstatal contexts is therefore evidence both of the cultural influence achieved by the operation of Roman institutions and, recursively, of the legitimacy accorded to those institutions and their procedures.

Consideration of the production, form, and use of records of proceedings provokes all sorts of historical questions about the development of stenography, about archival practice, about notions of truth in historical memory, and about the influence exercised on one another by different institutional cultures—Roman and local, statal and nonstatal, and so on. These are topics of very great interest and importance, and many of them might be generalized in such a way as to contribute to conversations about the legitimacy and power of institutions and the documents they produced. This is not to say that any genre of document can be a window onto every aspect of the challenges of evidence that historians of knowledge confront, that is, that any given genre is synecdochic of some whole. The particularity of documentary evidence—indeed, of premodern evidentiary regimes in general—often presents considerable challenges of aggregation, a topic that could use more sustained theoretical reflection than it generally receives. That said, I need now to sharpen and adjust the language I have just employed: the earliest documents that I discuss do not so much cite records of proceedings as they paraphrase the statements of parties before Roman institutions of inquiry. (The standard form taken by such paraphrases will be a concern below.) That legal judgments proceed overtly on the basis of such representations long before we have clear evidence for the production of stenographic records of proceedings is itself a historical fact worthy of study. The public esteem that such records received from institutions of great social power—and, one might suppose, of meaningful social authority—was a contributing factor in the universalization of the practice of recording proceedings in the operation of Roman and Romanizing public institutions across the Mediterranean.[4]

As it happens, records of proceedings have been the object of study in a small but diverse body of scholarship. There are papyrological and epigraphic literatures devoted to proceedings as genres of documents, as well as to stenographic practice, stenographic manuals, and the archival practices that allowed for the storage and use of proceedings.[5] Proceedings have also received at least limited attention from historians of Roman law—though this has occurred more regularly in cultures of scholarship interested in sociological approaches to historical legal study than in those invested in forms of dogmatic history. But *acta* receive their due attention in handbooks like Wenger's *Quellen des römischen Rechts*, even if his knowledge of the available papyrological material was less than perfect.[6] In addition, the practices of corporate bodies like the Roman Senate have been the object of very considerable study among historians of government and among a special subset of those interested in ceremony—because, of course, late records of the Roman Senate also record its acclamations; to that pool of interested scholars, one might append historiographers who inquire into the history and content of the *acta diurna* and the influence of the *acta senatus*.[7]

Finally, there is a very great literature on the councils of the church, though only a small portion of it is concerned with the mechanics of the recording of their proceedings in a technical way; the same might be said regarding the politics of knowledge production in councils narrowly or the church more generally, as symptoms of the cultures of knowledge production in society at large. To my mind, the great work in this field, which focused on the influence that Roman governmental practice had on the practice of the councils of the church, was written in the first decades of the twentieth century—by Pierre Batiffol and Francis Dvornik, above all, with some notable recent attention having been paid to these issues by Fergus Millar and Brent Shaw.[8]

For my part, I have written in the past about records of proceedings in two contexts. First, I reflected once upon a time on formal qualities of records of proceedings, urging that aspects of their protocols played an important role in affirming their truth content. The imitation of certain formal aspects of official texts in fake documents and subliterary cultural productions such as the *Acta Alexandrinorum* and the Christian martyr acts—like their citation in paideutic and historical contexts—testifies, I have urged, both to the way in which certain practices of Roman government came to function as cultural archetypes for the recording of public memory and, more broadly, to the legitimacy of the *procedures* of Roman government, if not to that of all its acts.[9] Second, I once wrote an essay on the culture of textuality visible in the records of Chalcedon.[10] The council of Chalcedon was called because a change of personnel on the throne of the empire occasioned a reversal in Christology, that being how truth in matters of religion was sometimes determined in those benighted times. But in this instance, the temporality of the change meant that many parties who had been present at the immediately prior council only two years earlier, the second council of Ephesus in 449, were on record as having sworn to an alternate formulation of the faith. In a bravura act of textuality, much of the proceedings of the second council of Ephesus, as well as records from the Home Synod in 448 and the first council of Ephesus in 431, were read into the record on the first day at Chalcedon. The result, in short, was that people were confronted with what the stenographic record said were their very own words. The last section of this chapter considers how this moment played out.

The chapter has four sections. In the first, I discuss some of the documentary forms and practices that gave rise to the knowledge culture in which the records of proceedings participated. In particular, I focus on the citation of adversarial argumentation in stipulations by executive or legislative authority, in which they enumerate the factual bases that justify the action that the document in question describes. The second section considers the conduct of hearings in the provinces, by Romans and those deputized by them. I there focus on the influence that records of those hearings—or, rather, the protocols of those hearings and records—exercised on notions of historical memory. In the third section, I turn to the role played by documents and documentary culture in the councils of Carthage between 401 and 411. (Councils took place outside Carthage in these years, and their acts were occasionally cited in proceedings in Carthage, but the ones from Carthage are best attested.) In the chapter's fourth and final section, I return to the council of Chalcedon.

I. Proceedings in the Epigraphic Record

Records of proceedings were technologies of institutional memory, not documents of autonomous normative power. There was, therefore, little reason to inscribe them on permanent media. Instead, the great bulk of records of proceedings are preserved on papyrus. This is not to say that proceedings are absent from the epigraphic records: the most famous instances are surely the hearing (*cognitio*) conducted by Caracalla into the case of the Goharieni and the so-called *angareia* inscription from Phrygia, which records a hearing before an imperial procurator over the division of responsibility between two villages for the maintenance of a road that passed between them.[11] But of course the practice of, and technology for, recording proceedings existed earlier, even if their origins cannot be located with precision. What is more, a large number of texts dating earlier than these third-century ones exhibit documentary instincts very closely aligned with those that, we may surmise, motivated the recording and archiving of proceedings. If we are to understand the culture in which the stenographic transcript of an official hearing—or, to put it differently, the paraphrase or quotation of speech in hearings—came to have both evidentiary value and cultural importance, we must inquire into the history and form of these derivative and related forms of official text.

In surveying this material, I want to draw attention to five features of these documents:

1. The documents are often generically hybrid. Letters from magistrates quote decrees of the Senate, for example; decisions by magistrates cite records of earlier proceedings in order to establish facts.
2. Read narrowly, the documents open windows onto the mechanics of hearings, including their rules of evidence. More generally, they shed great light on the procedures of Roman state institutions.
3. The texts represent (via paraphrase and indirect or direct speech) the

arguments of adversarial parties or, in the case of *cognitiones* (inquisitorial hearings before a magistrate), the interplay between a presiding official and the party or parties being questioned.

4. As a related matter, linguistic features distinguish the procedures and content of hearings from the documents in which the summary, paraphrase, or quotation of the hearing is embedded.
5. Finally, the documents reveal—or perhaps I should say, revel in—a constant interplay between oral and written, for one thing, and between what is efficacious as a matter of politics or law and what is dispositive at the level of memory, for another.

Finally, let me issue a caution. The documents that I discuss are sufficiently different in form, and they survive in sufficiently damaged condition, that it would be very risky to attempt to tell a developmental story about documentary culture on their basis. Indeed, the earliest surviving decrees of the Roman Senate already paraphrase the speech of parties before it as establishing the factual basis for its action, and they do so using linguistic protocols that will be standard ever after: "Whereas the Delphians spoke . . . , concerning this matter, it was decreed as follows" (περὶ ὧν . . . περὶ τούτου τοῦ πράγματος οὕτως ἔδοξεν; *RDGE* 1, document C, lines 3–5); "Likewise, whereas [the Thisbaians] spoke . . . , concerning this matter, it was decreed as follows" (ὡσαύτως περὶ ὧν . . . περὶ τούτου τοῦ πράγματος οὕτως ἔδοξεν; *RDGE* 2, lines 17–21). (It is important to distinguish this use and representation of speeches by nonsenators before the Senate from a more targeted inquiry that one might conduct into, for example, the speeches before the Senate of magistrates in the republic and principate or the submission of imperial *orationes* to the Senate as a guide to its culture of debate in the imperial period: these communications were subject to quite different formalities.)

Consider the letter of the consuls of 73 BCE to the magistrates, council, and people of Oropus concerning the tax status of the Amphiareion (*RDGE* 23). On even the simplest representation, the consuls quote the decree of the Senate (*senatus consultum*) that advised them to hear the case; the elaborated argument (*narratio*) that justifies their decision paraphrases the arguments of the two sides; the consuls' decision quotes the law of state contract and two decrees of Sulla, the second of which is validated by reference to a further decree of the Senate; and the letter closes by quoting a decree of the Senate affirming their decision. The *narratio* is both contextual and justificatory: that is, it explains what the case is about but does so by paraphrasing (in reported speech) only the elements of the arguments strictly relevant to their analysis ("whereas . . . whereas," περὶ ὧν . . . περὶ ὧν; lines 16, 24). Observe, in addition, that the paraphrase represents the arguments of the two parties as having an identical form: a causal claim is made via ἐπεί, "since," in reference to an issue of law and an issue of fact, followed by a consequential claim introduced by ὅπως, "in consequence <they maintained> that" (lines 19, 23, 25, 28).

That said, it is essential to observe that the inclusion of a summary of the adversarial argumentation is wholly in surfeit of need. It was possible for the magistrates to communicate only their decision, just as it was possible for the recipients—and other readers of such texts—to extract, quote, summarize, or adapt a decision or legal principle from them. Documents like the letter to Oropus, very broadly, or the record of the inquiry (the *cognitio*), more narrowly, contained many kinds of information, which meant that they could be used in many different ways; this flexibility goes a long way toward accounting for the many different forms in which the traces of records of proceedings come down to us. A useful and early comparandum is the decree of the Senate concerning Narthakion and Melitaia from ca. 140 BCE (*RDGE* 9): the sequence of stipulations cited by the Senate includes representations made by both sets of Greek ambassadors, who cite legal judgments made by third parties as well as a decree of Flamininus that had been confirmed by the Senate, to the point where the text loses grammatical coherence. That said, the form of the language asserts that all this material is cited to stipulate to the facts of the single and unitary matter under consideration and thereby to the Senate's mechanisms for recording and preserving them. That is to say, the decree of the Senate presents two stipulations—περὶ ὧν (line 14) . . . καὶ περὶ ὧν (line 36)—as background to its decree, while the actual decree is introduced by a retrospective deictic that refers back to those stipulations: "concerning this matter, it seemed best thus" (περὶ τούτου τοῦ πράγματος οὕτως ἔδοξεν). The Greek speakers are summarized as arguing in similar form: περὶ τούτου, "concerning this matter" (line 24); περὶ τούτου, "concerning this matter" (line 30); περί τε τούτων τῶν πραγμάτων, "concerning these matters" (lines 54–55). As in the text from Oropus, the parties are all *represented* as employing a form of argumentation that is formally mimetic of that employed by the Roman authorities in the text that frames, reports, and acts on the basis of those representations.

The letter to Oropus is not the earliest Roman documentary text in which a representation of adversarial argumentation survives. As it happens, the earliest surviving fragment of a senatorial decree, whose text was provided by the praetor Spurius Postumius to the people of Delphi in letters dated to 189 BCE, refers to the representations made by the Delphians to Rome in identical language (περὶ ὧν; *RDGE* no. 1, document C, line 3); and the action taken by the Senate is explicitly grounded in their claims (περὶ τούτου τοῦ π[ράγματος οὕτως] ἔδοξεν; lines 4–5)—though in this case, the argument before the Senate was not adversarial. The decree of the Senate in 129 BCE concerning Pergamene land is an obvious comparandum and is surely kindred in its hybrid form (*RDGE* 12). What is more, it seems clear that the text breaks off just as a paraphrase of the *cognitio* of Manius Aquillius, or just possibly a summary of its outcome, was to begin. That said, the text on Pergamum as we have it contains no representation of the exchange of speech in a formal hearing. The decree of the Senate of 112 BCE on the Dionysiac artists (*RDGE* 15 = *F.Delphes* III.2.70a) is in some respects a better parallel. It, too, establishes the problem to be addressed and the facts of the situation in which the Senate intervenes, by reference to representations made by the two parties, using the same language as the Greek text at Oropus (περὶ ὧν . . . καὶ περὶ ὧν): a statement by the Athenians from lines 6–28/29 and one by the Dionysiac artists from lines 29–53. In each case, a summary of the remarks of the envoys commences in indirect discourse before quoting their argumentation in *oratio recta* (using first-person verbs in the present tense). The logical succession to the judgment of the Senate is effected via a retrospective pronominal adjective, taking up the two parts of the *narratio*: περὶ τούτων τῶν πραγμάτων οὕτως ἔδοξεν. . . , "Concerning these matters, it thus seemed best . . ."

Understood in these terms, a very close parallel to these texts may be found in the decree of Lucius Helvius Agrippa, procuratorial governor of Sardinia in 69 CE, regarding a boundary dispute between the Patulcenses and Galillenses (*ILS* 5947). The text is framed as the decision of Agrippa in the matter. As with the Pergamene land and the Amphiareion, the process in Sardinia had unfolded in real time as a series of *cognitiones* before magistrates, and these are cited by Agrippa, who paraphrases both earlier decisions as well as an exchange between the Galillenses and an earlier procurator, Caecilius Simplex, but all in reported speech. Moreover, grammatically and logically, the decision of Agrippa cites this material in a sequence of *cum* clauses that include—without lexical differentiation—both normative claims about the principles motivating Agrippa's reasoning ("since it is necessary in view of the public welfare to abide by matters already judicially decided," *cum pro utilitate publica rebus iudicatis stare conveniat*) and factual statements about the history of the matter under dispute.

The words of the envoys to the Senate in the matter of the Dionysiac artists are reported in direct speech. It is, I suspect, impossible now to know whether the words as recorded in the inscription represent in full what the envoys said or, for that matter, whether the words were taken down during oral delivery or the envoys delivered to the archivist written copies of texts that they read aloud. These same questions arise in respect of the most famous genre of epigraphically preserved documents relevant to an inquiry into records of proceedings, namely, the acts of the imperial Senate and the *orationes* delivered there by emperors—often, however, in the form of texts read aloud by others. (I set aside the two extracts from the *acta senatus* preserved on papyrus.)[12] Many people have written about the ideological force of the representations contained in these texts, regarding the constitutional structure of the principate and the location of legislative power. For that reason, I speak here only about formal qualities of those texts. In the case of the letter of Marcus Aurelius and Commodus to Miletus, for example, not only does Marcus explain that he is forwarding an *oratio* delivered to the Senate, but the forwarded text changes language (Greek to Latin) and switches from addressing the Milesians in the second person to referring to them in the third, and so forth (*AE* 1977, 802 = Oliver, *Greek Constitutions*, no. 192). That is to say, the document that the emperors sent to Miletus ostentatiously displays its status as documentary; in so doing, it makes the Milesians into witnesses of the operations of Roman legislative institutions in real time, as it were. Similar analyses, both interpretive and formal, might be performed with regard to the inscriptions from Sardis and Italica containing the imperial *oratio* and senatorial *sententia prima* regarding the prices of gladiators (*AE* 1965, 137; *IGLSardis* I 16; see Oliver and Palmer 1955).

I close this review of historical material at the dawn of the third century with a few remarks on the acts of the Severan Saecular Games.[13] These not only cite many documents but do so in *oratio recta*. For example, the initial statement is delivered by the *magister* of the *XVviri sacris faciundis*, Manilius Fuscus, who reads from a notebook (*libellus*, I.5–6). The text purports to give his words as delivered, except for notarial interjections such as "he said" (*inquit*). His motion (*relatio*), moreover, is framed in the present subjunctive (I.21–22). The *sententia prima* is given by Calpurnius Maximus, *consularis*, who reads from a notepad (*ex manuario*, I.25). Later speakers include the emperors, who were not present and communicated by letter. The letters were read aloud, and the first-person voice of the letters, addressing the senators in the second person, is retained. The same might be said of the many edicts quoted verbatim: the mood and tense of verbs consistently reflects the original context of efficacy, not the status of their quotation, which is documentary (II.14–18, III.25–32; V^a.33–36; VIII^a.5–13).

Two conclusions to this section might usefully be drawn. First, the fact that some of the earliest documents attesting the recording of proceedings testify to the *use* of such records is surely significant. The texts about the Dionysiac artists and the Amphiareion and the Sardinian boundary dispute taught people not simply that proceedings were sites for the adjudication of facts, but also that records of proceedings were privileged means for motivating official action. That is what the citation of such records in *cum* and περὶ ὧν clauses means.

Second, it is striking how often records of proceedings reveal not only that cases were regularly appealed and relitigated, but also that records of earlier proceedings were cited to provide the factual basis or point of departure for the next trial. Something of that sort is true with regard to the senatus consultum on the Dionysiac artists, and this is emphatically the case with regard to the decree of Helvius Agrippa, the *angareia* inscription from Phrygia, and the petition of Dionysia (*P.Oxy.* II 237). As a preliminary conclusion, one might say that a technology intended to provide a kind of epistemic clarity to normative acts on the part of the state was accepted within social contexts as doing just that. At the very least, participants to hearings regularly made use of the records of earlier hearings. In doing so, they endorsed de facto the social efficacy of not simply the memories preserved by that technology but the *kind* of memory it preserved. What is more, widespread participation in Roman hearings was both constitutive and indicative of a broad-based acceptance of the legitimacy of state institutions and their procedures as fora for the adjudication of facts and not, that is, about the norms that would be deployed on the basis of those facts. In consequence, contests that might have been about norms became, instead, contests over the normative salience of particular facts. In the next section, I attempt to corroborate and elaborate this claim through examination of three bodies of evidence.

II. Proceedings of (Provincial) (Criminal) Hearings and Christian Memory

The paradigm of state institutions undoubtedly exercised much influence on the documentary culture of church councils. Many of the most important of those councils were organized by lay officials of the state, and some things that we call "councils" were in fact *cognitiones*, investigative hearings, such as the so-called council of Carthage in 411. But we should not forget that fundamental aspects of Christian Romans' attitude toward historical knowledge had long since been determined by the operation of official technologies of memory in criminal hearings.

In this domain, a historical turning point may have been the provincial edict of Antoninus Pius as governor of Asia, when he enjoined on local irenarchs that they should produce sealed, written reports of any interrogation they conducted of a criminal suspect, before turning that suspect over to Roman authorities. As emperor, Pius elaborated on this instruction: Roman authorities should not only question the suspect *ab initio* but interrogate the irenarch as well, to confirm the accuracy of the written report and the spirit in which it was prepared.[14] In other words, the use of the same technologies of memory and authentication employed by Roman authorities, or at least of ones isomorphic with these, was henceforth more or less enjoined on local officials, even in communities that were alien in respect of Rome in public law, whenever and wherever it was likely that a case might ultimately be transferred to or appealed to the jurisdiction of a Roman official.

But the influence of Roman technologies for the recording and authentication of knowledge within legal institutions did not turn on a normative act from above. Rather, it seems clear that the formal qualities of a wide range of provincial literatures concerned with group identity and communal memory—among which literatures of dissent are particularly important—chose to stake their own claim to truthfulness through their appropriation of the protocols that grounded both the claim to veracity and the social efficacy of official documents. I and others have made this argument elsewhere. The present argument demands a more narrow demonstration, concerning, first, the ways in which Roman technologies of memory were observed in those texts and, second, the influence they had on Christian historiography. I do this briefly here, solely to establish a context for my consideration of the councils.

To begin with, in the *Acta Apollonii*, when Apollonius is summoned before a senatorial court, the first stage of the hearing consists in the recitation of the transcript of the earlier interrogation, the one conducted by Perennes (ἀναγνωσθήτω τὰ ἄκτα Ἀπολλώ, *Acta Apollonii* 11). Likewise, in the *Acta Pionii*, when Pionius is summoned before the proconsular governor, the text observes that minutes were kept of the hearing (γενομένων ὑπομνημάτων τῶν ὑποτεταγμένων, *Acta Pionii* 19.1–2).

Christian authors subsequently demonstrate their faith in the operation of those techniques—in the ability of such technologies to record the truth about the past, to wit, to record words as they were actually spoken—when they ground truth claims about their own representations in the fundamental reliability of Roman institutions, even in the ages of persecution. So, for example, Eusebius cites Apollonius of Ephesus railing against the Montanist Alexander (Eusebius, *Eccl. hist.* 5.18.9): according to Apollonius, the lowness of Alexander's character may be known by the fact that he was convicted for banditry by the provincial governor, and any who wish to confirm this are invited to consult the public archives of the province of Asia (καὶ οἱ θέλοντες μαθεῖν τὰ κατ' αὐτὸν ἔχουσιν τὸ τῆς Ἀσίας δημόσιον ἀρχεῖον). Similarly, in his *Vita Cypriani*, at the crucial moment when Cyprian's faith was tested in the crucible of the state, Pontius declines to give his own account: "what the priest of God responded when the proconsul questioned him, there are the *acta* to give this information" (*et quid sacerdos Dei proconsule interrogante responderit, sunt acta quae referant, Vita Cypriani* 11.1).

Again, as quoted by Eusebius (*Eccl. hist.* 7.11.6), Dionysius of Alexandria, writing against one Germanus during the Valerianic persecution, affirmed the truth of his case by citing not his memory of his own actions but the documentary record of his own interrogation: "Listen to the things that each party said, as they were stenographically recorded" (Αὐτῶν δὲ ἐπακούσατε τῶν ὑπ' ἀμφοτέρων λεχθέντων ὡς ὑπεμνηματίσθη).

III. The Councils of Carthage

The final decades of the contest between Catholics and Donatists is as well documented as its first half-century is obscure, and the record of the last ten years, from the council of Carthage in 401 to the three *actiones* of the *cognitio* overseen by the imperial emissary Flavius Marcellinus in Carthage in 411, is simply remarkably detailed.[15] For an overall interpretation of this material, I can scarcely do better than Brent Shaw.[16] On his reading, the actions of the Catholics commencing already in the late 390s, but especially their documentary practices commencing in 401, amounted to a form of politics, and its audience was the imperial court. The Catholics sought to show themselves in close homology with the structures of state power and the operating principles of state institutions, to bring about an ideological alignment between themselves and the state. If they could achieve this, the Donatists would become, *per definitionem*, heretics and, perforce, enemies of the imperial order. The actions of the Catholic councils of 401 and 403 should thus be understood as having as their aim the legitimation, via documentation, of the argument advanced in the Catholic petition to Septiminus in September 404, namely, that the Donatists should be classified as heretics as the category had been established in imperial edict (i.e., *C.Th.* 16.5.21 of 392).

For my part, I want to draw attention to three aspects of the historical record: (1) the effort on the part of Catholics to coopt the role of state institutions in producing public memory; (2) the broad subscription of both sides to the same knowledge culture, at least in the records of the *cognitio* of 411; and (3) the form then taken by disputes over proof during that *cognitio*.

To begin with, the councils of 401, 403, and 404 are to a very large extent known on the basis of a curious text that circulates under the title *Regestri ecclesiae Carthaginensis excerpta*, purportedly compiled by one Dionysius Exiguus. Whatever the details of its production, the document testifies to the possibility of producing hybrid texts from records of proceedings, as the *Excerpta* extract rules and canons, as well as select speeches in *oratio recta*.

Second, between 401 and 403, the Catholics sought to coopt state institutions to two ends: to force the Donatists to accept their version of the history of the Maximianist schismatics and to employ that history as precedent, which is to say, as normative for their own situation. To this end, the Catholics resolved to write *ad iudices Africanos*, to seek their assistance in forcing the Donatists to subscribe to the contents of the public records (*gesta publica*), "because secure knowledge is necessary to all" (*propter firmam notitiam omnibus necessariam*).[17] On that basis, the Catholics would then make an overture of peace—or, rather, they would *be seen* to make an overture of peace. This would be made evident to all "through municipal record keeping, by means of the constancy of documents" (*per gesta . . . municipalia, propter documentorum firmitatem*), even as the Donatists themselves had done concerning their own Maximianist schismatics.[18]

For this latter claim, to wit, that Catholic practice against the Donatists mimicked that of the Donatists against their own schismatics, we largely rely on evidence supplied by the Catholics. But my point overall is that the epistemic commitments of both parties were overdetermined by the broad legitimacy accorded by the culture at large to the technology and operation of state institutions. This interpretation is widely confirmed by the records of the *cognitio* of Carthage of 411. For knowledge of this event, we rely on three texts above all: the *gesta* of the event, which do not survive in full (they break off part way through the third day, and there are slight textual problems even in the surviving material); a table of contents for the *gesta*, called the *capitula gestorum*, which is complete; and Augustine's three-book summary of the entire event, in the so-called *Breviculus conlationis cum Donatistarum*. Analysis of a few episodes will illustrate the themes that I outlined a moment ago.

Early on the first day, each side recited the *mandata*, the instructions of its own respective council—namely, the instructions given to the bishops representing it at the *collatio*. In each case, according to Augustine, "the entire case was given in brief compass" (*tota causa breviter conprehensa est*), all of which was "demonstrated via documents of certain provenance" (*certis documentis demonstraretur*).[19]

The third day opens with the *cognitor* Marcellinus seeking to confirm that each side has received a transcript of the first two days and assents to its content, and the assent of both sides is read into the record. On the actual occasion, each speaker initialed the record next to any representation of his own speech, which fact is given textual form in the notation "in another hand" (*et alia manu*) before the words of authentication.[20] Of course, the presiding official and his *officia* do not so operate.

Shortly thereafter, the Donatists walk into a Catholic trap. The Catholics claimed that the Donatists had assented to the *collatio* and even sought to bring it about. The *cognitor* heard the Donatists' objections and said, "The Catholics will have to prove this" (*hoc catholici probare debebunt*). After some wrangling, the Catholics do just that, by submitting "records of proceedings conducted in the hall of the prefecture" (*gesta habita in iudicio praefecturae, Breviculus* 3.5). The Donatists respond by submitting "records of proceedings of the proconsul and of the prefecture of the vicariate" (*gesta proconsularia et vicariae praefecturae*), seeking to demonstrate that the Catholics had created these so-called facts by manipulating the content of the records of municipal councils (*acta munici-*

palia, Breviculus 3.6). A remarkable debate follows, in which each side competes to have sections of the *gesta* read aloud, albeit the records from different days.

At one point, the sheer difficulty of manipulating the records is made apparent. The *cognitor* Marcellinus himself seeks to break an impasse by urging that the *gesta* be read aloud, to demonstrate which side had stood forth "in the role of plaintiff" (*petitoris loco, Gesta* 3.166). Navigius, an *adiutor*, begins on the wrong page. Alypius interrupts, "We submitted an earlier text." Marcellinus says, "Those *gesta* that are *antiquiora*, let them be read aloud" (3.169–70). Navigius begins again, this time with a proceeding from 406. Now Marcellinus interrupts, "Let the things that are earlier be brought forward by the *officium*" (3.171). The *scriba* Rufinianus interjects, "There are even earlier matters contained in a codex that has been submitted . . ." (3.172). Alypius interrupts, "Voilà, we submitted *antiquiora*" (3.173). Rufinianus continues as if Alypius had not spoken: "if, indeed, the codex contains the consulate of Theodosius and Rumoridus (403 CE), but it also contains the consulate of our Lord Arcadius VI and Probus" (3.173). Marcellinus responds (with relief, one imagines), "Let the things that are older be read aloud" (3.174).

Subsequently, the Catholics turn the tables, demanding that the Donatists prove an assertion. Alas, the text of the *gesta* are lost at this moment, but in Augustine's summary, the Donatists are described as reading *prolixissima gesta*, which do not, however, name either the prefect who presided or the place where the hearing was conducted (*Breviculus* 3.34). Without the appropriate protocols, the truth content of the document was immediately called into question. What is more, in Augustine's account, the imperial *cognitor* Marcellinus was himself suspicious: he marveled that one thing had been promised and another recited (*Breviculus* 3.34).

At another moment, Augustine reacted to an objection on the part of the Donatists. They asked that a claim be demonstrated (*demonstrari*) "by the sort of texts by which things are customarily proved" (*his documentis quibus solent*); otherwise, it should be *purgari*, struck from the record (*Gesta* 3.214). Marcellinus urged that the relevant *gesta* be read aloud. The *exceptor* Martialis began to read but was interrupted by Montanus, asking, "What is the title of the document?" (3.216). Marcellinus himself observes, "No title is appended to the *acta*" (3.216). Martialis resumes but is interrupted again, this time by Petilian, asking, "Whence does he bring this forward, from a public *scrinium* or his own?" (3.217). Augustine seeks to break the impasse: "Let it be read, and then demand of us confirmation of the text [*huius lectionis firmitatem*]" (3.218). Marcellinus objects, "Before reading the document out loud, show clearly the source whence you bring it forward" (3.219). Augustine bluffs, "If there is any doubt, consult the archives of the proconsul." Alas for the Donatists, Marcellinus falls for this, concluding, "Since you say that the things that are being recited are in the public archives, as he has begun, so let the *officium* recite everything" (3.220).

Both Catholics and Donatists assented to the legitimacy and efficacy of the Roman state's procedures and technologies for the recording and preservation of historical memory. This agreement is nowhere more palpable than in the forms taken by their disagreements, which focus on particulars, not principles: the authentication of particular texts via the degree to which their protocols adhere to the standards of the state; the critique of particular copies in light of their authentication, storage, and transmission; and so forth.

IV. Chalcedon

The acts of Chalcedon[21] represent, in many respects, a culmination of the currents that I have tried to chart: the subscription by all parties—Romans and subjects, Christians and pagans, Catholics and Donatists, and now monophysites and dyophysites—to the legitimacy and efficacy of the same practices for recording, storing, and retrieving historical memory. Indeed, all these parties made use of them, not least because they all brought their disputes before the organs of the state. This is, of course, an essential aspect of my story. These attitudes must also have shaped notions of what counted as worthy of memory altogether. If verbatim transcription is a privileged technology for conveying truth, then the facts that notaries are not present in all contexts, nor are all forms of social action given to transcription, are themselves historically significant information. In the terrain traversed by this chapter, some things were not recorded, and some contexts were disprivileged.

I have already explained that Chalcedon forms a noteworthy instance of the use of records of proceedings, because so many participants were confronted with a documentary record of their own words from the second council of Ephesus only two years before. Here, I highlight two ways in which arguments over the use and value of stenographic records now zeroed in very narrowly on technical issues in their production. The argument was emphatically not over whether such records could convey truth. Rather, the certainty that they could convey truth made it essential that everyone become skilled at impugning the security of any given transcript.

For example, early in the first *actio*, the so-called Oriental bishops respond to the submission of records by shouting, in unison, "No one concurred [with that statement of faith]; force was used; violence with blows. We signed blank paper" (εἰς ἄγραφον χάρτην ὑπεγράψαμεν; *in pura charta suscripsimus*, 1.52). They impugned the record later in the same *actio*, when they shouted, "No one said that!" (1.146). The possibility that the technology of witness and subscription could be made to attest to falsehood, via manipulation of book production, was a deeply knowing move.

In a similar fashion, when confronted with disputes over the accuracy of documents and the existence of multiple records, the assembled officials—the ἐνδοξότατοι ἄρχοντες καὶ ἡ ὑπερφυὴς σύγκλητος (the most glorious officials and the exalted Senate)—queried, "The record of the proceedings, in whose hand is it written?" (Τὰ ὑπομνήματα τίνος χειρὶ γέγραπται; *Monumenta gestorum cuius manu perscripta sunt*, 1.123). The answer provided by Dioscorus was that we each wrote through our own notary.

Despite these quibbles about particular moments, copies, and bits of information, the overall impression given by the acts is of tragedy and of human frailty when faced with the consequences of a revision in truth in consequence of a change in power. This reaches a particular low in the examination of Basil of Isaurian Seleucia, who is confronted with a transcript of his own words from two years earlier. At that time, he thinks he remembers, he himself had been repeating words that were recited by another party, to which each bishop had been ordered to assent; there was great shouting and confusion; and someone had interrupted, but Basil cannot remember who it was. But in his rambling Basil leads himself ultimately to the confession that in encountering the record of the minutes, he now knows what he himself said.[22] In this way, technology has triumphed even over knowledge of oneself.

The imperial officials at Chalcedon were, like Marcellinus the *cognitor* at Carthage in 411, not going to be the ones on the hook for errors in orthodoxy. They sought a resolution, and they were trained to see just the kind of clarity about past and future that only a written transcript and archival documents might provide. At the very close of the first *actio*, they therefore put forward a suggestion: "Let each of the devout bishops of the present holy synod set out in writing what he believes, without fright, placing only fear of god before his eyes" (1.1072 [Greek], 1075 [Latin]). Of course, a written statement of the faith—a written record of any statement on a matter of controversy—was precisely what the present council was teaching all to fear. Those in the ascendant at Chalcedon thus conspired throughout the council to hold private meetings—some at night, to prepare for the next day's *actio*—without notaries present. The suggestion that each write down his own statement of the faith was therefore twice rejected. In the first instance, the rationale was that no innovation beyond what the 318 bishops had said at Nicaea was permissible (2.3, 5, 7). Later, during the fifth *actio*, when Asclepiades, the deacon of the great church of Constantinople, finally read a definition aloud, "it was decided not to include it in the record of proceedings" (Ἀσκληπιάδης διάκονος τῆς μεγάλης ἐκκλησίας Κωνσταντινουπόλεως ἀνέγνω ὅρον, ὃν ἔδοξε μὴ ἐνταγῆναι τοῖσδε τοῖς ὑπομνήμασι, 5.3).

This was the end of this particular technology for producing truth: it had become a danger from which the powerful released themselves.

Notes

The title of this chapter, "The Certainty of Documents," translates the phrase *documentorum firmitas* from *Regestri ecclesiae Carthaginensis excerpta* (*CCSL* 149), section VII, *Notitia de gestis concilli Carthaginensis*, 13 September 401, §69.

Abbreviations employed in this chapter include *AE* = *L'Année Épigraphique*; *CCSL* = *Corpus Christianorum Series Latina*; *F.Delphes* = *Fouilles de Delphes*; *IGLSardis* = William H. Buckler and David M. Robinson, *Sardis*, vol. 7, *Greek and Latin Inscriptions*, pt. 1 (Leiden: Brill, 1932); *ILS* = *Inscriptiones Latinae Selectae*; *RDGE* = *Roman Documents from the Greek East*; *SEG* = *Supplementum Epigraphicum Graecum*.

1. In addition to the chapter by Nicolas Cornu Thénard in the present volume, see Clifford Ando, "Fact, Fiction, and Social Reality in Roman Law," in *Legal Fictions in Theory and Practice*, ed. Maksymilian del Mar and William Twining (Boston: Springer, 2015), 295–323.

2. The classic language of the formula offers the alternatives *sei parret* :: *sei non parret*, "If it appears" :: "If it does not so appear." See *Roman Statutes*, no. 28, the *lex de Gallia Cisalpina*, chap. 20; Gaius, *Inst.* 4.37.

3. Leanne Bablitz, *Actors and Audience in the Roman Courtroom* (New York: Routledge, 2007); Kaius Tuori and Laura Nissin, eds., *Public and Private in the Roman House and Society* (Portsmouth, RI: Journal of Roman Archaeology, 2015); Francesco de Angelis, ed., *Spaces of Justice in the Roman World* (Leiden: Brill, 2010); Amy Russell, *The Politics of Public Space in Republican Rome* (Cambridge: Cambridge University Press, 2016). See also Judith Resnik and Dennis Curtis, *Representing Justice: Invention, Controversy, and Rights in City-States and Democratic Courtrooms* (New Haven: Yale University Press, 2011).

4. For only the latest such instance of influence, see Georgy Kantor, "Local Courts of Chersonesus Taurica in the Roman Age," in *Epigraphical Approaches to the Post-Classical Polis*, ed. Paraskevi Martzavou and Nikolaos Papazarkadas (Oxford: Oxford University Press, 2012), 69–86, at 79. Kantor suggests that the practice of recording the names of witnesses who affixed their seal on the recording of a decree of the council of Chersonesus may have developed in imitation of the practice of the Roman Senate, which recorded the names of those present at the writing down of the official text of its decrees.

5. H. J. M. Milne, *Greek Shorthand Manuals: Syllabary and Commentary* (London: Egypt Exploration Society, 1934); R. Coles, *Reports of Proceedings in Papyri*, Papyrologica Bruxellensia 4 (Brussels, 1966); H. C. Teitler, Notarii *and* Exceptores, Dutch Monographs on Ancient History and Archaeology 1 (Amsterdam: Gieben, 1985); G. A. Bisbee, *Pre-Decian Acts of Martyrs and Commentarii*, Harvard Dissertations in Religion 22 (Philadelphia: Fortress, 1988); Rudolf Haensch, "Das Statthalterarchiv," *Zeitschrift der Savigny-Stiftung für Rechtsgeschichte: Romanistische Abteilung* 109 (1992): 209–317; Sofía Torallas Tovar and K. A. Worp, *To the Origins of Greek Stenography: P.Monts.Roca 1* (Barcelona: Publicacions de l'Abadia de Monserrat, 2006).

6. Leopold Wenger, *Die Quellen des römischen Rechts* (Vienna: Österreichische Akademie der Wissenschaften, 1953), 388–95, "Akten des römischen Senats und anderer Körperschaften."

7. Barry Baldwin, "The *acta diurna*," *Chiron* 9 (1979): 189–203; Richard J. A. Talbert, *The Senate of Imperial Rome* (Princeton: Princeton University Press, 1984), 303–37; Marianne Coudry, "Sénatus-consultes et *acta senatus*: Rédaction, conservation et archivage des documents émanant du sénat, de l'époque de César à celle des Sévères," in *La mémoire perdue: À la recherche des archives oubliées, publiques et privées, de la Rome antique*, ed. Ségolène Demougin, CNRS—Série Histoire Ancienne et Médiévale 30 (Paris: Sorbonne, 1994), 65–102; Peter White, "Julius Caesar and the Publication of *Acta* in Late Republican Rome," *Chiron* 27 (1997): 73–84.

8. Pierre Batiffol, "Le règlement des premiers conciles africains et le règlement du sénat romain," *Bulletin d'ancienne littérature et d'archéologie chrétiennes* 3 (1913): 3–19; Francis Dvornik, "Emperors, Popes, and Councils," *Dumbarton Oaks Papers* 6 (1951): 3–23; Fergus Millar, *A Greek Roman Empire: Power and Belief under Theodosius II (408–450)* (Berkeley: University of California Press, 2006), 235–59; Brent D. Shaw, *Sacred Violence: African Christians and Sectarian Hatred in the Age of Augustine* (Cambridge: Cambridge University Press, 2011).

9. Clifford Ando, *Imperial Ideology and Provincial Loyalty in the Roman Empire* (Berkeley: University of California Press, 2000), 73–130; Andrew Harker, *Loyalty and Dissidence in Roman Egypt: The Case of the "Acta Alexandrinorum"* (Cambridge: Cambridge University Press, 2008). More broadly, see Luca Fezzi, *Falsificazione di documenti pubblici nella Roma tardorepubblicana (133–31 a.C.)* (Florence: Le Monnier, 2003).

10. Clifford Ando, "Scripture, Authority and Exegesis, Augustine to Chalcedon," in

Dans le laboratoire de l'historien des religions: Mélanges offerts à Philippe Borgeaud, ed. Francesca Prescendi and Youri Volokhine (Geneva: Labor et Fides, 2011), 213–26.

11. The Goharieni proceeding before Caracalla from Dmeir is *SEG* XVII 759. The *angareia* inscription from Phrygia is *SEG* XVI 754. I know only of a partial English translation of the Dmeir inscription, in A. Arthur Schiller, *Roman Law: Mechanisms of Development* (New York: Mouton, 1978), 486. Still valuable is the initial publication of the *angareia* inscription, in W. H. C. Frend, "A Third-Century Inscription Relating to *Angareia* in Phrygia," *Journal of Roman Studies* 46 (1956): 46–56. For a convenient translation, see Barbara Levick, *The Government of the Roman Empire: A Sourcebook*, 2nd ed. (New York: Routledge, 2000), 63–64.

12. Richard J. A. Talbert, "Commodus as Diplomat in an Extract from the *acta senatus*," *Zeitschrift für Papyrologie und Epigraphik* 71 (1988): 137–47.

13. The text of the *acta* of the Secular Games is cited from G. B. Pighi, ed., *De ludis saecularibus populi Romani quiritium libri sex*, 2nd ed. (Amsterdam: Schippers, 1965).

14. *Dig.* 48.3.6.1. On this text, see Clifford Ando, "Substantive Justice in Provincial and Roman Legal Argument," in *The Impact of Justice on the Roman Empire*, ed. Olivier Hekster and Koen Verboven (Leiden: Brill, 2019), 138–56.

15. Serge Lancel provides an indispensable guide to this material in his edition, *Gesta Conlationis Carthaginiensis anno 411*, *CCSL* 149A (Turnhout: Brepols, 1974), vii–xxxvi; see also E. Lamirande, ed., *Traités anti-donatistes*, vol. 5, Œuvres de Saint Augustin 32 (Paris: Études Augustiniennes, 1965), 9–90.

16. Shaw, *Sacred Violence*.

17. *Regestri ecclesiae Carthaginensis excerpta* (*CCSL* 149), section VII, *Notitia de gestis concilii Carthaginensis*, 13 September 401, §67.

18. *Regestri ecclesiae Carthaginensis excerpta* (*CCSL* 149), section VII, *Notitia de gestis concilii Carthaginensis*, 13 September 401, §69.

19. Augustine, *Breviculus* 1.10; see also *Gesta* 3.51, 141.

20. E.g., *Gesta* 3.7–10. Cf. 3.29, where the emperor subscribed *divina manu* (in his own hand) to a document.

21. For a brief guide to the acts of the eastern councils, see Millar, *Greek Roman Empire*, 235–47. On Chalcedon in particular, all modern readers are indebted to the introduction and translation by Richard Price and Michael Gaddis, *The Acts of the Council of Chalcedon*, 3 vols. (Liverpool: Liverpool University Press, 2005). See also André Jean Festugière's *Ephèse et Chalcédoine: Acts des conciles* (Paris: Beauchesne, 1982) and *Actes du Concile de Chalcédoine* (Geneva: P. Cramer, 1983). I cite the Greek and Latin texts from the edition by Eduard Schwartz, *Acta conciliorum oecumenicorum*, vol. 2 (Berlin: De Gruyter, 1933–1937).

22. *Acts of the Council of Chalcedon* 1:176 (trans. Price and Gaddis): "As reading of the minutes has reminded me, I then said. . . ."

CHAPTER 8

Fact as Law

An Archaeology of Legal Realism

Pierre Thévenin

The semantic versatility of the word *fact* stems not only from its widespread use in both common parlance and academic discourse but also from the uneasy way in which that word intertwines descriptive and normative senses. In its descriptive sense, the word *fact* presupposes a general distinction between propositions and their referents in the world. A proposition, or theory, is a set of words or thoughts that purports to represent reality; a fact presents itself as an element of reality. Of course, the distinction between words and worlds, propositions and facts, is not as simple as that broad-brush description suggests. Confronted with poets' insistence that "language is not outside of the world" but is "as concrete as a sandbag falling on your head,"[1] philosophers discuss several conflicting conceptions of fact: nominalist, constructivist, and realist.[2] The descriptive sense of *fact* seems to sit right at the crossroads of all three of these philosophical conceptions. In keeping with the "attempt" of modern knowledge "to describe the world to the extent that it is independent of our thought and action,"[3] facts are expected to stay immaculate, untouched by the discursive schemes that people, with our knack for talking, keep on devising.

That the term *fact* also has a normative sense is apparent from the way in which social scientists influenced by Weber[4] and philosophers with an interest in ethics[5] have discussed the "fact/value" distinction. The normative implications of the notion of fact are most clearly apparent in legal practice. In law, making a judicial decision necessarily entails finding facts. Identified by the law of evidence with "the object of judiciary proof-taking,"[6] this "factual segment" is ascertained through a variety of practical means, which depend on the types of evidence that are admissible under positive law and on the form of procedure—adversarial or not—used to present evidence in court. Just as a negative is integral to a photograph, facts are the negative of law. A judicial decision is always carefully separated into legal and factual "segments," yet the "truth about the fact," or *veritas rei*,[7] is an integral ingredient of law.

How do these two meanings of *fact*—descriptive and normative—relate to one another? Determining the relationship between the normative sense of *fact*, as defined by the law of evidence, and the descriptive sense of *fact*, as expressed in the epistemological distinction between propositions and facts, is not easy. The question implicates the relationship between jurisprudence and modern science. It may also elicit diverging views on the autonomy of law, the legal relevance of empirical research, or the construction of a deductive system of legal ideas.

In this chapter, I reassess the far-reaching relationship between these two senses of *fact* by taking an archaeological approach. In particular, picking up on a claim made by historians of science that the modern scientific concept of fact had legal origins, I reexamine the role that Roman law and its reception played in shaping the idea of fact and consider some unexplored implications of that role for contemporary jurisprudence. To show that a reconsideration of classical Roman law and its medieval reception can provide a fresh perspective on the notion of fact, I draw a contrast between two key moments in the evolution of the concept: the idea of *factum* in classical Roman legal thought and the idea of fact invoked by American legal realists in twentieth-century jurisprudence.

Balancing Two Meanings of Fact

Although the extent of its diffusion may have blurred its remote origins, the term *fact* is a characteristic product of classical Roman law. The word bears the stamp of morphological and semantic developments in the Latin language, which first allowed for the substantive use of the past participle of the verb *facio*, then provided it with a specific meaning in Roman courts. This specialized meaning stemmed from the sharp distinction that ancient *iurisperiti* drew between *ius* (law) and *factum* (a thing done or achieved), to "isolate" legal from nonlegal matters.[8] Although we should not exaggerate the importance of Rome for Western legal culture,[9] we must still recognize that the concept of fact originated in Rome, as a specific feature of the legal mindset. In ancient Greece, Athenian courts distinguished between τὰ πράγματα (*ta pragmata*) and ὁ νόμος (*ho nomos*), a distinction that bears some similarity to the *ius/factum* divide. But the Athenians never developed this nuanced pairing into a sharp disjunction.[10] Elsewhere, the "prelegal" thinking of Western culture before Rome and civilizations outside the West never gave rise to a concept that is equivalent to the Roman *factum*. Indeed, the idea of the fact as something that is the negative of law necessarily depends on a conceptual "isolation" of law from the ethical, religious, and social domains.[11] In that sense, the specifically Roman development of the concept of fact is an important element of what Rudolf von Jhering called the "inner awakening into consciousness" of Roman law as a whole.[12]

It is unlikely that a contemporary legal scholar, when asked about the word *fact*, would recall the Latin concept of *factum* and its diffusion in European culture along with the rest of Roman law. If anything, should that scholar turn his or her thoughts toward history at all, he or she would be more likely to think of the word *fact* in the phrase "law as fact"—one of the maxims of legal realism, a movement in jurisprudential thought that emerged in the first decades of the twentieth century. In this line of legal thought—a line that continues to mark out large parts of contemporary socio-legal scholarship—legal issues are fundamentally reducible to empirical terms. Legal cases should be decided through the identification of relevant legal rules and their correct interpretation; the correctness of the identification and interpretation depends on a process of fact-driven analysis.

How much of legal realists' modern understanding of the term *fact* can be said to echo the specific meaning given to the word *factum* by ancient Roman *iurisperiti*? The difficulty of answering that question arises not only from the historical distance that separates classical Roman lawyers from legal realists but, at a theoretical level, from the alteration of the balance between the descriptive and normative senses of the word *fact*. As the present analysis will show, this alteration stems from the development of a "factual sensibility" in modern science. Indeed, the development of this sensibility constitutes the dividing line between the ancient Roman normative sense of the term *fact* and its modern descriptive sense.

An Extended Tableau of the Factual Sensibility

In its descriptive, epistemological sense, the word *fact* designates the occurrence of an event having the capacity to corroborate or verify a hypothesis that the scientific community has framed to explain a phenomenon.[13] Certainly not all facts verify or corroborate a hypothesis. Some facts are "recalcitrant," in that they make it necessary either to shift to a new theory or to draw subsidiary hypotheses preserving the initial one. How does this scientific notion of observational facts, either corroborative or recalcitrant, relate to the legal domain? Legal realists, embracing an attitude toward facts that they saw as typical of modern science, answered this question by promoting the study of law itself as an observational, descriptive fact. Historians of science underscored the importance of the descriptive/normative divide. The descriptive notion of fact, the latter suggested, derives directly from the normative one.

The suggestion that scientists actually borrowed their conception of the fact from lawyers had a special theoretical resonance among philosophers of science. It upset the assumption that the two senses of the word *fact* belonged to the two separate functional systems of science and law.[14] In so doing, it appealed to many theorists of science for whom the association of facts with the passive part of our knowledge had been unsatisfying.[15] It also fleshed out the meaning of the terse claim, made by philosophers, that "no fact is ontologically fundamental."[16] It thus prepared the way for a new understanding of *fact* as an "elevator-word," whose "use is not oriented to the description of any entity of the world, but at expressing how we think about the world."[17] But if the word *fact* works as an "elevator," at how many floors does it stop?

One answer to that question was given by historians of science. According to Gottlob Frege, the modern scientist who "wishes to emphasize the necessity of a firm foundation for science" cries "Facts! Facts! Facts."[18] In the midst of the so-called science wars, some historians of science began to treat Frege's cry as a historical problem to be solved, turning the notion of fact itself into an object of historical inquiry. Those historians traced the genealogy of the term *fact* to a "factual sensibility" that they saw reflected in the cornucopia-like collections of sixteenth- and seventeenth-century cabinets of curiosities. The startling assemblages of uncongealed crystals with distorting mirrors in such cabinets "bequeathed to natural philosophy," according to the historians of science, "an enduring ideal of factuality."[19] The historians associated this factual sensibility with another new intellectual practice, an "epistemological decorum" that made research produced by others—"those surprising matters of fact which had been naturally found or artificially produced"—a legitimate source of knowledge about the natural world.[20] Most important, historians of science, following the lead of Michel Foucault,[21] traced the genealogy of the scientific fact back one step farther, claiming that the early modern "factual sensibility" and "epistemological decorum" both had roots in a judicial context. The concept of fact, they explained, "was established in law long before it appeared in science," so that we can "trace its movement from its old home in law to its new home in natural philosophy."[22]

A hodgepodge of legal-historical arguments was deployed to justify this new genealogy of the fact. Most scholars scrutinized the connections between the scientific fact and the reasonable-doubt doctrine developed to regulate jury verdicts in English law, where proof, testimony, and findings of facts were all central issues. Other scholars focused on the possible linkages between the scientific fact and the inquisitorial procedure applied by ecclesiastical courts and the lay jurisdictions of continental Europe.[23] Whatever the angle, particular attention was given to Francis Bacon's extensive use of judicial rhetoric in his essays in natural philosophy. Drawing on his practical experience as lord chancellor in the English Court of Chancery and as a clerk of the Star Chamber, Bacon formulated a series of judicial analogies that were integral to his call for an inductive method in natural philosophy. Just as the medieval Roman-canonical inquisitorial procedure called for a fine-grained examination of the *veritas facti* behind the defendant's claims, inductivist modern philosophers would try to compel "Nature," who likes to "hide herself," to confess "her secrets."

> For like as a man's disposition is never well known or proved till he be crossed, so nature exhibits herself more clearly under the trials and vexations of art than when left to herself.[24]

The apparent reference to cross-examination and confession, both forensic techniques of determining facts, is far from anecdotal here. Into the scientific revolution of the early seventeenth century, it transposes the attitude toward facts that had blossomed in the course of an older revolution, the "medieval revolution of inquisition."[25]

Indeed, during the emergence of inquisitorial procedure that began in the thirteenth century and continued through the late fourteenth century, a new insistence was put on facts and on the necessity of reaching the "truth." Arising partly as a result of the rediscovery of Justinian's *Corpus iuris* in central Italy in the late eleventh century, the new forms of procedure stood in sharp contrast with the forms of trial that had prevailed during the early Middle Ages. In early medieval ordeals and duels, the restoration of concord between opposing parties (in effect, armed families) mattered more than the public illumination of any sort of "truth." The *révolution de l'inquisitoire*, influenced by Roman law, reversed this prioritization: at least from the thirteenth century onward, every judicial decision was to be based on a fine-grained examination of facts.[26]

The new procedures did not simply respond to the "widespread demand to ascertain the facts in a juridical key" that the historian Massimo Vallerani has documented in medieval Italy.[27] Rather, they created such a demand, by diffusing the idea that it was technically possible and politically desirable to establish the *veritas facti* of a dispute by dedicated institutional means. Such means included, from the thirteenth century onward, both accusatorial (adversarial) and inquisitorial (nonadversarial) procedures. The degree of factual certainty that could be established varied depending on the form of procedure. The objective of accusatorial procedure was to determine the probable truth—that is, facts of relative certainty; the objective of inquisitorial procedure was to determine the "absolute and theoretical truth."[28] In each procedure, a fixed order of procedural steps (*ordo iudiciarius*) provided a road map for ascertaining the facts. In close keeping with the activity of tribunals experimenting with these procedures,[29] medieval scholars created a specific genre of legal treatise setting forth that *ordo*. The treatises discussed matters ranging from the organization of the judicial proceeding itself to the forensic operation of cross-examination and confession.[30] That doctrinal discussion of the *ordo* of trial made it possible to inquire into facts.

The entertainment of an equivalent possibility within natural science was the true stake of Francis Bacon's program. Following the legal parlance in which he was proficient, Bacon coined the new inductivist method as an *inquisitio facti ipsius* (inquisition of the fact itself).[31] More than a rhetorical whim,[32] this method was a powerful means of obliterating the Aristotelian conception of knowledge that had permeated natural philosophy for nearly five centuries. For Aristotle, knowledge sprang from an appetite of the soul; thought, for him, was "moved by the intelligible" (νοῦς δὲ ὑπὸ τοῦ νοητοῦ κινεῖται).[33] Bacon's new method of learning provided a kind of administrative process of knowledge formation. Science would no longer rest on a natural process, one aimed to fulfill the stellar desires of cosmic perfection supposedly implanted within the contemplative mind. Modeled on medieval administration of justice, which had come to depend on the formalized proceedings of a court of law, the new science would depend on the "trials and vexations of art." As the legal machinery was aimed at the command of men, the scientific machinery was aimed at the command of nature.

A Natural Science of Law (as Fact)

Natural science is one of the floors served by the elevator-word *fact*. Unraveling the historical passage from the normative meaning of the Roman *factum* to the descriptive ambit of facts cried out by modern scientists, historians of science set out to recover the intellectual linkages between medieval law and the modern ideal of inductive science. More often than not, the historians would proceed to use those analogies as indicators of the brittle foundation of the modern ideal of science. The corresponding line of research eventually fell short of the philosophical expectations that had seemed to surround it at first. The historians' research had aimed at changing the minds of philosophers of science, whose assumptions the research was intended to call into question.[34] But its ultimate outcome, as it faded away in the 2000s, was simply to reinforce the preexisting divide between science-friendly fact lovers and postmodern "factish" breakers.[35]

Few historians in this debate realized that the elevator could move in both directions—not only down, from law to science, but up, from science back to law.[36] From the perspective of a "historian of the fact," it is noteworthy enough that a movement called "legal realism" should have emerged in the first half of the twentieth century, with the expression "law as fact" as its motto and with an eponymous essay as one of its foremost manifestos.[37] Consideration of this recent chapter in the history of legal thought becomes even more relevant when one observes its implications for the relationship between the descriptive and normative meanings of the term *fact*.

An outline of the basic tenets of legal realist thought makes this apparent. Differences make it difficult to present legal realism as a unified school: it is best described as a diverse movement, divided between a Scandinavian branch and an American one, with roots in late nineteenth-century European antiformalist thought.[38] Yet we may say that legal realists share a preoccupation with the interdependence of law and reality. Shunning any approach to the law as a world of its own, they insist, as the Swedish legal realist Karl Olivecrona put it, that

> only the metaphysical conceptions have engendered the doctrine that legal science should move within another sphere of reality than science in general.[39]

Just as the natural sciences, in the course of their development since the seventeenth century, broke away from metaphysical ideas, the legal realists argued that it was high time for lawyers to do the same for their discipline and to acknowledge that law is a social and political phenomenon. By different means and to varying extents, all legal realists have sought to entertain the possibility of looking at law itself as a mundane reality, a series of facts, expected to be empirically verifiable and statistically predictable.

A new parallel was drawn between the lawyer's and the modern scientist's missions. Just as it is the modern scientist's task to substitute metaphysics and debunk superstition, the legal realist must expose the magical features of the legal rules with which he or she is confronted. The legal realist's first concern is to dissipate the heady fumes that legal rules have been diffusing ever since the Roman law of possession, which Olivecrona held to be a paradigmatic illustration of the fact that

> all rules of law are rules about the acquisition and transference of supernatural powers over a thing or a person, derived from a sort of magic.[40]

The fact-driven model of legal analysis is meant as a remedy against any tendency to enhance this legal magic. It stands against two assumptions that have been pivotal to the historical development of legal scholarship.

The first assumption is the long-standing view that law consists of a set of legal rules and legal ideas. To a realist, this is far from evident. Legal rules and ideas are not a sui generis phenomenon but are epiphenomena of larger practices and forces: political moves, social turmoil, economic calculations, and (possibly) judicial decisions. Legal rules certainly matter, but they are not all that matter. Only a metaphysics-laden kind of legal thinking would see them as the material of which law is made.

A second assumption the legal-realist stance upsets is the common expectation that legal rules should form a body and fall in a closed system of legal ideas. Legal realists oppose the conceptualist agenda that entrusts legal science with the task of illuminating or looking after law as a system. To them, the scientific quality claimed by the conceptualist approach to legal rules is simply a formalist facade.[41] Far from being "scientific" in any appropriate sense of the word, any longing for a legal system effectually stimulates the metaphysical representation of law as a reality of its own, a transcendent realm whose hold on "natural" reality amounts to a sort of magic.

Critical of this conceptualist agenda, legal realists insist that legal thinking must follow suit from inductivist science. "They want," as Karl Llewellyn put it, "to check ideas, and rules, and formulas by facts, to keep them close to facts."[42] The use of the verb *check* in Llewellyn's formulation speaks to a typically descriptive representation of facts as epistemological assets, endowed with a capacity to corroborate a statement. The true meaning of the "law-as-fact" mantra surfaces here. It is an incentive to treat legal rules and legal ideas in the exact fashion in which a modern scientist would treat a hypothesis. As William Twining puts it, legal realists do not merely "conceptualize law in terms of . . . fact"; they call for a profound reorganization of legal studies so that legal scholars and practitioners "take . . . facts seriously."[43] How else could we be protected from the supernatural aura of legal rules? As soon as the experimental creed of inductivist science was accommodated by legal scholars, facts began to appear everywhere in law. The examination of facts—social, economic, and political—would help to "check" legal ideas and legal rules, while a nascent "natural science of the law"[44] would help to improve the law machine.

A Circular Archaeology of the Fact

The development of the parallel between legal and scientific missions should count as an important chapter in the history of the concept of fact. The core tenet of the legal realists can be read as a call for applying back to legal scholarship the very method that historians of the fact had analyzed as a modern derivation from the judicial sphere. If that suggestion is correct, the archaeology of the fact takes on a sort of circular form. Just as adding one story to a building disrupts the equilibrium among its initial components, altering its overall appearance, the integration of the "law-as-fact" stance forces us to rearrange our archaeological scenario.

In an initial stage, brought about by the rediscovery of the Justinianic *Corpus iuris*, a technical distinction between *quaestiones facti* (questions of fact) and *quaestiones iuris* (questions of law) resurfaced in the High Middle Ages. Although this technical distinction was originally the work of the classical Roman lawyers, achieving its greatest elaboration in the second century CE[45] and in a distinctive orientation toward the "isolation" of legal thinking,[46] the medieval lawyers gave the distinction new dimensions. On the one hand, they used it to set up an "inquiry into the fact itself," as part of the new inquisitorial (nonadversarial) procedure of the thirteenth century. On the other hand, they used it in adversarial forms of procedure, to allocate decision-making authority between judges, responsible for questions of law, and jurors, responsible for questions of fact. In medieval English law, this distinction is readily apparent in the oath by which jurors deliberating an *assize of novel disseisin* swore to reach a *veritatis dictum* by looking exclusively at questions of fact, leaving it to the judges to examine issues of law.[47]

In a second stage, seventeenth-century philosophers with high-level legal experience drew on these judicial patterns (long established by then) to flesh out a new ideal for the advancement of learning. Recasting science as an *inquisitio naturae*, instead of a contemplation of ideas motivated by cosmic desires, they paved the way for the modern experimentalist's contention that "matters of fact ought to be brought to trial."[48]

Then, in a third and final stage, a movement within Scandinavian and American legal scholarship, beginning in the late nineteenth century[49] and reaching its acme in the 1920s and 1930s, applied this new model of scientific inquiry back to jurisprudence itself. A "natural science of the law" was put forth to reabsorb (so to speak) this scientific model and thereby to keep "legal rules and formulas close to facts."[50]

Each of the steps in this sequence is certainly complex enough to raise problems of historical interpretation. I focus here on the archeological scenario that brings them together and on the consequences of this loop-like, circular movement of the concept of the fact, from law to science and from science back to law. One immediate consequence of the circle is to complicate the question of just how close legal rules and formulas can come to facts and reality. We need to circumvent the philosophical tendency to see the "law-as-fact" mantra as a matter of defining what law is—that is, a matter of providing an answer to a general inquiry into the nature of law.[51] Instead of leaving it up to philosophers to settle this question (e.g., asking whether "we may think of the jurisprudence the Realists advocated as a naturalized jurisprudence on the model of Quine's naturalized epistemology"),[52] we should commit ourselves to the practice of a different jurisprudence, more sensitive to the far-reaching echoes of the concept of fact. This concept continues to play a major part in philosophical debates on law's relationship to reality.[53] Yet only a historical[54] and exploratory[55] jurisprudence can make sense of the circular genealogy that I have been describing: on the one hand is the ancient Roman legal concept of the *factum*, which has had practical relevance to lawyers ever since it was put to use to shape judicial procedures; on the other hand is the modern Baconian "matter of fact" associated with the "factual sensibility" and the "epistemological decorum" of seventeenth-century natural philosophy, which Quine might well be said to have brought to a late stage of philosophical refinery.

As this circle indicates, the relationship of law and reality promises to be intricate indeed. A crux of the issue is not only that the Baconian concept of the fact is, at whatever remove, an inheritance from Roman legal vocabulary, as cultural historians of the 1990s documented, but that the development of legal realism into a branch of jurisprudence marked a sort of double-entry jurisprudential book keeping, allowing for the preservation of the normative notion of *factum* in legal practice,[56] while making use of the descriptive notion of facts in a "natural science of the law." Was this enough to conflate the two archeologically distinct layers of the word *fact*?

America's "Intimate Connection" with Roman Law

Inasmuch as it provides the archeology of facts with its most ancient touchstone, Roman law offers a fruitful ground for answering the question posed at the end of the preceding section. If legal realists claimed to develop a "natural science of law," can we take them at their word and understand them as having indeed conflated the normative and descriptive notions of fact? In other words, did they absorb the Roman legal *factum* used in judicial practice into the Baconian concept of facts as premises for inductive reasoning?

A preliminary discussion of the relationship between legal realism and Roman law may help us engage with this issue. That there is such a relationship at all might be surprising at first blush. Despite historians' long-standing efforts to understand it as a product of the broader social dynamics of Roman history,[57] Roman law is commonly associated with the conceptualist approach to legal thinking as a closed system.[58] Roman legal thought thus seems to be at odds with legal realism, which is, in Max Radin's words, "the sworn foe of conceptualism as a legal ideal."[59] Moreover, if the "closed-system" model of law is, as Karl Llewellyn writes, "nowhere to be found in the USA," where a high degree of judicial discretion has always predominated,[60] why should Roman law and this American strand of twentieth-century legal thought be related to one another in the first place? Significantly, the most authoritative survey of the teaching of Roman law in the United States ends in the 1930s, at the exact moment when legal realists are commonly described as having gained scholarly and political prominence.[61] Was it indeed the case that the rise of legal realism corresponded to an eclipse of Roman law?

The understanding of Roman law as a backdrop for the promotion of a conceptualist ideal of legal science surfaces clearly in discussions of the legacy of late nineteenth-century American legal science. Praising its "desire for legal clarity and certainty,"[62] upholders of this classical form of American legal thought suggest that it was deeply indebted to the European tradition of civil law. "Unlike the common law with its mass of particular cases," explains Charles Barzun, "the civil law, derived from the ancient Roman Law, was a distillation of clearly-written first principles from which rules could be easily deduced."[63] On that account, the scientific character of civil law systems is a result of their "derivation from" Roman law. American scholars' interest in Roman law in the late nineteenth and early twentieth centuries was thus largely collateral to and contingent on their admiration for the deductive, highly conceptualist European legal science of the nineteenth century. As a relic of the age of "classical legal thought,"[64] the study of Roman law declined together with the "geometric paradigm" of law that harked back to Leibniz, himself an admirer of the geometrical quality of Roman law.[65] This geometrical conception of Roman law fits, in turn, with Karl Llewellyn's description of the closed-system model of jurisprudence, one that legal realists contested.

> The Law exists as a given; not a tool, but a master to be served. It is the constant from which one deduces the correct answer; it therefore stands upon its own self-sufficient ground—superior, not subordinate, to Life.[66]

That Llewellyn's description corresponds to the German *Rechtswissenschaft* of the mid-nineteenth century is certain. In Savigny's view, the Law (capital *L*) was not subordinate to any Life (again, capital *L*). As a coherent, deductive, and closed system of legal ideas—a system that Savigny laid out in his 1840 *System des heutigen römischen Rechts* (System of contemporary Roman law),[67] Law was granted a life of its own. Law was, in Savigny's conception, an "organic" emanation of the popular spirit of the people—the mysterious and romantic *Volksgeist*, where Savigny located the primeval source of all law. In his polemic *Vom Beruf unsrer Zeit für Gesetzgebung und Rechtswissenschaft* (On the vocation of our time for legislation and jurisprudence), his most famous programmatic writing, Savigny wrote, "Like language, law *lives* in the consciousness of the people" (emphasis added).[68] Based on a romantic approach to both national law and idiom, Savigny's vision—of a sophisticated, conceptual schema of private law based in Roman law and arising out of the historical depth of the *Volk*'s psyche[69]—gave German *Rechtswissenschaft* its basic creed for the rest of the nineteenth century. But how much of this description really fits Roman law?

There are many reasons to suspect that the lens through which nineteenth-century legal scholars saw the Roman legal sources biased their understanding.[70] We should, at minimum, be cautious of ascribing to Roman lawyers the conceptualistic views of nineteenth-century geometric lawyers. Were the legal realists who were most familiar with Roman law not especially aware of the discrepancy between nineteenth-century jurisprudence and classical Roman law? One could perhaps argue that Roscoe Pound, although a formative figure for the American legal realists, was still writing under the spell of conceptualism when he wrote that "law, in a modern sense, [began] with the Romans."[71] But can the same be said of Max Radin? An important exponent of American legal realism, best known for his essay on statutory interpretation, Radin was a Roman law specialist and expert in philology, whom Spanish legal historian Carlos Petit praises as "the American legal scholar with the most connections in Europe."[72] Like Roscoe Pound, but with a degree of historical precision that Pound could not attain, Radin argued that American law had an "intimate and direct" connection with Roman law.

Was it not a "mischievous error," argued Radin, to view the *Corpus iuris*, for instance, as an authoritative code? Although modern civilians might have been eager to see the Justinianic corpus as a statute of sorts, Radin compared it to a collection of legal precedents, similar to those with which common lawyers work.

> In dealing with this [Justinianic] material, men trained in the Common law have a very real advantage. Much the larger part of it consists of decisions in concrete issues, not distinguishable in character from those decisions that begin with the Year Books and end with the current issue of the advance sheets.[73]

No statement could have contrasted more sharply with the opinion that then prevailed in the United States, modeled on Thomas Scrutton's imperialistic confidence that English common law had no share in the "sea of waves" formed by civil law systems influenced by Roman law.[74] Clearly, Radin knew that it was necessary to distinguish between, on the one hand, the original thought-world of classical Roman law and, on the other hand, the conceptualistic, closed system of law that his fellow professors wrongly associated with Roman law. Radin followed suit with his *Handbook of Roman Law* in 1927, the same year in which he teamed up with Karl Llewellyn to defend Sacco and Vanzetti, an episode that revealed legal realism's force as a political movement. Such an interest in Roman law, held by such an exponent of legal realism, could hardly have come from an admiration for the civil law tradition and its "geometrical" perfection. On the contrary, it points to a flaw in the prevailing historical narrative, according to which Roman law and European civil law fade into one another.

Factum fictum

That an original approach to Roman law might have developed under the umbrella of American legal realism[75] sheds more light on our circular archeology of facts. This new light—a signal that those two distant lines in the history of legal thought might actually intersect—prompts us to question divisionist accounts of the geography and history of legal thought. But to what extent does it help us to elucidate the balance between the descriptive and normative meanings of the term *fact*? The best way of delineating any line of answer to this issue is to spot the occasions on which the legal realists' approach to facts—as a specific blend of judicial *factum* and Baconian matters of fact—confronted the original Roman approach to *quaestiones facti*.

Legal fictions (*fictiones legis*)—one of the distinctive features of the Roman lawyers' mode of thought—were one occasion for this confrontation. At a time when Rome had grown from a city-state into an empire, Roman lawyers devised legal fictions as work-arounds to statutory law, aimed at closing the gap that "yawned between contemporary practice and statute law that notionally governed that practice."[76] Because they allowed legal innovation while "honoring the principles articulated in earlier legislation,"[77] legal fictions ranked among the praetor's favorite interpretative techniques.

Is it possible to give a legal-realist account of this feature of Roman law? We can begin by noting the instrumentalist, means-to-end character of Roman legal fictions.[78] In that sense, Roman fictions exemplified the technical dimension that legal realists deemed essential to legal thought in general. The realists distinguished between technical considerations, "which restrict themselves to limited goals," and theoretical knowledge, "which comes up when thoughts are ordered in accordance with a sense of unity."[79] To a legal realist, all legal knowledge is technical and should pursue "limited goals." Roman legal fictions, as technicalities par excellence, dovetail neatly with this crucial tenet of legal realism—the reluctance to ascribe to the lawyer a mission to order legal thought "in accordance with a sense of unity." Roman fictions can serve as an archaeological touchstone for any legal scholar with a preference for technique over formal, deductivist, and systematical science.

Indeed, before Jerome Frank made a splash in 1930 by claiming that "all legal rules, principles, precepts, concepts, standards are fictions,"[80] Roman *fictiones legis* had already been identified as a paradigmatic instance of fact-oriented legal thinking. This is precisely what Roscoe Pound himself had done in 1910, when he formulated the famous distinction between law in books and law in action, which would be so influential in the development of socio-legal studies. This distinction derived, in Pound's terms, from the practical need to "adjust the letter of the law to the demands of administration in concrete cases."[81] Pound, an acknowledged connoisseur of Roman law, almost certainly had in mind the distinctively Roman *legis fictiones* when he presented the necessity of that adjustment as "one of the earliest discoveries of the law." As he explained,

> We are by no means so much wiser than our fathers as we sometimes assume. While we have few of the old fictions of procedure left, we can make new ones of our own upon occasion in the like spirit.[82]

If my reading of Pound is correct, the main contribution of the legal realists to jurisprudence was, basically, to recover the technical dimension of Roman legal fictions and to extend it to law as a whole, at the expense of any conceptualistic approach to jurisprudence. When Jerome Frank presents all legal ideas as fictions and when Karl Llewellyn insists that rules and law itself should be regarded as "means to ends,"[83] they invite the twentieth-century lawyer to develop technical work-arounds to statutory law that resemble those of the Roman praetors.

It may seem paradoxical to present Roman legal fictions as prefigurations of a movement aimed at equating law and fact. Our circular archaeology warns us to distinguish between ancient lawyers and their twentieth-century counterparts. Inasmuch as the division of the term *fact* into separate descriptive and normative senses was contingent on the "factual sensibility" of early modern science, Roman lawyers and twentieth-century legal realists cannot be taken to operate within identical discursive parameters. Although Roman legal fictions might have served as "convenient shorthands,"[84] they would also, more often than not, bring about "epistemic and ontological conundrums."[85] Precisely this metaphysical dimension prompted Hans Vaihinger and Hans Kelsen to broach the subject of legal fictions, at about the same time as Roscoe Pound published the papers from which I have quoted. In Kelsen's view, fictions are "contradictory to reality." They consist of "an adulteration or a detour of thought."[86] As legal anthropologist Annelise Riles has noted, legal fictions may even legitimate an artificialist reading of law that is at odds with "naturalized" jurisprudence. From an artificialist point of view,

> far from just helping to order social, political or economic phenomena [i.e., the legal realists' understanding of fictions] legal fictions actually constitute those phenomena.[87]

As Riles pointedly remarks, this conception of legal fictions implies that fictions create "virtual facts," that is, "factual modes which transcend actual factual reality."[88] But if legal fictions can be seen as extreme illustrations of the distinction between "legal" facts and "natural" facts, how could Roman legal fictions have inspired legal scholars intent on keeping legal rules "close to the facts"?

The circular dimension of our archaeology may suggest another approach to the problem.[89] Rather than asking which theoretical reading is more apt to capture the essence of legal fictions, we should ask how this particular form of legal thinking managed to climb its way up the multilayered archaeology of the fact, from its Roman origins up to its adoption by the legal realists. As Yan Thomas has shown, the legal fictions embedded in the Roman tradition were precisely a mixture of metaphysical conundrums and convenient shorthands.[90] Roman lawyers' use of fictions combined sophisticated conceptualization and down-to-earth practical thinking. On the one hand, such fictions could be taken as evidence for the capacity of law to create "virtual facts"—facts completely contrary to reality, which exist as facts only by operation of law. On the other hand, fictions could serve the purpose of a natural science of law. Would recognition of this ambivalent nature not be in keeping with the circular, loop-like movement that we have associated with the "discovery" of the fact?

It is certainly tempting to endorse the artificialist idea that legal fictions "actually constitute" facts. Would it not provide a straightforward answer to the philosophical puzzle that this formulation encapsulates? Facts were not only originally a Roman, judicial invention; they are also a revelation of law's power to make worlds and to construct social reality. This conception of fact as the product of artifice is also compatible with a postmodernist account of fact, in which even facts that are not created by the legal system may exist only as "mere illusions."[91] This postmodernist account, too, would obliterate the archaeological distance that separates the ancient, normative sense of *factum* and its modern, Baconian descriptive sense, as if we had to make a choice between the two and take the side of either the artificialists or the realists.

Words

I conclude this analysis by sketching an escape route from this forced choice between the normative and descriptive senses of the term *fact*. I focus here on the second floor served by that "elevator-word": the moment when the rediscovery of Roman law in the Middle Ages caused a reconfiguration of judicial practice. Interestingly, the Middle Ages stand at a point along our archaeological circle when "facts" are not yet an object of interest for natural philosophy but when the sources of Roman law were already being studied with an eye toward systematization. Such a concern for law as a system was arguably absent from ancient Roman lawyers' thinking about law, at least if we follow a legal-realist approach to Roman law, like that of Max Radin.[92]

This medieval moment was marked by a distinctive attitude toward words. Indeed, words play a large part in the divide between the different branches of jurisprudence that I have outlined so far. Lon Fuller's analysis of legal fictions, for instance, establishes a clear distinction between the practical merits of fiction as a technique and its metaphysical connotations. While favoring the technical dimension of legal fictions, Fuller also takes care to explain why fictions stirred enthusiasm among lawyers who were metaphysically minded. Fuller then refers to Jhering's explanation, according to which this line of thought originated in a fascination with the "all-pervading power of the word" and the "mysterious influence exercised by names and symbols."[93] The legal realists, we could say, were essentially lawyers who resisted that fascination for words. Llewellyn typifies this resistance when he describes law in books as threatened by a tendency to "turn into words—placid, lifeless, like some old canal."

Whereas legal practice is compared to a vigorous river, legal science aspires to have the river "spill and flood into the canal of stagnant words." As Llewellyn puts it, legal realists "want law to deal with things, with people, with tangibles—not with words alone."[94]

The medieval interpretations of Roman law offer the sort of "archive" that we need in order to reassess this vision.[95] Medieval legal scholasticism was certainly infused with an intense fascination for words. As a genre, the gloss itself was thoroughly literal and exclusively oriented to the text, as the legal historian Ennio Cortese has accurately remarked.

> Because it is oriented at a literal explanation [*alla comprensione della lettera*] [of the *Corpus iuris*], Irnerius' method of exegesis also prepares for the establishment of the text. Technical legal analysis and philological endeavor are the two sides of the same coin. The first [medieval] approach to [the Byzantine compilation of classical legal material established by Emperor] Justinian developed along those two complementary dimensions. This theorical and fairly abstract approach had the text as its substantial core and the gloss as its typical literary outcome.[96]

Medieval glosses on Roman law offer the historical example par excellence of "law in books," to pick up on Roscoe Pound's seminal expression.[97] Yet words, in the medieval jurists' conception, were not at all opposed to dealing "with things, with people, with tangibles." In the medieval understanding, words were neither stagnant nor lifeless. There was a tangible quality to them, a quality on which Ezra Pound touched when he said that one can never understand what literature meant in the Middle Ages if one forgets the amount of work that it cost to copy a manuscript by hand.

That the same goes for legal literature as for poetry is apparent in the prologue of a twelfth-century collection of disputed legal problems known as the *Questiones de iuris subtilitatibus* (Questions on the subtleties of the law).[98] Borrowing a literary image from the scene depicting the dream of Scipio in Cicero's *De re publica*, the author describes visiting the Temple of Justice (*templum iustitiae*) while taking a stroll in the countryside. A deified Justice sits in the middle of the temple. Inscribed in letters of gold on the surface of the glass walls of the temple is the entire Justinianic corpus of Roman law (*litteris aureis inscriptus est totus librorum legalium textus*). The author catches a glimpse of Justice through the legal words, that is, through the blank unfilled spaces apparent within and between the written letters—literally, in the gaps of the law. More important, Justice herself perceives the surrounding world through the same blank spaces.

Such a peculiar phenomenology stands in some contrast with the realists' view of words, facts, and fictions. Not only is the perception of the facts strictly dependent on the letter of the *libri legales*, as in the formula *ex iure oritur factum*,[99] but the letter itself is moving. Indeed, in the dream, Justice is surrounded by the six civic virtues. Among them, Equity leads a group of professors, whose task is to reposition the different *leges* apparent on the temple's glass walls. This scholarly activity therefore results in an ever-shifting combination of textual patterns.

This twelfth-century image offers quite an accurate picture of what the law is all about even today. Max Radin assumed that the scholastic method was essentially a way of "dispensing with reality."[100] His distinction between words and facts, however, relied on the modern, descriptive notion of the fact, itself a sly naturalization of the Roman legal *factum*. In truth, medieval jurists read law books in a much more poietic, creative manner. Recovering this medieval approach to law would yield the sort of "man-made irrealities" that Ernst Kantorowicz outlined in his study *The King's Two Bodies*, which drew extensively on *ius commune* and is dedicated, significantly, to Max Radin.[101] It would combine law in books and law in action, concepts and techniques, forms and facts, in a manner that it seems important to keep on exploring, should one care to assess, in all its historical complexity, law's relationship to reality.

Notes

1. Christophe Tarkos, "Entretien avec Christophe Verdier," in *Ecrits poétiques* (Paris: P.O.L., 2008), 357 (insisting that "words have no reference").

2. For a milestone of such philosophical puzzles, see Nelson Goodman, *Fact, Fiction, and Forecast* (Cambridge, MA: Harvard University Press, 1955).

3. Werner Heisenberg, "Goethe and Newton on Colour," in *Philosophic Problems of Nuclear Science: Eight Lectures by Werner Heisenberg*, trans. F. C. Hayes (London: Faber and Faber, 1952), 60–76.

4. Max Weber, *The Methodology of the Social Sciences*, ed. and trans. Edward A. Shils and Henry A. Finch (Glencoe, IL: Free Press, 1949). On this topic, see the symposium "Facts, Values, and Social Science," ed. Philip S. Gorski, *Society* 50 (2013): 543–609. Gorski's introduction ("Beyond the Fact/Value Distinction: Ethical Naturalism and the Social Sciences," 543–53) briefly places Weber in an intellectual context. For an alternative account also embracing Hume but proceeding via the sciences of political economy without

regard for law, see Mary Poovey, *A History of the Modern Fact: Problems of Knowledge in the Sciences of Wealth and Society* (Chicago: University of Chicago Press, 1998).

5. Hilary Putnam, *The Collapse of the Fact-Value Dichotomy, and Other Essays* (Cambridge, MA: Harvard University Press, 2004).

6. Mirjan Damaška, "Presentation of Evidence and Factfinding Precision," *University of Pennsylvania Law Review* 123 (1975): 1083–1106, at 1086.

7. A propos of English medieval legal proceedings, James Bradley Thayer referred to the "stream of questions as to the reality, the *rei veritas*, the fact, of what was alleged before the jurors . . . constantly [pouring] in," in "'Law and Fact' in Jury Trials," *Harvard Law Review* 4 (1890): 147–75.

8. On the concept of "isolation," see Rudolf von Jhering, *Geist des römischen Rechts auf den verschiedenen Stufen seiner Entwicklung* (Leipzig: Breitkopf and Härtel, 1854), 2:47–55; Fritz Schulz, *Principles of Roman Law* (Oxford: Clarendon, 1936), 19; Yan Thomas, "Mommsen et l'*Isolierung* du droit: Rome, l'Allemagne et l'État," foreword to *Droit public romain*, by Theodor Mommsen (Paris: De Boccard, 1984), 1:iii–xlviii. For a reminder of the influence that rhetoric had on Roman lawyers' ability to "arrive at the facts of a case" through a technical process of *inventio*, see Caroline Humfress, "Telling Stories about (Roman) Law: Rules and Concepts in Legal Discourse," in *Legalism: Rules and Categories*, ed. Paul Dresch and Judith Scheele (Oxford: Oxford University Press, 2015), 80.

9. There is a growing conviction that "cosmopolitan" and "multinormative" narratives might best equip us to address law's "fading" historical and geographical "coordinates." On cosmopolitanism, see William Twining, preface to *General Jurisprudence* (Cambridge: Cambridge University Press, 2009), xi; on multinormativity, see Thomas Duve, "Was ist 'Multinormativität'?—Einführende Bemerkungen," *Rechtsgeschichte—Legal History* 25 (2017): 88–101; on contemporary law's lack of situatedness, see Neil Walker, "Out of Place and Out of Time: Law's Fading Co-ordinates" (University of Edinburgh School of Law Working Paper 2009/01, https://doi.org/10.2139/ssrn.1367591).

10. On the looseness of the law/fact distinction in Athens and its epistemic backdrop, see the contributions by Adriaan Lanni and Daniela Cammack, respectively, in the present volume. The institutional context for which the most vigorous case might be made for the development of a stronger version of the law/fact distinction at Athens is the maritime courts: see Adriaan Lanni, "'Verdict Most Just': The Modes of Athenian Classical Justice," *Yale Journal of Law and the Humanities* 16 (2004): 312–21.

11. Rudolf von Jhering (*Geist*, 48) singles the development of Roman law out of "oriental law," marked by a primitive confusion between law and ethics. This line of thought extends through the German school of legal ethnology, keen to analyze primitive law as a "consequence [*Angebinde*] of religious representations" (Josef Kohler and Leopold Wenger, *Allgemeine Rechtsgeschichte* [Leipzig: Teubner, 1914], 1:4), up to Aldo Schiavone's *The Invention of Law in the West*, trans. Jeremy Carden and Antony Shugaar

(Cambridge, MA: Harvard University Press, 2012). For a classic statement of an alternative history for Jewish law see David Daube, *Studies in Biblical Law* (Cambridge: Cambridge University Press, 1947), 1–73; Daube urges that the theological portrait of Hebrew society in the Pentateuch is built on a foundation of preexisting legal concepts.

12. Jhering, *Geist*, 47: "Ein innerliches Zu-Sich-Kommen des Rechts."

13. In Karl Popper's conception, for instance, the term *occurrence* refers to a class of equivalent singular statements, while the term *event* denotes "what may be typical or universal about an occurrence" (*The Logic of Scientific Discovery* [London: Routledge, 1992], 89).

14. I am indebted to Anton Schütz for his helpful remarks on this point.

15. As Ludwig Fleck has pointed out in his preface to *Genesis and Development of a Scientific Fact* (Chicago: University of Chicago Press, 1979), xxii, the common notion of fact crystallizes our "complete passivity in the face of a power that is independent of us; a power we call 'existence' or 'reality.'"

16. Kevin Mulligan, "Facts, Formal Objects and Ontology," in *Modes of Existence: Papers in Ontology and Philosophical Logic*, ed. Andrea Bottani and Richard Davies (Heusenstamm: Ontos Verlag, 2006), 40.

17. Ian Hacking, *The Social Construction of What?* (Cambridge, MA: Harvard University Press, 1999), 22–23.

18. Gottlob Frege, "Der Gedanke: Eine logische Untersuchung," in *Beiträge zur Philosophie des deutschen Idealismus* (Erfurt: Deutsche Philosophische Gesellschaft, 1918–19), 2:74: "'Tatsachen! Tatsachen! Tatsachen!'"; trans. P. Geach, in "Thought: A Logical Inquiry," *Mind* 259 (1956): 307.

19. Lorraine Daston, "The Factual Sensibility," *Isis* 79 (1988): 464.

20. Steven Shapin, *A Social History of Truth: Civility and Science in Seventeenth-Century England* (Chicago: University of Chicago Press, 1994), 200.

21. Michel Foucault, "Truth and Juridical Forms," in *Power: Essential Works of Foucault, 1954–1984*, vol. 3, ed. James D. Faubion (New York: New Press, 2000), 31–45 (hinting, en passant, at the entanglement of truth and judicial forms, to unveil the survival of Roman Catholic forms of confession within psychoanalysis).

22. Barbara Shapiro, "The Concept 'Fact': Legal Origins and Cultural Diffusion," *Albion* 26 (1994): 14. By the same author, see also "Fact and Proof of Fact in Anglo-American Law, 1500–1850," in *How Law Knows*, ed. A. Sarat, L. Douglas, and M. M. Umphrey (Stanford: Stanford University Press, 2007), 25–71.

23. In "Scientific Experiment and Legal Expertise: The Way of Experience in Seventeenth-Century England," *Studies in the History and Philosophy of Science* 20 (1989): 19–45, Rose-Mary Sargent focuses on the trial by jury of the English common law, as does Barbara Shapiro, to a lesser extent, in "Concept 'Fact.'" For a convincing restatement of the influence of Roman-canonical law, see Eleonora Montuschi, "The 'Inquisition' of Nature: Francis Bacon's View of Scientific Enquiry" (LSE, Centre for Philosophy of Natural and Social Science, Discussion Paper 48/00, 2000).

24. Francis Bacon, "On the Advancement of Learning," in *The Works of Francis Bacon*, ed. James Spedding, et al. (London: Longmans, 1887), 3:333.

25. This formulation is a translation from Julien Théry's "*Fama*: L'opinion publique comme preuve judiciaire; Aperçu sur la révolution médiévale de l'inquisitoire (XIIè–XIVè s.)," in *La preuve en justice de l'Antiquité à nos jours*, ed. Bruno Lemesle (Rennes: Presses Universitaires de Rennes, 2003), 119–48. Théry's analysis of how *fama*/fame was framed by medieval lawyers as factual evidence links up interestingly with Esther Eidinow's contribution to the present volume.

26. Julien Théry, "Fama"; Alain Wijffels, "La procédure romano-canonique: Un algorithme médiéval?," in *"In principio erat Verbum": Mélanges offerts en hommage à Paul Tombeur par des anciens étudiants à l'occasion de son éméritat*, ed. Benoît-Michel Tock (Turnhout: Brepols, 2005), 431–65.

27. Massimo Vallerani, *Medieval Public Justice*, trans. Sarah Rubin Blanshei (Washington: Catholic University of America Press, 2012), 77.

28. Alessandro Giuliani, "Le rôle du fait dans la controverse: À propos du binome rhétorique-procédure judiciaire," *Archives de philosophie du droit* 39 (1995): 229–37.

29. Massimo Vallerani, *Medieval Justice*, 77.

30. Linda Fowler-Magerl, *Ordo iudiciorum vel ordo iudicarius: Begriff und Litteraturgattung* (Frankfurt am Main: Vittorio Klostermann, 1984).

31. *The Works of Francis Bacon*, 4:123, quoted by Shapiro, "Concept 'Fact,'" 14.

32. Eleonora Montuschi ("Inquisition") is oversimplifying the debate, I believe, when she states that Bacon "used legal terminology" as an "illustration of what the inquiring attitude of the natural philosopher amounts to."

33. Arist. *Metaph.* 1072a.

34. The entry for *fact* in the online *Stanford Encyclopedia of Philosophy* fails to mention either this research or the importance of the notion of fact in legal practice and discourse (Kevin Mulligan and Fabrice Correia, "Facts," *The Stanford Encyclopedia of Philosophy* [Winter 2017 ed.], ed. Edward N. Zalta, https://plato.stanford.edu/archives/win2017/entries/facts/).

35. "Factish" translates Bruno Latour's *faitiche*, a punning neologism that melds the paronomastic French words for "fact" and "fetish"; see his *On the Modern Cult of the Factish Gods* (Durham: Duke University Press, 2010). Characteristic of a historicist approach that gives no attention to legal culture is Mary Poovey's *History of the Modern Fact*. On the other side of the fence, see Ian Hacking's final profession as a "fact-lover," in *Social Construction of What?*

36. Some scholars have looked into aspects of this reverse movement, such as the patchy influence of philosophical empiricism on the doctrine of probable cause; see Barbara Shapiro, *Beyond Reasonable Doubt and Probable Cause: Historical Perspectives on the Anglo-American Law of Evidence* (Berkeley: University of California Press, 1991). However, the period under consideration in these works was too far back in time to include the years of the twentieth century in which law itself came to be treated as a fact.

37. Karl Olivecrona, *Law as Fact* (London: Stevens, 1971).

38. James E. Hegert and Stephen Wallace, "The German Free Law Movement as the Source of American Legal Realism," *Virginia Law Review* 73 (1987): 399–455. In "Understanding Legal Realism," *Texas Law Review* 87 (2009): 734, Brian Z. Tamanaha raises doubts about the distinctiveness of American legal realists as a group. For a classic survey of American legal realism, see Morton Horwitz, *The Transformation of American Law, 1870–1960: The Crisis of Legal Orthodoxy* (New York: Oxford University Press, 1992).

39. Karl Olivecrona, *Law as Fact*, 55.

40. Karl Olivecrona, *The Acquisition of Possession in Roman Law* (Lund: C. W. K. Gleerup, 1938), 34. On the paradigmatic importance of this sequence of Roman law in the history of law and philosophy, see Pierre Thévenin, *Le monde sur mesure: Une archéologie juridique des faits* (Paris: Classiques Garnier, 2017).

41. As the term *science* has also been put forward by conceptualists, it is useful to discriminate, drawing on Max Weber's terminology, between a formal legal science, exemplified by Savigny's and Kelsen's versions of *Rechtswissenschaft* (with their reciprocal and equally systematic focus on the system of legal ideas and legal norms), and the empirical legal science that the legal realists have in mind.

42. Karl Llewellyn, "Some Realism about Realism," *Harvard Law Review* 44 (1931): 1223.

43. William Twining, *Karl Llewellyn and the Realist Movement* (Cambridge: Cambridge University Press, 2012), 441.

44. Karl N. Llewellyn, *The Case Law System in America* (Chicago: University of Chicago Press, 1989), 5.

45. See Filippo Vassalli, "L'antitesi '*ius—factum*' nelle fonti giustinianee," *Annali della Facoltà di giurisprudenza dell'Università di Perugia* 28 (1914): 3–53. See also Nicolas Cornu Thénard's contribution to the present volume.

46. See, earlier in the present chapter, my remarks under "Balancing Two Meanings of Fact," as well as n. 11.

47. Thayer, "Law and Fact," 147. The Elizabethan adage *ad quaestionem facti non respondent judices, ad quaestionem juris non respondent juratores*, on which Barbara Shapiro focuses ("Concept 'Fact,'" 2), is just a way of encapsulating this medieval principle at a later stage of its development.

48. Robert Boyle, *Hydrostatical Paradoxes*, 2:742–44, quoted in Rose-Mary Sargent, "Scientific Experiment and Legal Expertise."

49. Hegert and Wallace, "German Free Law Movement."

50. This is Llewellyn's formulation, quoted in the preceding section of this chapter.

51. Herbert L. A. Hart, *The Concept of Law* (Oxford: Clarendon Press, 1961).

52. Brian Leiter, "Naturalizing Jurisprudence: Three Approaches" (University of Chicago Public Law and Legal Theory Working Paper 246, 2008), 10.

53. For two different perspectives instantiating the great part that the notion of fact

often plays here, see Patrick Nerhot, "The Fact of Law," in *Autopoietic Law: A New Approach in Law and Society*, ed. Gunther Teubner (Berlin: Walter de Gruyter, 1988), 312–34; Lech Morawski, "Law, Fact and Legal Language," *Law and Philosophy* 18 (1999): 461–73.

54. For an invitation to resist the "disciplinary amnesia" affecting legal theory, see Nicola Lacey, "Jurisprudence, History, and the Institutional Quality of Law," *Virginia Law Review* 101 (2015): 919–45.

55. I borrow this formulation from Roger Cotterrell, "Why Jurisprudence Is Not Legal Philosophy," *Jurisprudence* 5 (2014): 41. Cotterrell rightly opposes the tendency of many legal theorists "to view jurisprudence, insofar as it is not legal philosophy [in the sense of a branch of philosophy], as unworthy of serious scholarly attention."

56. This preservation is apparent in Karl Llewellyn's brilliant didactic account of the discrepancy between facts that are legally relevant and facts tout court, in *The Bramble Bush: On Our Law and Its Study* (New York: Oceana Publications, 1991), 47. On this passage, see Twining, *Karl Llewellyn*, 233.

57. See, e.g., John Crook, *Law and Life in Rome* (Ithaca: Cornell University Press, 1967).

58. See John W. Cairns and Paul J. du Plessis, introduction to *Beyond Dogmatics: Law and Society in the Roman World* (Edinburgh: Edinburgh University Press, 2007), 3. For further bibliography, see Clifford Ando, "Roman Law," in *The Oxford Handbook of Legal History*, ed. Markus Dubber and Christopher Tomlins (Oxford: Oxford University Press, 2018), 663–79.

59. Max Radin, "Legal Realism," *Columbia Law Review* 24 (1931): 826.

60. Llewellyn, *Case Law System*, 3.

61. M. H. Hoeflich, *Roman and Civil Law and the Development of Anglo-American Jurisprudence in the Nineteenth Century* (Athens: University of Georgia Press, 1997). See also Clifford Ando, "Il diritto romano e i giuristi romani nella cultura giuridica americana," in *Giuristi romani e storiografia moderna dalla "Palingenesia iuris civilis" agli "Scriptores iuris Romani,"* ed. Aldo Schiavone (Turin: G. Giappichelli, 2018), 99–111.

62. Charles Barzun, "Common Sense and Legal Science," *Virginia Law Review* 90 (2004): 1057, here following Hoeflich, *Roman and Civil Law*.

63. Barzun, "Common Sense," 1057.

64. I am picking up on the conceptualization of classical legal science that is apparent in Duncan Kennedy, "Savigny's Family/Patrimony Distinction and Its Place in the Global Genealogy of Classical Legal Thought," *American Journal of Comparative Law* 58 (2010): 811–42.

65. Michael H. Hoeflich, "Law and Geometry: Legal Science from Leibniz to Langdell," *American Journal of Legal History* 30 (1986): 113.

66. Llewellyn, *Case Law*, 3.

67. Friedrich Carl von Savigny, *System des heutigen römischen Rechts*, 8 vols. (Berlin: Veit und Comp., 1840–49).

68. Friedrich Carl von Savigny, *Vom Beruf unsrer Zeit für Gesetzgebung und Rechtswissenschaft* (Heidelberg: Mohr and Zimmer, 1840), 8: "das Recht wie die Sprache im Bewußtsein des Volkes lebt" (emphasis added in translation in text).

69. See James Q. Whitman, *The Legacy of Roman Law in the German Romantic Era: Historical Vision and Legal Change* (Princeton: Princeton University Press, 1990).

70. That the same lens still prejudices our understanding today is argued by Kaius Tuori in *Ancient Roman Lawyers and Modern Legal Ideals: Studies on the Impact of Contemporary Concerns in the Interpretation of Ancient Roman Legal History* (Frankfurt am Main: Vittorio Klostermann, 2007).

71. Roscoe Pound, "The End of Law as Developed through Juristic Thought," *Harvard Law Review* 7 (1914): 605–28, at 605.

72. Carlos Petit, *Max Radin: Cartas Romanisticas, 1923–1950* (Naples: Jovene, 2001), 20.

73. Max Radin, "Fundamental Concepts of the Roman Law," *California Law Review* 12 (1924): 396.

74. "Sea of waves" is Edward Coke's construction, quoted by Thomas E. Scrutton in *The Influence of the Roman Law on the Law of England* (Cambridge: Cambridge University Press, 1885), 129.

75. That the Scandinavian branch of legal realism also took an interest in Roman law is indicated by Olivecrona's direct acquaintance with Roman sources (see above, n. 39) and Axel Hägerström's seminal importance to the movement. Hägerström's approach to Roman law appears in *Der römische Obligationsbegriff im Lichte der allgemeinen römischen Rechtsanschauung*, 2 vols. (Uppsala: Skrifter utgivna av K. Humanistiska Vetenskapssamfundet i Uppsala, 1927).

76. Clifford Ando, "Fact, Fiction, and Social Reality in Roman Law," in *Legal Fiction in Theory and Practice*, ed. Maksymilian Del Mar and William Twining (Berlin: Springer Verlag, 2015), 295–323.

77. Ando, "Fact."

78. See Jhering's account of "dogmatic legal fictions" as a creative "chemistry." A reference to that positive interpretation of *fictiones legis* by Jhering appears in, e.g., Roscoe Pound, *Interpretations of Legal History* (Cambridge: Cambridge University Press, 1923), 136.

79. Rudolf Stammler, *Lehrbuch der Rechtsphilosophie* (Berlin: Walter de Gruyter, 1922), 262: "Wenn die Gedanken nach einer unbedingt einheitlichen Weise geordnet sind."

80. Jerome K. Frank, *Law and the Modern Mind* (1930; reprint, Gloucester, MA: Peter Smith, 1970), 179. For a discussion without reference to Roman *fictiones*, see Charles Barzun, "Jerome Frank and the Modern Mind," (University of Virginia School of Law, Public Law and Legal Theory Research Paper 2009-01, 2009).

81. Roscoe Pound, "Law in Books, Law in Action," *American Law Review* 44 (1910): 12–36.

82. Roscoe Pound, "The End of Law as Developed through Juristic Thought," *Harvard Law Review* 7 (1914): 605–28.

83. Llewellyn, "Some Realism," 1223.

84. Lon Fuller, *Legal Fiction* (Stanford: Stanford University Press, 1967).

85. Ando, "Fact," 313.

86. Hans Kelsen, "Zur Theorie der juristischen Fiktionen: Mit besonderer Berücksichtigung von Vaihingers Philosophie des Als Ob," in *Annalen der Philosophie und philosophische Kritik*, ed. Hans Vaihinger (Leipzig: Felix Meiner, 1919), 631: "Eine Fälschung, ein Umweg des Denkens."

87. Annelise Riles, "Is the Law Hopeful?" (Cornell Law Faculty Working Paper 68, 2010), 4.

88. Riles, "Is the Law Hopeful?," 4.

89. A sign that this debate could be oversimplified is the immediate influence that Vaihinger's analysis of legal fictions had on Jerome Frank's 1930 essay. See Charles Barzun, "Jerome Frank," 10.

90. Yan Thomas, "*Fictio legis*: L'empire de la fiction romaine et ses limites médiévales," *Droits, revue française de théorie juridique* 21 (1995): 17–63.

91. Massimo Vallerani writes, "Questa visione di una realtà pregiuridica dei fatti è illusoria," in "I fatti nella logica del processo medievale: Note introduttive," *Quaderni storici* 108 (2001): 665–93, hinting at Carlo Ginzburg, *Threads and Traces: True, False, Fictive* (Berkeley: University of California Press, 2012).

92. Radin, "Fundamental Concepts." See also Thomas, "Mommsen."

93. Fuller, *Legal Fictions*, 11.

94. Llewellyn, "Some Realism," 44. One could probably understand the rise of critical legal studies in the late 1970s as a reengagement with language and *écriture* in the wake of legal realism.

95. An anthropological plea for an exploration of the archives of Western legal thinking appears in Alain Pottage, "Law after Anthropology: Object and Technique in Roman Law," *Theory, Culture and Society* 3 (2014): 147–66.

96. Ennio Cortese, "Alle origini della scuola di Bologna," *Rivista Internazionale di Diritto Comune* 5 (1993): 29.

97. Pound, "Law in Books, Law in Action." See discussion at note 81.

98. *Questiones de Iuris Subtilitatibus*, ed. Ginevra Zanetti (Florence: La Nuova Italia, 1958).

99. That the brocard *ex facto ius oritur* may have appeared for the first time in Guillaume de Cun's commentary to *Dig.* 9.2.52, in the first half of the fourteenth century, is postulated in B. Brandi, *Notizie intorno a Guillelmus de Cunio, le sue Opere e il suo Insegnamento a Tolosa* (Rome: Forzani, 1892), 110. In its original context, the brocard referred to the treatment of the content of customary law as a question of fact, rather than a question of law; in this sense, norms of customary law "arose" from fact. See O. Condorelli, "'*Quum sunt facti et in facto consistent*,' note su consuetudini e statuti in margine

a una costitutione di Bonifacio VIII (*licet Romanis Pontifex*, VI, 1, 2, 1)," in *Rivista internazionale di Diritto Comune* 10 (1999): 205–15. The brocard was turned upside down by Max Radin in "*Ex facto ius, ex iure factum*," in *Interpretations of Modern Legal Philosophies: Essays in Honor of Roscoe Pound* (New York: Oxford University Press, 1947), 578–88, providing the title of the present essay with a model.

100. Radin, "Legal Realism," 826.

101. Ernst Kantorowicz, *The King's Two Bodies: A Study in Medieval Political Theology* (Princeton: Princeton University Press, 1957).

Contributors

Clifford Ando is Professor of Classics, History, and Law and the David B. and Clara E. Stern Professor at the University of Chicago and a research fellow in the Department of Biblical and Ancient Studies at the University of South Africa. He is a historian of government, law, and religion in the Roman Empire and the Roman tradition. His publications include *Imperial Ideology and Provincial Loyalty in the Roman Empire* (2000), *Law, Language, and Empire in the Roman Tradition* (2011), and *Roman Social Imaginaries: Language and Thought in Contexts of Empire* (2015).

Daniela Cammack joined the University of California, Berkeley, as Assistant Professor of Political Science in 2019. Prior to that, she was a junior fellow in the Harvard Society of Fellows and taught for three years at Yale University. She works primarily on ancient Greek politics and philosophy and on the history and theory of democracy, and her research has appeared or is forthcoming in *Political Theory*, *Polis*, *History of Political Thought*, *Classical Quarterly*, *Classical Philology*, and the *Journal of Political Philosophy*. She is currently writing a monograph on ancient Greek democracy.

Nicolas Cornu Thénard is Professor of Roman Law and Legal History at Université Paris II Panthéon-Assas and General Secretary of the Société de Législation Comparée. He studies Roman civil procedure, history of argumentation, and legal philosophy. His publications include *The Distinction between Fact and Law in Roman Jurists' Thought* (forthcoming). As a member of the Institut universitaire de France, he is working on a research project dedicated to the autonomy of legal argument and is the cofounder of the law review *Tribonien*.

Esther Eidinow is Professor of Ancient History at the University of Bristol. She specializes in ancient Greek history, with particular interest in magic and religion. Her publications include *Oracles, Curses, and Risk among the Ancient Greeks* (2007), *Luck, Fate and Fortune: Antiquity and Its Legacy* (2011), and *Envy, Poison, and Death: Women on Trial in Classical Athens* (2016).

Nicole Giannella is Assistant Professor of Classics at Cornell University. She specializes in slavery studies, Roman law, and Latin prose literature. She is currently writing a book about slavery and the limits of ownership in Roman law and society.

Adriaan Lanni is the Touroff-Glueck Professor of Law at Harvard Law School. Her research focuses on ancient law and modern criminal procedure. Her publications include *Law and Justice in the Courts of Classical Athens* (2006) and *Law and Order in Ancient Athens* (2016).

David M. Lewis is Lecturer in Greek History and Culture at the University of Edinburgh, Scotland. He works on the socioeconomic history of ancient Greece, particularly the history of labor, in its broader Eastern Mediterranean setting. He is the author of *Greek Slave Systems in Their Eastern Mediterranean Context, c. 800–146 BC* (2018) and coeditor of *The Ancient Greek Economy: Markets, Households and City-States* (2016).

William P. Sullivan is the Drinan Research Fellow at Boston College Law School and an associate at Three Crowns LLP in Washington, DC. The focus of his research is the comparative history of procedure, with a special emphasis on the Roman legal tradition.

Pierre Thévenin is a CNRS tenured researcher in Legal Studies at the Ecole Normale Superieure Paris-Saclay. He looks at Roman-canonical law as a resource for philosophy. He is the author of *Le monde sur mesure: Une archéologie juridique des faits* (2017).

Index

Printed and bound by CPI Group (UK) Ltd, Croydon, CR0 4YY
16/09/2026
14963491-0001